MODERN ITALIAN COOKING

Biba Caggiano

Illustrated by Melanie Parks

A Fireside Book
Published by Simon & Schuster
New York   London   Toronto   Sydney   Tokyo   Singapore

F

FIRESIDE

Rockefeller Center
1230 Avenue of the Americas
New York, New York 10020
Copyright © 1987 by Biba Caggiano
All rights reserved
including the right of reproduction
in whole or in part in any form.
First Fireside Edition 1992
FIRESIDE and colophon are registered trademarks
of Simon & Schuster Inc.
Designed by Irving Perkins Associates
Manufactured in the United States of America
10 9 8 7 6 5 4 3 2 1
10 9 8 7 6   Pbk.

Library of Congress Cataloging in Publication Data
Caggiano, Biba.
    Modern Italian cooking.

    Includes index.
    1. Cookery, Italian.   I. Title.
TX723.C25   1987   641.5945   86-29737
ISBN: 0-671-55330-5
ISBN: 0-671-75445-9 Pbk.

To Vincent, Carla and Paola

con tanto amore

Contents

List of Recipes

Stuffed Mushrooms
Mozzarella Marinated in Oil and Oregano
Carpaccio with Parmigiano, Capers, and Olive Oil

Pasta

Spinach Ravioli Stuffed with Sea Bass
Fettuccine with Ham, Peas, and Egg Sauce
Angel's Hair with Prosciutto, Cream, and
   Lemon Sauce
Shells with Wild Mushrooms and Anchovy Sauce
Fettuccine with Creamy Gorgonzola Sauce
Pasta with Roasted Peppers and Anchovies
Bucatini with Onion Sauce
Pasta with Broiled Eggplants, Zucchini, and Crookneck
   Squash
Pennette 3 Vasselle Style
Linguine with Pesto, Potatoes, and Peas
Spaghetti with Squid
Whole Wheat Spaghetti with Cauliflower and
   Red Pepper
Noodles with Leeks

Soups

Cream of Summer Vegetables
Cold Vegetable Soup with Pesto
Chilled Springtime Lettuce Soup
Zucchini Soup

Risotti

Risotto with Lobster
Risotto with Artichokes
Risotto with Zucchini and Zucchini Blossoms
Risotto with Fresh Peas and Chives
Green Risotto
Risotto with Mint
Springtime Risotto

Meat and Poultry

Mixed Roasted Meats
Broiled Filet of Beef with Balsamic Vinegar
Cold Roast Beef with Capers and Anchovies
Cold Pork in Tuna–Pickled Vegetable Sauce

Pork Tenderloin with Cherries
Pork Chops Cooked in Milk
Veal Chops with Tomato–Onion Sauce
Veal Chops Sautéed with Butter and Sage
Veal Scaloppine with White Wine Sauce
Springtime Veal Stew
Stuffed Veal Roast
Roasted Rabbit with Juniper Berries
Chicken with Herbs
Sautéed Marinated Chicken Breast
Chicken Skewers with Wine and Worcestershire
    Sauce
Fillet of Turkey Breast with Apples

Seafood

Sea Bass Poached with Fresh Tomatoes
Broiled Swordfish with Green Sorrel and Pepper
    Sauce
Stuffed Swordfish Bundles
Broiled Trout
Turbot with Vinegar–Mint Sauce
Skewers of Mixed Broiled Fish
Shrimp with Fresh Tomatoes
Broiled Lobster Tails
Scallops with Parsley, Garlic, and Wine Sauce
Clams with Savory Tomato Sauce

Salads

Mushroom, Ham, and Cheese Salad
Warm Roasted Eggplant, Pepper, and Tomato
    Salad   00
Rice Salad the Sicilian Way
Shells Salad with Broccoli, Anchovies, and Capers
Salad of Roasted Meat and Red Onions
Salad of Marinated Capon Breast
Roasted Turkey, Potato, and Peas Salad
Rice and Shellfish Salad
Mixed Seafood Salad
Shrimp and Red Pepper Salad

Eggs

Frittata with Tomatoes and Anchovies
Frittata with Mint and Parsley

Vegetables and Simple Salads

Artichokes with Peas and Prosciutto
Asparagus with Fried Eggs
Fava Beans with Bacon and Tomatoes
Carrots with Marsala
Broiled Eggplant with Garlic and Fresh Oregano
Sautéed Peas with Leeks
Potatoes with Fresh Sage and Garlic
Sautéed Swiss Chard with Oil and Lemon
Glazed Spring Vegetables
Salad of Roasted Red Peppers and Yellow
   Tomatoes
String Bean, Potato, and Pancetta Salad
String Bean Salad with Lemon

Desserts

Strawberry and Orange Tart
Apple Roll with Raisins, Pine Nuts, and Jam
Strawberries with Balsamic Vinegar
Fig Tart
Ugly but Good Hazelnut Cookies
Carla's Yogurt and Raisin Cake
Peach Mousse
Three-Flavor Ice Cream Bombe
Stuffed Ice Cream Bombe
Apple Fritters with Raspberry Sauce
Roberta's Molded Custard with Caramel Glaze
Frozen Zabaglione Mousse with Raspberry Sauce
Peaches Marinated in Red Wine
Espresso Granita

Wonderful Autumn and Winter Fare

Appetizers

Stuffed Baked Mussels
Eggplants Stuffed with Fontina and Sun-Dried
   Tomatoes
Crostini of Polenta with Mushrooms
Eggplant Mousse
Medley of Sweet and Sour Eggplants, Raisins, Pine
   Nuts, and Tomatoes
Stuffed Artichoke Bottoms
Marinated Deep-Fried Scallops
Broiled Bread and Cheese Skewers
Crostini of Spicy Eggplant

Pasta

Large Ravioli with Taleggio Cheese Sauce
Spaghetti with Shellfish Baked in Aluminum Foil
Tortelloni Stuffed with Parsleyed Eggplants and
    Ricotta
Fettuccine with Mushrooms, Sausage, and Cream
Green Lasagne with Mushrooms
Pasta Roll Stuffed with Spinach and Cheese
Pumpkin Tortelli
Linguine with Lobster Sauce
Fusilli with Meat Sauce Neapolitan Style
Rigatoni with Mushrooms, Prosciutto, and Cream
Penne with Red Pepper Sauce
Penne with Pepper Sauce in Foil
Tricolor Pasta
Bucatini with Stewed Beans

Soups

Taglioline in Broth
Egg Soup Roman Style
Franca's Country Bean Soup
Cabbage Soup Val d'Aosta Style
Pasta and Chick-pea Soup
Easy Lentil Soup
Cream of Pumpkin Soup
Cabbage and Rice Soup
Mushroom Soup with Porcini

Gnocchi

Squash and Cheese Gnocchi
Cavatelli with Butter and Cheese
Green Potato Gnocchi with Pancetta and Fresh
    Sage

Polenta

Basic Polenta
Polenta with Dried Wild Mushrooms and
    Pancetta
Polenta with Mascarpone
Polenta with Gorgonzola

Risotti

Risotto with Cream of Seafood
Baked Molded Risotto with Mushrooms and Peas

Meat and Poultry

Mixed Boiled Meats
Skewers of Mixed Broiled Meats
Braised Beef with String Beans
Stuffed Savory Beef Bundles
Roasted Leg of Pork Marinated in Beer
Pork Chops in Piquant Sauce
Sweet and Sour Medallions of Pork
Fried Sausage with Broccoli and Hot Pepper
Pan-Roasted Veal with Porcini Mushrooms
Veal Shanks with Red Pepper Sauce
Veal Chops with Cheese Parma Style
Fast Stuffed Veal Bundles
Veal with Prosciutto and Sage
Roasted Leg of Lamb the Tuscan Way
Lamb Stew with Small Onions and Carrots
Lamb in Egg–Lemon Sauce
Lamb Skewers with Balsamic Vinegar
Rabbit with Tomatoes and Olives
Rabbit in Piquant Sauce
Paola's Boned Roasted Rabbit
Quails and Polenta in a Savory Tomato Sauce
Chicken with Peppers and Tomatoes the Roman
    Way
Chicken Breasts with Vermouth Sauce
Roasted Capon with Potatoes

Seafood

Fried Cod Roman Style
Swordfish Sicilian Style
Steamed Trout Fillets
Spicy Mussel Soup

Eggs

Spinach Frittata
Pasta Frittata
Onion Frittata

Vegetables

Baked Cauliflower with Onions and Cheese
Baked Celery with Butter and Cheese
Grilled Red Chicory
Fried Eggplants
Fried Fennel with Parmigiano
Glazed Small Onions
Stuffed Baked Onions
Mamma Lea's Roasted Potatoes
Fried Potatoes with Onions
Quick Broiled Tomatoes
Sweet and Sour Zucchini
Roasted Stuffed Peppers

Salads

Mixed Raw Salad
Radicchio and Pancetta Salad
Belgian Endive and Radicchio Salad
Radicchio and Pear Salad
Celery and Parmigiano Salad
Mushroom and Gorgonzola Salad
Orange and Fennel Salad
Cucumber and Pink Grapefruit Salad
Cauliflower with Parsley–Mustard Dressing

Desserts

Baked Pears with Marsala
Pear Tart
Family-Style Panettone
Sweet Pastry Ring from Bologna
Bolognese Fruitcake
Frozen Hazelnut Zabaglione Mousse with Hot
   Chocolate Sauce
Sorbet with Barolo Wine
Cantaloupe Sorbet
Neapolitan Honey Balls
Pears Poached in Wine and Lemon
Poached Pears with Champagne Zabaglione
Oranges with Marsala Syrup

Great, Fast Pasta Dishes Prepared in Less Than Twenty Minutes

Orecchiette with Tomatoes and Ricotta Cheese
Penne with Uncooked Tomato Sauce

Thin Spaghetti with Caviar
Bucatini with Fresh Tomatoes
Rigatoni with Porcini Mushrooms Genoa Style
Pennette with Cream–Tomato and Prosciutto
  Sauce
Pasta with Smoked Salmon and Cream
Spaghetti with Zucchini and Smoked Ham
Pasta with Eggplants
Linguine with Scallops and Anchovy Sauce
Spaghettini with Garlic and Oil
Bucatini with Mushrooms and Anchovy Sauce
Pasta with Broccoli, Anchovies, and Hot Chile
  Pepper

Pizza, Calzoni, Rustic Pies, and Savory Breads

Basic Pizza Dough
Pizza alla Napoletana
Pizza Margherita
Pizza with Ham
Pizza with Olives, Capers, and Anchovies
Pizza with Mushrooms
Pizza with Eggplant
Pizza with Eggplant and Tomatoes
Zucchini and Onion Tart
Eggplant Tart
Rustic Pie
Savory Pie with Four Tastes
Potato–Prosciutto and Cheese Cake
Calzone Stuffed with Cheese
Calzone with Red Onions
Calzoni with Ham and Cheese of Café San
  Domenico
Savory Bread with Onion, Pancetta, and Sun-Dried
  Tomatoes
Flat Bolognese Savory Bread with Bacon

Preface

The idea for this book came to me during one of my last trips to Italy. I had been noticing changes in food patterns for several years. Even within my family, Bolognesi for generations, these changes were quite evident. For example, when I was growing up in Bologna, Sunday meals were always special. My mother would spend extra time and take particular care when she cooked the Sunday meal and my father would select a special bottle of wine to go with the food. Then we would all congregate around the dinner table to enjoy the food and each other's company.

My parents are gone now, but my brother and sister still live in Bologna. On most Sundays, they leave the city with their respective families and drive to the hills or to the sea. They go fishing or hiking or simply lie on the beach. Sunday has become, for them, a day to relax and escape. A pattern has been broken. For them, as for many modern Italian families, the Sunday meal has become a thing of the past.

We all know that the world is getting smaller. Distances don't mean much anymore. We hop on a plane and within hours we are on a different continent. We are thirsty for new experiences and much more open to new ideas and trends. As I see it, even the Italian kitchen is in a state of transition. Old and new concepts are walking hand in hand, taking, giving, and mixing styles, allowing the modern cook more freedom than ever before.

With this book, I attempt to show the reality of the Italian kitchen of today. Some of the recipes that I have selected, tested, and retested in my own kitchen have stood the test of time and are as valid today as they were years ago. Others have been slightly adapted to fit the modern kitchen; some are simply new, fresh interpretations by modern cooks and chefs.

The food of the modern Italian kitchen makes more sense today than ever before, because it is guided by tradition, but not ruled by rigid dogmas. It relies on pure, fresh basic ingredients and is adaptable, straightforward, often inexpensive, and truly exquisite.

The Modern Italian Kitchen

Until not too long ago, the food of Italy was defined regionally to the extent that the term "Italian cooking" was a generalization seldom used by Italians themselves. One cooked "alla Bolognese" or "alla Fiorentina," rather than "alla Italiana." Each region would show, through its food, a rich history, a uniqueness and character of its own. Even within a region there were many noticeable differences: Each town had its own variation of a stew, a soup, or a pasta dish. Similarly, the restaurants and trattorias specialized in the local food. Only on rare occasions would one find a dish that belonged to another region.

So much has changed. There is no doubt that Italian cooking is going through a slow transition and that, in a not-too-far distant future, Italian food will lose a lot of its regional diversity. Cities, towns, and hamlets that once were virtually isolated are now connected by super freeways. Italians have become very mobile, settling, mingling, and marrying outside of their regions, and mixing culinary styles. Food can now be transported easily and quickly from one part of Italy to another. A Bolognese can now enjoy fresh fish from Sicily almost on a daily basis, and freshly made tortellini can reach a Sicilian table without spoiling within the same day. What was once an agricultural society is now becoming a fast-paced industrialized country. As a result, the Italian kitchen of today, though simpler and less traditional, is multifaceted and even more versatile than ever before.

Classic regional food can still be found, especially in the homes of the smaller towns and hamlets and in the deep South, as well as in regions where food is of particular importance, such as in Emilia-Romagna. But there is also the food of the fast-paced mobile society, of the great cities and modern households, where work is a priority for both husband and wife. The daily meals are generally lighter and often improvised on the spur of the moment, with little fuss or complication and they don't generally follow a classic pattern. A plate of pasta can be whipped up in a short amount of time and topped by a light, fresh sauce. Some rice might be served alongside a broiled chop. A salad can become a whole meal when leftover meat or fish are added to it, and some soup might be thawed, reheated, and served simply with some crusty bread. The approach to daily cooking is uncomplicated. Often the decision as to what to cook is made at the last moment at the market with the selection of some fresh ingredient.

We all know that Italian food is, and has always been, straightforward and uncomplicated. The tradition of excellent, uncontrived home cooking is still there. What has changed is the everyday way of eating. We eat differently today because we live differently than we did years ago. We have become affluent and sedentary. When I was growing up in Bologna, the streets of my city were clogged with bicycles and pedestrians. One would walk or bike almost anywhere. Today, we leave the bikes in the garage and drive to work. Everything seems to be mechanical and automated. We take elevators to go to the second floor. We have machines that do our dishes and our laundry and machines that scrub, buff, and vacuum our floors. We have machines that make our pasta and our ice creams and electrical gadgets that open our cans and grind our coffee. With so little physical effort on our part, it is difficult to justify four-course meals on a regular basis.

A lighter cooking approach is evident everywhere. Even in northern Italy, traditionally butter country, one sees some changes: lighter sauces; less use of butter and cream and more use of olive oil; an increase in the use of vegetables and fresh fish as active ingredients in dishes or solely by themselves. Even the way we eat pasta is changing: The portions are smaller. We tend to prefer plain shapes of pasta over stuffed, filling concoctions. Vegetable sauces for pasta are becoming more and more popular both at home and in restaurants. Of course, vegetable sauce for pasta is not a new idea. During the Renaissance, vegetables and herbs were cooked together to produce sauces, and Sicilians have used vegetables on their pasta for centuries. In fact, Sicily, beautiful but poor, unconsciously developed what may be the healthiest diet in all of Italy. Fruits and cereals, pasta made with superlative wheat, vegetables, fish, and extraordinary olive oil are all important staples of Sicilian cooking.

Dishes from many regions that were once labeled "poor man's food" have now been rediscovered and readapted. Polenta, for example, a staple with many northern Italians, has taken on a new identity. In many elegant restaurants, polenta is now served as an appetizer: It is cut into small *crostini*, topped with Gorgonzola cheese or wild mushrooms and then broiled. Polenta has even found its way into the trendy "California cuisine": Jeremiah Tower, whose restaurant Stars is among the most popular in San Francisco, has served warm polenta over an avocado half with a sauce containing goat cheese and ancho chiles. Dishes made with beans, onions, and lentils that once were considered "peasant" are now praised for their wholesome and healthy qualities.

New food trends and changes can be seen almost everywhere, but especially in restaurants. The humble trattoria, generally tucked away in peripheral parts of town, might still offer the more honest and authentic fare, but more and more restaurants are now offering national, rather than regional, dishes, catering to an ever-increasing number of foreign patrons. And several high-class restaurants offer the *Nuova Cucina Italiana*, in which the principles of the *nuova* cuisine are applied to Italian ingredients. Whatever sort of restaurant they choose, Italians today eat out more than ever before. They hunt for good restaurants with the same intensity and determination they would hunt for gold.

The realities of modern life have also affected the Italian home kitchen. Once the Italian woman married, raised children, and took care of the home. She became a baker, a pasta maker, and a skilled cook. Her interests outside the home were few. Today, things are quite different, especially in the more industrialized North. Many women work outside the home, and many more will join the working force in the years to come. They have children to raise, families to run, and new challenges to meet. Life is faster and more demanding. Time, that cherished commodity, is becoming increasingly scarce, with less time to devote to the daily pleasures and demands of the multi-course meal cooked at home.

Proof of these changes can be seen in the increasing numbers of supermarkets in Italy, where once there were none, and in the proliferation of new Salumerie and Rosticcerie and take-out gourmet food shops that have spurted up all over the large cities. Row upon row of magnificently prepared dishes are strategically displayed in full view of customers. In the early evening, these shops are virtually mobbed by people returning from work. The increased popularity of cookbooks, food magazines, and television cooking shows also indicates a change in the Italian interest in food. Once, very few households owned cookbooks. The heritage of fine food was handed down through the centuries from mother to daughter by teaching, observation, or badly scribbled recipes. Using local ingredients and with a keen feeling for tradition, the cook would reproduce, day after day and year after year, the same wonderful, yet parochial, food. Today's cook has less time at her disposal, but is possessed by a more acute curiosity, one that is not limited to the food of her own region. Paradoxically, she also needs to know more about food to do it well and quickly.

About ten years ago only a few non-professional cooking schools existed in Italy. These schools were intended primarily for foreign visitors to Italy, especially Americans. Today, the number of schools has increased dramatically, and many Italians attend these courses as well. This was absolutely unheard of only a generation ago. The walls of the Italian kitchen have now expanded and the potential for new ideas and new challenges is there. Even the most prestigious and venerable food magazine *La Cucina Italiana* has, in the last year or so, added a new feature: "La cucina rapida" or fast cooking, which acknowledges the need of the modern woman who wants to prepare good food in a relatively short time. And, should she find herself without a clue as to what to cook on any particular day, she can simply pick up the phone and the Italian phone company will provide her with the recipe of the day as well as with a special dietetic recipe.

So, within a certain classic structure, the modern Italian cook can now move around as freely as a pianist improvising a sonata.

She can choose and adapt, she can revive an old recipe or create a new one, and with the choice of superlative raw materials available to her now from every corner of Italy, she can prepare a small masterpiece of a simple dish.

Italians still love to eat, perhaps more than any other people in the world, and they adore the conviviality of the table and the intimacy that comes from sharing food with family and friends. Today, however, the food at hand may be a specialty from any region, a simple, streamlined creation from the modern home kitchen, or a highly original dish from the *Nuova Cucina Italiana*, as well, of course, as an old family favorite. In any case, it is always heartily appreciated. Not all cooking traditions have been lost. Sometimes they have just simply been set aside. It is comforting and reassuring to know they are there, ready to be rediscovered or, perhaps, lightened and readapted.

What Food Means to Me

I am very grateful for the good fortune of having been born and raised in Bologna, for this city, with its heritage of great food, gave me an early appreciation of excellent cooking. My mother was a superb regional cook as were my grandmother and my aunt; in fact, there were thousands of homemakers scattered around Bologna who were also superb cooks. This was taken for granted: Food in Bologna was such an integral part of one's life that being a skilled cook was nothing to boast about. I remember coming home from school in the middle of the afternoon, walking into our large kitchen, and seeing my mother routinely intent on preparing our evening meal. The aromas, the reassuring disarray of pots and pans, of flour and eggs scattered on the large kitchen table, always gave me an instant feeling of well-being. In affluent times, my mother prepared the most heavenly tortellini and Bollito Misto. She would roast veal, chicken, and pork to perfection. With modest cuts of meats she would prepare the most incredible broth—light, but full of flavor. In leaner times, she would cook big pots of beans or lentils, and combine them with small pasta soups or enormous platters of polenta dressed only with a bit of ragù or olive oil. Every morning at dawn, she would go to Bologna's open market to take advantage of the fresh, special ingredients. Sometimes, especially after the war, we didn't have meat on our table for weeks. Then she would send my sister, my brother, and me to visit an aunt who had a small farm outside Bologna. *Zia* Rina would give us some of the precious ingredients that she kept hidden away in the cellar, flour, eggs, butter, and fresh vegetables. The miracles that my mother performed with those special ingredients are still so clear and vivid in my mind. Perhaps that is why I grew up loving food, for it was an extension of my mother's love.

It really doesn't matter whether we cook a lot or only a little, whether we spend a fortune on the food we put on our table or we must select ingredients on a tight budget. It is what we do with that food that really counts. Sometimes my day can be quite hectic and I might suddenly realize that it is 6 o'clock and I don't have the foggiest idea what to cook that night. So, I improvise. Perhaps I make a frittata or whip up an easy plate of pasta or try to do with whatever I have around. However, no matter how impromptu the meal, I always set a nice table because the half hour or so we spend around the dinner table is very important. The sense of family can be strengthened in this daily sharing and turn the act of eating into a civilized, loving experience.

A Word About Pasta

The proliferation of pasta books on the market, written by luminaries of American Food, has convinced me that pasta is, in this country, the "discovery" of the eighties. However, I became more certain that pasta is, indeed, the food of the eighties when I found boxes of "homemade" fettuccine amidst the peppers, eggplants, and tomatoes while I was shopping at my favorite produce ranch here in Sacramento. The ranch is owned by a nice Asian family. They told me that the fettuccine had been made by a relative. Pasta, I think, is here to stay.

As a good Italian I never get tired of pasta. My daughters and my husband never get tired of pasta. My friends, when they come to dinner at my house, always expect pasta. What is it that makes this particular food so appealing? Perhaps because it is a highly satisfying food or because the numerous pasta shapes and sauces are so intriguing. Or maybe we like it because it is economical and easy to prepare. And, now that we have been told that pasta is good for us, we like it even more.

The image of pasta in this country has changed

considerably in the last twenty years. Once considered a poor man's staple, pasta has become a very "in" food today. Nutritionists tell us now that we should eat more pasta and less meat, for pasta is high in energy-producing carbohydrates and low in fat. Every month a food magazine goes to great lengths to depict the virtues of pasta and restaurant chefs strive to create wonderful and absolutely "new" pasta dishes.

Fresh pasta stores are sprouting up all over the country. They not only offer conventional pasta, but multicolored and multiflavored pasta as well. Pasta machines are sold like hotcakes. The simple hand-cranked machine of some years ago is now being outsold by other machines that make "instant pasta." "Simply put in eggs and flour," the instructions say, "and push the button." Then, as if by magic, this space-age appliance produces pasta of any kind. But as in all things that are suddenly popular, there are negative aspects to consider as well. There is also, I find, a great deal of confusion. The following short discussion and "do's" and "don'ts" of pasta making, equipment, ingredients, and pasta fads are meant to clarify the preparation of pasta at home.

Is Homemade Pasta Better Than Factory-Made Pasta?

I read the following in a recent brochure sent to me by a cooking school: "Making pasta at home is easy and fun and the result is so superior to dry pasta, you will never buy it again." There are two incorrect statements here.

First, while making pasta at home is fun, it is not all that easy. Good homemade pasta requires more than just flour and eggs to be outstanding. It also takes skill that can

be obtained only by those who are willing to put in a certain amount of time in the pursuit of a craft.

Second, one should not compare homemade pasta with factory-made pasta, unless the comparison is intended only toward commercially made egg pasta. Simply, these are two different products no more comparable than veal and beef. Just as veal and beef share the same beginning but develop into a light and delicate meat on the one hand, and a savory and robust one on the other, so it is with pasta. With soft white flour and eggs, one can make a nice, soft dough, perfect for tender noodles and delicate stuffed pasta dishes. With hard durum wheat (semolina flour), water, and large commercial pasta machines, a more consistent, firmer dough is produced best suited for spaghetti, perciatelli, ziti, and so on.

While homemade pasta is more popular in northern Italy, southern Italians need their daily dose of spaghetti and maccheroni. Now, however, that Italians have less time to cook, the homemade product is in sharp decline and the consumption of factory-made pasta has increased even in the North. Fifty-five million Italians enjoy commercial pasta on a regular basis.

Delicate, homemade fettuccine can be absolutely heavenly, but a steaming plate of penne with a zesty sauce can also be heavenly. Frankly, I would personally buy good commercial pasta any time over some of the sad looking so-called "fresh pasta" that is now available.

Flour to Use for Homemade Pasta

All the recipes for homemade pasta in this book are made with all-purpose unbleached flour. This is closest to Italian flour. Contrary to what many cookbooks written by non-Italians state, semolina flour is almost *never* used in Italy for homemade pasta.

Eggs

The eggs in these recipes are large eggs. If smaller or extra-large eggs are used, the amount of flour should be adjusted accordingly.

Proportions

I have made pasta all my life and when I must give exact proportions I always hesitate. There are so many variables that it is almost impossible to be exact. The proportions I use are a little more than half a cup of flour for each large egg. On a rainy, humid day I will need a little more flour. The temperature of the kitchen, the altitude, the size of the eggs, all will have an effect on how much flour will be needed. It makes sense to start with a scanter amount, for you can easily add as you work out your dough.

Equipment Needed for Making Pasta

It used to be easy. Once there was only the rolling pin and the precious tools of our hands. Today, there are so many machines on the market for pasta making that it is often difficult to decide what we really need.

To Make Pasta Dough by Hand

A large wooden board is definitely the first choice, because wood is porous and will impart to the dough a porous surface that will absorb the sauce. Formica or marble can also be used, though marble is more slippery.

A fork to mix the flour with the eggs. A long rolling pin, ideally an Italian rolling pin, 32 inches long and approximately 1½ inches in diameter to roll out the dough.

A dough scraper which you will need to collect all the sticky pieces from the board and to clean the board.

A pastry wheel, straight-edged or, better yet, scalloped to cut pasta into shapes.

To Make Pasta Dough by Machine

A food processor or an electric mixer. (Keep in mind that making pasta by machine requires a little bit less flour.)

An electric or hand-cranked pasta rolling machine. I like my little electric Bialetti. The dough is put through two cylindrical plastic rollers and it is rolled out several times until a long, thin sheet of pasta is produced. The only drawback to this machine is the noise—it is almost like having an airplane taking off over your head!

The dough can also be rolled out through a hand-cranked rolling machine which works on the same principle as the electric one. It is silent and less expensive. It produces a dough that is, however, more "slippery" because the rollers are made of stainless steel. It is also helpful to have a dough scraper nearby and a pastry wheel that you will use to cut stuffed pasta.

A wonderful compromise can be achieved by kneading the dough by hand and rolling it out by machine. Let's face it, rolling out pasta by hand is not easy. It takes considerable time, patience, and skill; making pasta entirely by machine saves time, but robs us of a first-class product. If we take 10 minutes to knead the dough by hand, we can roll it through the machine in a breeze. I assure you that the end product will be more wonderful.

Cutting the Dough

Once this wonderful sheet of dough has been produced, it must be cut into the shape of your choice. Both electric and hand-cranked machines have two cutting attachments to produce either wide or narrow noodles. The dough can also be cut by hand by simply folding the sheet of dough loosely, jelly roll style, and cutting it horizontally with a sharp knife, into the noodles of your choice.

In my opinion, a ravioli attachment is not necessary, unless you love gadgets. Once you have developed your pasta-making skill, not only ravioli, but also ravioloni, tortelli, lasagne, and fettuccine can be made in no time at all.

What About Extrusion Machines?

There are some kitchen appliances that have become essential for most of us. For me they are: a food processor, large mixer, and an electric rolling pasta machine. If the new extruders were making superlative pasta, better than homemade or factory-made, I probably would have one sitting on my counter. It doesn't make sense to me to buy a machine only because it makes "fresh" pasta. The key question here should be not whether the pasta is "fresh" but whether it is "good." To my mind, the extruders simply do not produce a first-rate product.

Cooking Pasta

My mother used to say "Pasta does not wait for anyone," and she was right! Precooked pasta, that sits with or without a sauce, becomes limp and cannot be reheated without becoming overcooked. Pasta, except that being used in salads, should always be cooked at the last moment.

For 1 pound of pasta you will need approximately 5 quarts of water. The large amount of water is critical to ensure even cooking and to prevent some of the pasta from sticking together. Stir the pasta a few times as it cooks. The amount of time needed to cook pasta depends on the type and shape: Fresh, homemade pasta, such as noodles, cooks virtually in a matter of seconds. Fresh stuffed pasta generally needs a little longer cooking, since it has a double thickness.

Factory-made pasta might cook within 5 to 12 minutes, depending on the brand and the shape of pasta you choose. The best and safest way is to taste as you go along. Make sure *not* to overcook your pasta. "Al dente" is a term that has been used, abused, and misspelled. However, it is the perfect definition for how pasta should taste: "tender but firm to the bite." As soon as the pasta is cooked and drained, put it in a warm bowl with its sauce and serve at once.

Should Pasta Be Rinsed?

One of my students once said to me "I rinse my pasta to get rid of the excessive starch (?)" It seems to me that, if one is afraid of starch, one should forget about eating pasta. Another student said, "I rinse my pasta because it sticks together." If you cook it with plenty of water it won't stick.

Do not rinse your pasta unless you are planning to use it in a salad, *or* you plan to stuff it and bake it (such as lasagne, canelloni, or stuffed pasta roll). These are the only instances when pasta is quickly precooked, rinsed to stop the cooking, and dried before it is stuffed and baked.

How Much Pasta to Serve?

One pound of pasta will serve 4 to 6 as a first course. For 4, the portions will be generous; for 6, the portions will be moderate.

In Italy, pasta is always served as a first course, especially at a formal dinner, logically following the "antipasti." In this case, portions should be moderate, as other courses will follow. However, these rules are much more relaxed at home and often a nice plate of pasta topped by a multiingredient sauce can become the whole meal. Pasta is *never* served as a side dish.

Storing Homemade Pasta

Homemade noodles, properly dried, can be kept for several weeks. Prepare your noodles, put them in bundles on a kitchen towel, and leave them to dry, uncovered, for 24 hours. Transfer the noodles to plastic bags or large jars and store them in your pantry just like any ordinary dried pasta. They will keep well for 3 to 4 weeks.

Generally, stuffed pasta does not keep very long. Often the filling for stuffed pasta is very moist and, if left to stand, will make the dough soggy. Ideally, stuffed pasta should be used the same day it is made. Personally I never freeze stuffed pasta, because freezing changes its texture and consistency. Whenever possible, stuffed pasta should be used the day it is made and as promptly as possible. If necessary, it will keep in the refrigerator, covered with a kitchen towel for one day more.

Pasta Fads

Italians have been making and eating pasta for centuries and yet "colored" pasta—with the exception of spinach pasta and, on occasion, beet pasta—is almost nonexistent in Italy. Perhaps we are dull! Or, perhaps, we take the role of pasta very seriously. Colored pasta might be fun to look at, but do we really "yearn" for carrot or cinnamon pasta when we are hungry? Perhaps the innovators who, striving for originality, produce multicolored pasta forget that it is the neutrality of pasta that makes it the best vehicle for sauces. What sauce could we put on cinnamon pasta? And should we eat cinnamon pasta as a first course or as a dessert? I *know* that "plain" pasta will be around for years to come; I am not so sure, however, about colored pasta.

Your Food Processor and Modern Italian Cooking

When the first food processor appeared on the market several years ago, a friend of mine who had every imaginable gadget in her kitchen asked me why, with all the cooking I was doing, I still didn't own one. With a certain amount of superiority, I told her that I could work with my knife quite fast and didn't need a new toy on my countertop. My snobbish attitude deflated instantly the first time I had a chance to try out one of these machines. I might have been snobbish, but I was not dumb. So, the same day I went out and bought myself a lovely food processor.

I don't have to convince anyone about the virtues of the food processor. We all know that it slices and chops at high speed, that it kneads, makes pastry dough, and purées with efficiency. It also can help us save money, because leftover meats can be turned into tasty morsels, forgotten vegetables

33

into creamy soups, old bread into bread crumbs, and ripe fruit into healthy, refreshing drinks.

Thanks to the food processor, we can be more efficient in the kitchen because we can do so much more in considerably less time. Without my food processor, I could not possibly make all those batches of pesto every year, or the sauce for vitello tonnato, or the spur-of-the-moment green sauce for boiled meats. Without my food processor, I could never start a soup at 6 o'clock and hope to have it ready for dinner in an hour.

When I teach my classes these days, after demonstrating the art of pasta making by hand, I also show how to knead the dough in the food processor, mainly because I am asked to do so. Years ago I would have fainted at the idea of pasta made with a food processor. Even though it is definitely not my first choice, I must admit, however, that the food processor has introduced homemade pasta to people who would never have made it by hand.

Food processors have become standard items even in Italian kitchens. Both my sister and my sister-in-law in Bologna have processors and use them regularly.

In this book, you will find recipes for pasta made by hand and by food processor. Using the food processor is an option in many other recipes—piecrusts, pizza dough, sauces, soups, and even in old classic dessert recipes such as Struffoli (page 284). Every time that I was able to retain the quality and the texture of the dish, I have given the option to use a food processor.

I am sure that women of one or two generations ago would have loved to have some of the "options" we have today.

About Some Basic Ingredients and Methods

The secret of "authentic" ethnic cooking is fidelity to its ingredients.

Once, while I was in Boston promoting my first book, *Northern Italian Cooking*, on a local television show, the host of the show told me about an Italian restaurant in the area that was making the ultimate, very best Fettuccine all'Alfredo. When I asked him how the dish was prepared he said, "But of course, with butter, cream, and cream cheese." Possibly those fettuccine were as outstanding as he professed they were. But they were Fettuccine alla Boston, not the authentic all'Alfredo.

Not so long ago, many Italian ingredients were virtually unavailable in this country. Fortunately, this is not the case anymore. So, let's start cooking Italian food with Italian ingredients. Only through a precise process will you be able to understand the soul of Italian food; then you can begin to relax, to experiment, and to fully enjoy your creations.

Tomatoes

How often do we see in the market meaty, red, fragrantly ripe tomatoes? We all know the answer. No wonder, then, that when we try to duplicate a sauce we had in Italy, we invariably find it flat and lacking in substance. Because we cannot all grow our own tomatoes and hand-pick them when they are perfectly ripe, we must rely on good-quality imported tomatoes. The best Italian canned tomatoes come from San Marzano in southern Italy. These tomatoes are deep red, ripe, and flavorful. I always keep a large supply in my pantry, for they are excellent and quite handy to have around. (Sometimes after school my 13-year-old daughter, Paola, opens a can of tomatoes, prepares a sauce, and cooks some pasta for herself. What a wonderful snack!)

Garlic

Garlic is widely used in Italy but seldom abused. Many dishes need only a hint of garlic. A clove or two of garlic cooked gently into a stew, will become very sweet and impart to the stew a delicious nonoffensive aroma. With garlic, as with most things in life, the secret is moderation; for the most part, garlic is not used for its own sake but rather because its flavor or the hint of its flavor belongs in a dish. As a general rule, the heartier the dish, the more emphatic is the presence of garlic.

To freshen the breath after eating food that is too spicy or garlicky, munch on some parsley or coffee beans.

Capers

Capers are the unopened buds of nasturtiums that grow wild around the Mediterranean. They come large and small and they are generally preserved in vinegar. These delicious buds are used to flavor pasta sauces, pizza, mixed composed salads, and antipasti. They are thoroughly appetizing. Add a tablespoon of capers and a handful of fresh basil to some fresh tomato chunks and you'll have a delicious, quick pasta sauce.

Funghi Porcini

Porcini are wild Italian mushrooms. These succulent, woodsy mushrooms are one of the glorious elements of Italian gastronomy. Porcini grow under chestnut trees and are abundant in the spring and fall. Perhaps one of the reasons why I choose to take my annual trip to Italy in the fall is because, besides avoiding the hordes of tourists, I am able to eat fresh porcini every day if I choose to. If you have the opportunity to go to Italy in the fall, make sure you taste "Porcini alla Griglia"—fresh porcini dressed with garlic, parsley, and good olive oil—an absolute experience.

Even though fresh porcini can be found in this country by the few who know how to hunt for them, they are not common in local markets. What are available here are dried porcini imported from Italy. These dried mushrooms have a wonderful, intense, and concentrated flavor. When fresh porcini are unavailable, Italians use dried porcini to flavor risotti, sauces, and stews. Dried porcini can be found in Italian markets and specialty food stores. Make sure that the package contains nice, large, meaty pieces of mushrooms. If a dish calls for porcini, do not substitute any other type of mushroom for the porcini or the flavor of the dish will not be authentically Italian.

Rice

Italian rice is short and thick grained. It is the perfect rice for the delicious, unique preparation called risotto. Years ago it was almost impossible to find Italian rice in California or in most other parts of this country. Today, the best and most widely exported grain variety, Arborio, is widely available. Substitute California short-grain pearl rice if Italian rice is available. In a pinch, you can also use a good brand of converted rice. I hope, however, that you will go the extra mile to secure the ingredient that is so vital to a perfect risotto.

Anchovies

Anchovies find their way into many southern Italian dishes, but just as with garlic, anchovies should not be abused. Fresh anchovies are delicious. Canned anchovies, preserved in oil, are generally used as a condiment. A hint of anchovy on a pizza or a few chopped anchovies in a sauce can liven up the flavor of the dish. They are available in tins in supermarkets.

Wine

If a wine is good enough for cooking it is also good enough to drink. Every little ingredient we put into a dish affects its quality, and wine is no different. Therefore, using a little bit of good wine will improve the quality of your dish and of your mood, as you will probably be sipping a little as you cook.

Marsala wine

This wonderful aromatic wine comes from Marsala, Sicily. Most Italian families have a standard supply of Marsala wine in their pantry. A bit of Marsala can turn a veal dish into a delicacy and can enrich and flavor an otherwise plain sauce. Marsala wine comes sweet and dry. Always use dry Marsala for cooking. Of the imported brands, Florio and Pellegrino, both produced in Marsala, are the best. Domestic Marsala is a long-lost relative of the real thing; it should be put at the very back of your pantry and used if nothing else is available.

Vinegar

Use a good, unflavored wine vinegar.

Aceto Balsamico

Balsamic vinegar is synonymous with Modena, a small, lovely city in Emilia-Romagna which dates back to the year 1046. In the sixteenth century, balsamic vinegar was considered so precious that it was often made a part of a legacy in a will.

Balsamic vinegar is made from the boiled-down must of white Trebbiano grapes. It is aged in a series of barrels of different woods and diminishing sizes, all of which give a different fragrance to the vinegar. By law, this vinegar has to be at least ten years old before it can be marketed. The most precious, however, are seventy, eighty, or even ninety years old, extremely expensive and very rare. In Modena, such balsamic vinegar still can be found among some families which have been making it for generations, or it can be obtained through some of the few remaining artisans who still make it for sale. Most of the balsamic vinegar available in this country now is mass-produced. In using it, keep in mind that it varies in strength. The older the vinegar, the more concentrated and aromatic it becomes and the less you need to use.

Broth

Good broth is not only nourishing, but also an important element of Italian cooking. As our sauces are basically only the extension of what we cook, we tend to maximize those pan juices with the addition of some liquid which is quickly brought to a thick consistency over high heat. This liquid could be wine, cream, tomato sauce, or broth. Good broth is also vital to risotto and to innumerable soups. Add a ladle of broth to a stew or a braised meat and it will be enriched with additional flavor.

In the chapter "Some Basic Recipes," you will find a Meat Broth which is made with scraps of mixed meats and bones. The variation of this dish also shows you how to prepare a chicken broth, which I like to use to cook my risotto as well as in making soup. Another, richer and more intensely flavored broth can be produced with several cuts of first-quality meats. This broth is the direct result of preparing the classic Bollito Misto (see page 218).

Canned Broth

Because we cannot prepare homemade broth on the spur of the moment, it is useful to keep a certain amount of good canned broth in the pantry. Keep in mind that it varies in strength, depending on the brand. Even more important, some canned broth is also quite salty and often it should be diluted with water; certainly, salt should not be added to the dish until after the broth has been incorporated.

Pork Products

Prosciutto

Prosciutto is unsmoked, salted, and air-cured ham. The best and sweetest pro-

sciutto is Parma ham, which is cured in the nearby hilly town of Langhirano. This prosciutto, aged a minimum of one year, is deliciously sweet. It is widely used in Italian cooking, as well as served as an appetizer with ripe figs or cantaloupe. Unfortunately, Italian prosciutto cannot be imported into this country. Most American prosciutto is not aged long enough, is saltier than the Italian product, and is cured with nitrite. In my opinion, the best American-made prosciuttos are Volpi, Daniele, and Citterio.

Pancetta

Pancetta is widely used in Italian cooking, and its flavor is essential to many northern Italian dishes. Pancetta is the same cut of pork as bacon. However, unlike bacon, it is not smoked but cured in salt and spices; it comes rolled up like a salami. Good pancetta should have approximately the same amount of lean and fat meat.

Oil

Olive Oil

Good olive oil, which should have the greenish color and fragrance of olives, comes in three basic grades:

Extra virgin oil, made from olives that are slightly underripe, is produced by using an exclusively physical means (stone crushing and cold pressing). This oil, often made in farmhouses and small estates, has the lowest acidity—under 1.0 percent. Produced without chemical means (rectification), it is the highest-quality and most flavorful olive oil.

Virgin olive oil, made from olives that are riper than those used in extra virgin oil, is produced in the same manner as extra virgin olive oil. It has a slightly higher acidity, which can be up to 4.0 percent.

Pure olive oil is the most common grade. It is rectified (deodorized, deacidified, and decolorized by chemical means) and contains only olive oil, without the blending of seed oil, hence the name "pure." Highly advertised brands, available in most supermarkets, generally fall in the category of "pure olive oil."

I generally use extra virgin olive oil for salads and for dishes where the flavor of the oil is essential, and pure olive oil for dishes where an emphatic olive oil flavor is not needed. Some of the best Italian olive oils come from Tuscany, Umbria, Liguria, and Puglia. Each of these regions produces oils that have different flavor characteristics. Experiment and you may find that you like to keep a few types on hand for different dishes. Store olive oil in a tightly sealed bottle (not plastic) and place it in the coolest, darkest part of your pantry—do not refrigerate it. Once opened, the oil should keep well for 2 to 3 months.

Oil for Frying

Use any light-flavored vegetable oil. My preference is for corn or peanut oil. For an olive flavor, some olive oil can be added to the pan or to the finished dish.

Butter

Italians use unsalted butter, which is, in fact, the only kind available; more unsalted butter is consumed in the North than in the South. Unsalted butter can be found in supermarkets, though you might have to look in the freezer section.

Cheeses

Parmigiano-Reggiano

A champion among cheeses, Parmigiano-Reggiano is, unquestionably, the finest and most widely used cheese of Italy. Italian cooking would be greatly handicapped without parmigiano. This noble cheese gets into innumerable dishes. Pasta, rich dishes, and soups are rarely served without it. Parmigiano is also an active and vital ingredient in savory pies, frittatas, appetizers, and even salads. As a table cheese, it is second to none. A chunk of perfectly aged Parmigiano-Reggiano paired with ripe pears, figs, or grapes is simply outstanding.

Genuine Parmigiano-Reggiano is made with milk produced between the first of April and the eleventh of November only in the provinces of Parma, Reggio, Modena, Mantua, and Bologna. This superlative cheese, made by hand by artisan cheese makers, follows a cheese-making tradition that has remained unaltered for seven centuries. In all, 1,200 cheese-making dairies produce the cheese, a figure that is the proof of individual craftsmanship that goes into the making of Parmigiano-Reggiano.

Parmigiano-Reggiano is made under very strict regulations and does not contain any artificial additives. It has a long, natural method of maturation under constant supervision and must age a minimum of eighteen months before it is sold.

When buying parmigiano, look for the words "Parmigiano-Reggiano" etched in tiny dots on the rind of the cheese. The cheese should be straw yellow, crumbly, and moist inside. It is expensive, but a little goes a long way. Buy a piece and grate it as needed. Wrap the parmigiano in foil and store it in the refrigerator. If the cheese dries out a little, wrap it in a piece of damp cheesecloth and leave it in the coolest part of your refrigerator. Then remove the cloth and wrap the cheese in foil. As Parmigiano-Reggiano is vital to authentic Italian cooking, do not substitute it for the domestic parmigiano or the grated "parmesan" sold in jars in supermarkets. Parmigiano-Reggiano is now readily available in most Italian markets as well as in gourmet markets across the country.

Parmigiano should always be grated, never shredded. Use a hand grater or grate in the food processor using a metal blade.

Parmigiano-Reggiano is a low-fat cheese with a high-protein content. Figures from the Consortium of Parmigiano-Reggiano offer some interesting comparisons. One hundred grams of Parmigiano-Reggiano corresponds in protein content to, approximately, any one of the following:

    160 grams of raw ham
    206 grams of beef
    214 grams of pork
    300 grams of trout
    914 grams of milk
    5 eggs

Grana Padana

Grana Padana is similar to Parmigiano-Reggiano; it is produced near, but outside, the restricted area. It is a good substitute.

Gorgonzola

This is a lovely blue-veined cheese that comes from Lombardy. A cow's milk cheese, gorgonzola is injected in its early stage with a mold. During its maturation, the cheese is pricked so that air can enter the cheese and speed up the development of the mold. A mature gorgonzola is about 5 to 6 months old with a pungent, sharp taste. Younger, milder, and sweeter gorgonzola is now also available. Gorgonzola has a high fat content; it is delicious as a table cheese and is also used more and more frequently in cooking, especially for creamy, delicate pasta sauces.

Mozzarella

The best mozzarella is made from the curd of water buffalo. It is generally sold in water and is quite perishable. Buffalo mozzarella imported from Italy is now more easily available than in the past; it can be found in Italian and specialty food stores across the country. Cow's milk mozzarella can also be quite good. In the Italian neighborhoods of some of the larger cities, good, locally made cow's milk mozzarella is now available. Check your local Italian grocers. However, steer away from the factory-made product on the supermarket shelves; it is a distant, unhappy relative of the real thing.

Ricotta

Ricotta, made from whey, can be an absolute treat when properly made and fresh. Unfortunately, what we can find in supermarkets still leaves a lot to be desired. This cheese byproduct is used extensively in Italian cooking, from a topping for pasta to luscious desserts. I love to eat good fresh ricotta simply sprinkled with a bit of sugar. Ricotta is also very perishable. Again, check your local Italian markets for the fresh product. Today, we can find some locally made products that are a definite improvement over mass-produced ricotta that was available only a few years ago.

Pecorino

Pecorino is made from sheep's milk. This cheese varies greatly in taste and texture, depending on the area where it is made. Tuscany makes outstanding pecorino, mild and tender, a wonderful table cheese to eat at the end of a meal. The Italian pecorino we are familiar with in this country is Pecorino Romano, a sharp, assertive hard cheese from Rome, which is used primarily to be grated over hearty southern Italian dishes.

Fontina

This tender, mild cheese is made in Val d'Aosta in Piedmont, in the northwest corner of Italy. Italian fontina is much milder and more delicate than Danish fontina. This cheese is used considerably in Italian cooking because of its soft, melting quality. It is also a superlative table cheese.

Herbs

The use of herbs in Italian cooking goes beyond the whims of fashion. Since ancient times, herbs have been widely used by those who live amidst nature. There is no doubt that a touch of fresh herbs can significantly improve a dish. Be cautious, however, in the use of dried herbs: Some might be too assertive and others might lack aroma and be musty and old.

To fully appreciate the taste of fresh herbs, add them to a dish only at the last moment and do not go overboard: The moderate use of herbs will enhance a dish; too much will overpower it.

Basil

One of the most popular herbs, widely used especially in the cooking of Liguria. Basil's sweet, pungent taste can enrich a dish with the fragrance and perfume of summer. Fresh basil can be preserved between layers of coarse salt in tightly sealed jars—the color will fade but the aroma will remain—or in olive oil. I generally chop the basil, put it in a jar, and cover it with oil. Then I use it when I need a bit of basil taste. I personally do not like dried basil, for I find it flavorless.

Basil can be cut up or chopped and kept in olive oil, ready to use whenever needed in soups, salads, sauces, and in preparing meat and fish.

Rosemary

This wonderful aromatic herb is perfect for roasted meats and fowls, for marinades and savory breads. Dried rosemary is perfectly acceptable.

Sage

Sage is great for game cooking, savory breads, marinades, and roasted potatoes (roasted potatoes with fresh sage and garlic are simply tantalizing). Use dry sage sparingly because its flavor can be overwhelmingly strong.

Oregano

Oregano is as popular in southern Italian cooking as basil is in the North. Fresh oregano is mild and sweet and beautifully aromatic. It can impart a delicious flavor to fresh tomato sauces. Use dry oregano in moderation.

Parsley

Perhaps because parsley seems to be such an intricate part of the vegetable section of supermarkets, we tend to forget that parsley is in reality an herb used regularly in Italian cooking. If possible, use the flat-leafed Italian parsley which has a stronger fragrance than curly parsley. Parsley is a good source of vitamins A and C and also iron.

Some Basic Recipes and Sauces

This is a short chapter of recipes basic to good, everyday Italian home cooking. Here are the tomato sauces for pasta dishes, the broths that form the backbone of endless soups, and the simple pan sauces typically served with meat, fish, or poultry. Finally, I have a recipe for pastry dough that can be used for every type of pie and tart, sweet or savory.

This collection is deceptively small, but well worth mastering, for it barely hints at the endless ways these recipes can be incorporated into an imaginative home cook's repertoire.

Basic Homemade Meat Broth

For me, homemade meat broth is essential to everyday cooking and the basis of many good soups. A good, basic meat broth can be prepared with a variety of bones and meat scraps along with some vegetables for added flavor. The best bones for broth should come from beef, chicken, and veal and so should the scraps of meat. In Italy, we don't use lamb or pork in broth because of their aggressive flavor. This broth simmers gently for 2½ to 3 hours in order to extract every bit of flavor from the bones and scraps of meat. Sometimes I add a whole chicken to the pot to increase the flavor of the broth. (The chicken is then eaten as a second course with some mashed potatoes or a green sauce.) When I use the chicken I try to remove as much fat as possible from the broth before using it.

If time allows, I prepare the broth a day ahead, strain it, and then refrigerate it for several hours or overnight. The day after, I remove all the fat that has solidified on the surface and I am left with a flavorful, fat-free broth for soups, risotti, and as an added ingredient to many recipes. (The chicken can be reheated in the broth.) As you accumulate scraps of meat, bones of chickens, and so forth, freeze them and then on the first rainy day—or when your child develops a cold—you can promptly and inexpensively prepare a wonderful, aromatic broth from scratch.

*3½ to 4 pounds bones and meat scraps
   from beef, chicken, and veal*
A few parsley sprigs
2 carrots, cut into chunks
2 celery stalks, cut into chunks
1 small onion, quartered
1 ripe tomato, quartered
Salt (optional)

MAKES APPROXIMATELY 2½ QUARTS OF
   BROTH

Put all the ingredients, except salt, in a large stockpot. Cover them with cold water (the water should be 2 or 3 inches above the bones, meat, and vegetables). Cover the stockpot and bring the water to a gentle boil. Lower the heat and simmer gently for 2½ to 3 hours. During the first 10 minutes of simmering, skim the scum that comes to the surface of the liquid. Add salt to taste during the last few minutes of cooking.

Strain the broth and use it while hot, or cool it completely before refrigerating or freezing it.

Basic Chicken Broth

Follow the proportions and instructions for the Basic Meat Broth recipe. After the broth has simmered for about 1½ hours, add a whole, plump 3- to 3½-pound chicken to the stockpot. Add enough water to cover the chicken completely and simmer for 1 to 1½ hours longer. Use the broth while hot or cool it and refrigerate it. Serve the chicken hot with mashed potatoes or a Salsa Verde (page 47).

Pasta Frolla

Sweet Pie Pastry (Short Pastry)

This is a simple, but very good dough to use for sweet tarts. Omit the sugar and add a pinch of salt when using it for savory pies.

In a medium-size bowl or in the bowl of a food processor fitted with a metal blade, mix the flour and butter until crumbly. Add the egg, sugar, and wine. Mix until the dough is gathered all around the blade before it turns into a ball. If you are making the dough by hand, knead very briefly, just enough to make it into a ball.

Put the dough on a work surface and divide it into 2 balls; wrap each ball separately in aluminum foil and refrigerate or freeze until ready to use.

2 cups all-purpose unbleached flour
4 ounces plus 1 tablespoon unsalted butter at room temperature for hand mixing, or cold and in small pieces for a food processor
1 large egg
1 tablespoon sugar
2 to 3 tablespoons chilled white wine or cold water

MAKES ENOUGH DOUGH FOR TWO 10-INCH TART PANS WITH REMOVABLE BOTTOMS

When you prepare the crust for a pie, double or triple the amount you need and freeze what you don't need. It will come in handy when you want to prepare a dessert on the spur of the moment.

Besciamella

Basic White Sauce

Besciamella or balsamella is a basic white sauce that Italians claim was their own long before it was called béchamel by the French. As I am not a food historian, I leave the dispute to the more scholarly-inclined. I am glad, however, that someone invented this lovely, versatile sauce, which is essential to many Italian dishes.

3 cups milk
4 tablespoons unsalted butter
5 tablespoons all-purpose unbleached flour
Salt to taste

MAKES APPROXIMATELY 2½ CUPS

Heat the milk in a saucepan over low heat until bubbles appear around the side of the pan. Melt the butter in a medium-size saucepan. When the butter foams, stir in the flour. Lower the heat and stir the mixture with a wire whisk. Cook for a few minutes, without letting the flour turn brown.

Remove the saucepan from the heat and add milk all at once. Whisk energetically to prevent lumps. Put the saucepan back over low heat, season the mixture with salt, and cook gently for 3 to 5 minutes, whisking constantly until the sauce has a medium-thick consistency.

If not using immediately, cover the sauce with a piece of buttered wax paper. Leave at room temperature until ready to use. Besciamella can also be refrigerated. When you are ready to serve, heat the sauce over low heat. If it seems too thick, add a bit of milk and stir to bring it back to the original, smooth consistency.

Besciamella can also be seasoned with some ground nutmeg or parmigiano or enriched with the addition of 1 or 2 egg yolks. (To add the egg yolks, remove the sauce from the heat and cool it slightly. Then whisk in 2 slightly beaten egg yolks until they are well incorporated.

Salsa Verde

Piquant Green Sauce

Salsa Verde is the perfect accompaniment to Bollito Misto (page 218). Besides the basic ingredients that are always part of this sauce, I also add a diced sweet red or yellow pepper whenever possible: The sweetness blends beautifully with the piquancy of the sauce. Salsa Verde is also delicious served with steamed or simply baked fish. In this case, substitute lemon juice for the vinegar. As the sauce is quite flavorful and is served as a condiment, use only 1 to 2 tablespoons for each serving. Salsa Verde keeps well in the refrigerator for about a week if stored in a tightly covered container.

Put the parsley, garlic, anchovies, and capers in the bowl of a food processor fitted with a metal blade. Process until smooth. Add the sweet pepper, salt and pepper, vinegar, and sugar and process again, turning the machine on and off. The peppers should be finely diced, but not puréed. Add the oil and process briefly to incorporate it. Taste and adjust the seasoning. Transfer to a bowl, cover, and refrigerate until ready to use. Serve at room temperature.

2 cups loosely packed fresh parsley leaves
2 garlic cloves
2 flat anchovy fillets
2 tablespoons rinsed and dried capers
1 sweet yellow or red pepper, cut into
*   pieces*
Salt and freshly ground black pepper
2 tablespoons good red wine vinegar
1 teaspoon sugar
½ cup olive oil

MAKES ABOUT ¾ CUP SAUCE

Salse Semplici di Pomodoro

Four Simple Tomato Sauces

In some parts of this country people still hold the notion that Italian to-mato sauces should be thick, pasty, and spicy. Nothing could be farther from the truth. With the exception of sauces that result from braising meats, most tomato sauces are cooked for only a short time, so that they can retain the essence and freshness of tomatoes. A good, basic tomato sauce is essential to most Italian kitchens. Often, ingredients such as onions, anchovies, garlic, capers, and herbs are added, depending on the personal preference of the cook. To produce a good tomato sauce we need, first and foremost, good, ripe juicy tomatoes. During the summer months, when tomatoes are at their best, scan your local market for the best tomatoes you can find. Look first for plum tomatoes or any other variety of tomatoes that are deep red in color and soft to the touch. When such tomatoes are nowhere to be seen, we must then rely on a good brand of canned tomatoes. San Marzano tomatoes are, in my opinion, the best imported Italian tomatoes.

Here we have three variations of a basic tomato sauce: Two are made with fresh tomatoes and one with canned tomatoes. I have also included my own recipe for the ambitious cook who wants to take advantage of summer's bounty and put up a winter's worth of sauce. They are all extremely simple to prepare, but merely dress a plate of pasta with one and you'll be instantly gratified.

Double or triple any sauce for pasta that can be frozen. You will be happy to have it when you are pressed for time.

Chunky Fresh Tomato Sauce Using Fresh Tomatoes

Serve over any type of factory-made pasta, such as spaghetti or bucatini or short shapes (ziti, penne, etc.).

Bring a large saucepan of water to a boil. Add tomatoes. Cook for 30 to 40 seconds, or until tomato skin begins to split. Transfer the tomatoes to a bowl of cold water. Peel, seed, and dice tomatoes as soon as you can handle them. Put the tomato pieces into a sieve over a bowl to drain off some of the excess juices. Leave for 10 minutes.

Heat the oil in a medium-size skillet or saucepan (the wider the surface of the skillet, the faster the moisture of the tomatoes will evaporate). Add the garlic and sauté gently until the garlic begins to color. Add the tomatoes and season with salt and pepper. Cook over high heat, uncovered, for 7 to 8 minutes, or until the tomatoes lose their excessive watery juices. Stir in the parsley.

6 large juicy ripe tomatoes
4 tablespoons olive oil
2 garlic cloves, finely chopped
Salt and freshly ground black pepper
1 tablespoon chopped fresh parsley leaves, or a handful of fresh basil leaves, cut into pieces

SERVES 4

Smooth Tomato Sauce Using Fresh Tomatoes

This fragrant fresh tomato sauce can be served over spaghetti, spaghettini, or homemade noodles. Or, with the addition of a few tablespoons of cream and 2 additional minutes of cooking, this is an ideal sauce for any stuffed shape, such as tortellini or ravioli.

Boil the tomatoes as directed in Chunky Fresh Tomato Sauce. Peel and seed the tomatoes and cut them into large pieces. Put the tomato pieces into a sieve over a bowl to drain off some of the excess juices. Purée the tomatoes through a food mill or a sieve.

Heat the oil in a medium-size skillet or saucepan together with the garlic. Discard the garlic when it turns golden brown. Add the tomatoes and season with salt and pepper. Cook over medium heat, uncovered, for 10 to 12 minutes, or until sauce has a medium-thick consistency.

6 large juicy ripe tomatoes
2 tablespoons olive oil
2 tablespoons unsalted butter
1 garlic clove
Salt and freshly ground black pepper

SERVES 4

Basic Simple Tomato Sauce Using Canned Tomatoes

You have the good canned tomatoes from San Marzano if you are really fortunate in your pantry. You are tired and hungry. This is what a lot of Italian women in your situation would do.

1 28-ounce can imported Italian plum tomatoes with their juices
4 tablespoons olive oil
2 garlic cloves, finely chopped
3 anchovy fillets, chopped
Salt and freshly ground black pepper
1 tablespoon chopped fresh parsley leaves

SERVES 4 TO 6

Put the tomatoes through a strainer or a food mill to remove the seeds.

Heat the oil in a medium-size skillet or saucepan. Add the garlic and anchovies. Sauté over medium heat until the garlic begins to color. Add the tomatoes and season with salt and pepper. Cook over medium heat, uncovered, 15 to 20 minutes. Stir in the parsley. Taste and adjust the seasoning. Serve over spaghetti, spaghettini, linguine, or bucatini.

La Mia Salsa di Pomodoro

My Own Tomato Sauce

Last summer, at the invitation of a friend whose husband is a tomato grower, I went to pick tomatoes. Clusters and clusters of beautifully ripe tomatoes were sprawled over acres and acres of sun-drenched land. It was a magnificent sight. Aided by my youngest daughter Paola, and by my friend Bernice, we started picking and selecting the most beautiful ones, marveling at the sight of such glorious abundance. We picked euphorically for more than 2 hours, filled 5 large boxes, and then struggled to pick up the heavy boxes and put them in the trunk of my car. We arrived home dirty but exhilarated. Then it occurred to me that I had to do something with all those tomatoes . . . so I decided to make a sauce and can it. For two and a half days, patiently and diligently I washed and cut up about 200 pounds of tomatoes, cooked them, strained them, bottled and sterilized the jars. Then exhausted, I sat down, looked at the 40 quarts of tomato sauce I had made, looked at the incredible mess that my kitchen was, and didn't know whether to cry or rejoice.

Now I am enjoying the result of all that work and so are all my friends. This is the recipe, in case you, too, have a moment of madness in which you decide to pick 200 pounds of perfectly sun-ripened tomatoes.

Wash and dry the tomatoes and cut them into large chunks. Put the chunks into a large stockpot. Add the salt, onion, celery, and basil leaves, if using. Bring the sauce to a boil. Cook over medium heat, uncovered, for 15 to 20 minutes. Put the tomatoes through a food mill and then return them to the pot. Cook for 10 minutes longer.

Wash your canning jars in your dishwasher (this way they will also be sterilized) and your lids and bands in a pot of boiling water.

Fill each jar with tomato sauce leaving about ½ inch of headspace at the top of each jar. Place a few basil leaves into each jar and secure the jar with the lid.

Place the jars on the rack of a canner. Fill the canner halfway with water and bring the water to a slow simmer. Lift the rack with the jars into the simmering water. Add more water, if necessary, to cover jars completely. Cover the canner and boil gently for 20 to 25 minutes.

Remove jars with canner's tongs and place them on a counter covered with kitchen towels. Let the jars cool completely overnight. When cooled, test the lids: Press the center of the lid. If it stays firm and tight, store the jars in the coolest and darkest part of your pantry or cellar. If the lid springs back at your touch, it means the jars were not properly sealed. Put them in the refrigerator and use the sauce within a week.

Equipment needed for canning: Mason jars with two-part lids; a boiling water canner.

10 pounds very ripe tomatoes
1 tablespoon salt
1 large onion, sliced
1 celery stalk, cut into small pieces
½ cup loosely packed fresh basil leves (optional)
Additional basil for the jars

MAKES 8 TO 10 CUPS OF SAUCE

Food That I Crave in Spring and Summer

The joy and delight of summer eating can be summarized in two words: freshness and simplicity.

The same passion for food that has given us hearty comfort in winter is still with us. But just as a person sheds layers of clothing as the weather gets warmer, our cravings for food take on a new dimension. Forgotten are the steaming polentas and the winter stews. When it gets hot we go outdoors and smell and breathe the fresh air; we reach for fresh fruit and wait expectantly for the new produce of the soil. The way we eat is simpler, the food we cook is fresher, often cooked out-of-doors. Our entertaining becomes less formal: buffet-style parties prevail over sit-down dinners. We want to look good and feel fit. Still, we also want to eat well.

In spring and summer food tastes better outdoors, or so it seems. Perhaps it is not by chance that so many restaurants and trattorias in Italy have outdoor dining, and the simplest meals seem special when shared in the garden or on the patio or terrace, or on a beach or under a tree.

For me one of the pleasures of summer is to organize a day of tennis matches with good friends and then end the day at my house over wonderfully uncomplicated good food, served informally outdoors.

Another joy of summer is the abundance of its harvest. I become totally mesmerized at the sight of the summer bounty. Sweet yellow and red peppers, fresh asparagus and sweet peas, sweet tender corn, young squash, small eggplants, tender new potatoes, and juicy ripe tomatoes. And then there is the abundance of fruit. The best way to enjoy these summer treats is to cook them as simply as possible. In the Italian style, vegetables are seldom covered with sauces. We want to bite into a tomato and taste all of its juicy ripeness. Perhaps more than any other season, summer celebrates ingredients, and this is the essence of fine Italian cooking. For instance, summertime sauces for pasta employ a rich variety of vegetables, most of them quick to prepare, fresh, and healthy, qualities that are becoming more and more important to the modern Italian cook. There is no doubt that pasta is an Italian treasure. It comes in myriads of shapes or sizes and it can be prepared literally in thousands of different ways. Now that we know that pasta is good for us, if it is eaten judiciously and with moderate amounts of sauce, we can enjoy it without guilt.

Another wonderful aspect of summer eating is the pleasure of eating cold dishes. Appetizingly refreshing, these cold dishes *must* be prepared ahead of time, which allows the cook greater freedom.

Also, in this section you will find several grilled dishes, but this is not because I want to follow a trend. Historically, grilling and cooking on an open spit is very much Italian. It was, and still is, one of the purest and oldest expressions of Italian cooking. Fishermen have always grilled their prize catch; the shepherds of Sicily and Sardinia still cook their suckling pigs, kids, and lamb on a spit next to an open fire and their fish and other meats on a grill. Skewered grilled meats and fish are as popular today as they were years ago. Innumerable countryside restaurants perpetuate the old tradition of cooking on a spit, and restaurants employ the use of grills constantly to satisfy the demand for lighter, simpler food. Tuscan cooking would not be what it is without all those wonderful aromatic grilled dishes.

In this section you will also find seafood salads, tasty appetizers, aromatic risotti, easy elegant dishes, great summer pasta, and tasty uncomplicated desserts.

Many of the recipes have been simplified so that you can enjoy an Italian feast with a minimum amount of work. I have supplied the recipes and the ideas. Now, for great Italian eating, I hope you will supply the exuberance and yearning for good food as well as a good appetite.

Appetizers

Mozzarella Fritta con Salsa di Pomodoro Estiva

Deep-Fried Mozzarella with Herbed Tomato–Anchovy Sauce

In this tasty appetizer, slices of mozzarella are dipped in eggs, coated with a bread crumb–parmigiano mixture and deep-fried. They are served piping hot and crisp with a dot of herbed tomato–anchovy sauce. Take care to coat the mozzarella slices thoroughly with bread crumbs or the cheese will melt out and stick to pan. And make sure your oil is very hot (375 degrees) for a quick-cooking crisp coating.

Use imported Italian canned tomatoes when fresh tomatoes are not at their best.

To prepare the tomato sauce, bring a large saucepan two-thirds full of water to a boil. Add the tomatoes. Boil gently until skins begin to split, no more than 2 minutes. Transfer the tomatoes to a bowl of cold water and peel them. Cut the tomatoes in half horizontally and remove the seeds. Cut tomatoes into chunks and purée through a food mill or in a food processor.

Heat the oil in a medium-size skillet. Add the garlic and anchovies. Cook gently for about 1 minute. Before the garlic begins to color, add the tomatoes and season with salt and pepper. Cook, uncovered, for 10 to 12 minutes. Stir in the oregano. Keep warm over very low heat while you prepare mozzarella.

Cut the mozzarella into ½-inch-thick slices. In a shallow dish, beat the eggs and salt and pepper. Put the bread crumbs in another shallow dish. Add the parmigiano and mix to combine.

Dip the mozzarella slices into the beaten eggs. Coat well with the bread crumbs, pressing the crumbs with the palm of your hand. Put the coated slices on a platter and refrigerate for 10 to 15 minutes.

Pour oil into a skillet to a depth of 2 inches. Heat the oil. Test the oil by dropping in a bit of bread; if it sizzles and turns golden right away, the oil is hot enough for frying. Use a slotted spoon to lower the mozzarella into the hot oil one slice at a time. Fry only a few slices at one time. When the slices are golden, turn and cook on the other side. Transfer to paper towels. Arrange the slices on individual serving dishes. Dribble a dot of herbed tomato sauce over each slice and serve at once.

For the Herbed Tomato-Anchovy Sauce

4 large juicy ripe tomatoes
2 tablespoons olive oil
1 garlic clove, finely chopped
2 anchovy fillets, finely chopped
Salt and freshly ground black pepper
⅓ cup loosely packed fresh oregano leaves, basil leaves cut into pieces, or 1 tablespoon chopped fresh parsley leaves

For the Mozzarella

1 pound mozzarella
2 large eggs
Salt and freshly ground black pepper
2 cups dry unseasoned bread crumbs
½ cup freshly grated parmigiano
Frying oil

SERVES 4

Crostini Appetitosi

Crostini with Mozzarella, Tomatoes, and Herbs

A great way to start an informal meal. These crostini are so appetizing that the only difficulty you'll have will be to stop eating them. They can be prepared in a matter of minutes and are delicious whether mozzarella or fontina is used.

1 baguette Italian or French bread
4 juicy ripe tomatoes, peeled and seeded
  (page 55)
1 tablespoon olive oil
2 tablespoons rinsed and dried capers
2 anchovy fillets, diced
¼ cup roughly chopped fresh oregano, basil
  or parsley leaves
Salt and freshly ground black pepper
¼ pound mozzarella or imported Italian
  fontina, sliced

SERVES 4 TO 6

Cut the bread into ½-inch-thick slices. Cut the peeled and seeded tomatoes into rough strips. Put the tomato strips in a strainer over a bowl to drain off the excess juices. (Reserve the juices for soups or sauces, if you wish.) Preheat the broiler. Put the tomato pulp in a bowl. Add the olive oil, capers, anchovies, and oregano. Season lightly with salt and pepper and mix gently.

Cover bread slices with thin slices of mozzarella. Top the cheese with some tomato mixture. Place the crostini on a lightly oiled broiler pan and place the pan under the broiler about 4 inches from the heat source. Broil until the cheese has melted. Serve hot.

Crostini ai Pomodori Freschi e Pomodori Secchi

Crostini with Fresh and Sun-Dried Tomatoes

The crostini here have a somewhat classic topping, but with the addition of sun-dried tomatoes which are now available in many Italian markets. However, if you have to go fifty miles out of your way to obtain sun-dried tomatoes, simply forget about them and enjoy these tasty appetizers in their original state.

Peel and seed the tomatoes following the instructions on page 55. Chop the tomatoes coarsely. Put the tomato pieces in a colander and put the colander over a bowl to drain off the excess juices. The reserved juices can be used for sauces and soups.

Heat the oil in a medium-size skillet. Add the garlic and anchovies. Stir and cook for a few minutes, until the garlic begins to change color. Add the chopped fresh tomatoes and chopped sun-dried tomatoes. Cook over high heat for 5 to 6 minutes, or until the tomatoes have given up their juices. Add the capers and parsley. Cook a few minutes longer. Season with salt and several grindings of pepper. The sauce should now have a medium-thick consistency. Set aside.

Preheat the broiler. Put the bread slices on a broiler pan 4 to 5 inches from the heat source. Broil until golden on both sides. Spoon the tomato topping on each crostino and serve immediately.

Note: The topping for these crostini is equally delicious hot or at room temperature.

Crostini are slices of bread that are broiled, toasted, baked, or fried in butter and topped with a variety of ingredients. Shoppers might stop at midmorning in a café for a capuccino and a crostino. The student in between classes will devour a few. Friends will meet after work for an apéritif and a little treat of crostini. At home, crostini are generally served as appetizers.

In some regions of Italy, such as Tuscany and Lazio, crostini are very traditional. Made from hearty homemade bread slices, they are rubbed with garlic and dribbled with fragrant virgin olive oil. In other regions, truffles, wild mushrooms, gorgonzola, chicken livers, or tomatoes and anchovies are used for toppings. Restaurants and cafés all over Italy have their own versions of crostini.

16 juicy ripe tomatoes
3 tablespoons olive oil, preferably virgin olive oil
3 garlic cloves, finely chopped
2 anchovy fillets, finely chopped
4 to 5 sun-dried tomatoes, roughly chopped
3 tablespoons rinsed and dried capers
3 tablespoons chopped fresh parsley leaves
Salt and freshly ground black pepper
12 thick slices Italian bread, approximately 3 by 3 inches long and ½ inch thick

SERVES 6 TO 8

Crostini con Cape Sante Piccanti

Crostini with Spicy Scallops

In coastal towns and villages crostini are often topped by seafood. One of my favorites is this crostini with spicy scallops, but almost any kind of shellfish can be used for crostini.

This is traditionally a summer dish, but one cold, rainy night not too long ago, my husband and I opted to stay home and relax in front of the television. Because I was quite tired and didn't feel much like cooking, I made a batch of these crostini. We opened a good bottle of Chardonnay, kicked off our shoes, and indulged in some of the simple pleasures of life.

1 pound sea scallops
4 tablespoons olive oil
2 garlic cloves, finely chopped
A small piece of hot red chile pepper,
*   finely chopped*
2 tablespoons chopped fresh parsley leaves
1 cup dry white wine
1 cup canned imported Italian plum toma-
*   toes, strained to remove the seeds*
2 tablespoons seasoned bread crumbs
Salt to taste
Slices of Italian bread

SERVES 6 TO 8 AS AN APPETIZER

If the scallops are quite large, cut them in half or into quarters. Wash them under cold running water and pat them dry with paper towels.

Heat the oil in a large skillet. Add the garlic, hot pepper, and 1 tablespoon of the parsley. Sauté gently for 40 to 50 seconds. Add the scallops and raise the heat. Cook and stir for 1 to 2 minutes. Add ½ cup of the wine. Cook until the wine has evaporated, about 1 minute. Transfer the scallops to a bowl while you finish and reduce the sauce. Add the remaining wine to the skillet together with the tomatoes and bread crumbs. Season with salt. Cook over high heat until the sauce has a medium-thick consistency, about 3 to 4 minutes.

Return the scallops to the skillet. Add the remaining parsley and mix. Taste and adjust the seasoning. Cook for about 30 seconds, or until the scallops are thoroughly coated with the sauce. Serve over slices of broiled Italian bread.

Spuma di Peperoni Rossi con Salsa Fresca di Pomodoro

Red Pepper Mousse with Fresh Uncooked Tomato Sauce

This is a lovely, light appetizer that employs some of summer's nicest vegetables: red peppers, fresh tomatoes, and fragrant basil. My husband, who is not particularly fond of mousses, urges me to make this spuma whenever he sees the first crop of red peppers in our garden.

To prepare the peppers, roast them over an open flame or under a preheated broiler. When the skin is dark brown and blistered all over, transfer the peppers to a plastic bag and secure tightly. Leave the peppers in the bag for 30 minutes, or until they are cool and soft; then remove the skin and seeds. Put the peppers and pepper juices, if any, into a blender or food processor and process until smooth. Put the pepper purée into a bowl and season with salt and a bit of black pepper.

Dissolve the gelatin in ⅓ cup of lukewarm water and stir into peppers. Whip the cream until thick and fold it into the peppers. Cover the bowl and refrigerate for several hours or overnight.

Prepare the tomato sauce: Cut the tomatoes into chunks. Put the tomato chunks into a strainer over a bowl to drain off the excess juices. Put the tomatoes through a food mill and season with salt and pepper. Cover and refrigerate until ready to use.

Thirty minutes before serving, remove the mousse and the tomatoes from the refrigerator to bring them to room temperature. Cover the bottoms of 4 serving dishes lightly with the tomato sauce. Spoon some pepper mousse in the center of the sauce and shape it into a small mound. Garnish with a few fresh basil leaves and serve with slices of toasted bread cut into triangles, if you wish.

For the Peppers
4 sweet red peppers
Salt and freshly ground black pepper
1 envelope unflavored gelatin
½ cup whipping cream

For the Fresh Tomato Sauce
4 medium-size ripe tomatoes, peeled and
  seeded (page 55)
Several fresh basil leaves
Salt and freshly ground black pepper

Triangles of toasted bread (optional)

SERVES 4

Insalata di Sedano e Bresaola

Celery and Bresaola Salad

Bresaola is a specialty of the Valtellina, a beautiful valley at the foot of the Alps. This air-and-salt-cured beef is cut into thin slices, dressed with olive oil and lemon, and eaten as an appetizer. Bresaola is becoming more and more popular in Italian restaurants in this country and it is available in Italian specialty stores. Capocollo, salami, smoked ham, or prosciutto could be used if bresaola is not available.

2 bunches crisp celery
¼ cup olive oil
Juice of 1 lemon
Salt and freshly ground black pepper
½ pound sliced bresaola or capocollo

SERVES 4

Remove the green parts of the celery stalks and reserve them for another use. Slice the white celery hearts very thinly and put them in a salad bowl. Dress with the oil, lemon juice and salt and pepper. Mix thoroughly. Cover and refrigerate for 30 minutes.

Cut the bresaola into thin strips. When ready to serve, put the celery salad into 4 individual dishes. Place small mounds of the bresaola over the celery and serve.

Some of the dishes in this book are as good in summer as they are in winter. This is one of them.

Mozzarella Marinata

Mozzarella Marinated in Oil and Oregano

In this dish, mozzarella is cut into small pieces, dressed with virgin olive oil, salt and pepper, and chopped fresh oregano and left to marinate for a few hours. It is then served over a bed of finely sliced endives and radicchio. The result is a delicious dish of contrasting tastes. Good-quality mozzarella is imperative for this dish. Many Italian specialty stores now carry mozzarella imported from Italy or make their own right on the premises. Supermarket mozzarella is, in my judgment, not acceptable for this preparation. Pecorino Toscano or Pecorino Romano cheese could be used instead of mozzarella, but keep in mind that these cheeses are more aromatic and salty than mozzarella and they should not be so heavily seasoned.

Cut the mozzarella into pieces about the size of a small olive. Put the pieces in a bowl and dress them with the oil, oregano, and salt and pepper. Taste and adjust the seasoning. Cover the bowl and refrigerate until ready to use. Remove from the refrigerator at least 30 minutes before serving.

Put the endives and radicchio on individual plates. Put a small mound of marinated cheese on top of the lettuce, spoon a bit of the dressing over and serve.

For the Mozzarella
1 pound mozzarella
¼ cup olive oil, preferably virgin olive oil
2 tablespoons finely chopped fresh oregano
*   or parsley leaves*
Salt and freshly ground black pepper

To Complete the Dish
4 Belgian endives, finely sliced
Several radicchio or rucola leaves, if avail-
*   able, cut into small pieces*

SERVES 4

Funghi Ripieni

Stuffed Mushrooms

A lovely, firm large mushroom lends itself beautifully to stuffing. Here, savory ingredients are sautéed lightly together and then used to fill mushroom caps. In Italy, there seem to be as many versions of this dish as there are people. Serve these as a light appetizer or an accompaniment to broiled or grilled meat or fish.

Wipe the mushrooms clean with a damp cloth. Remove the stems and chop them very fine.

Heat the oil in a medium-size skillet. Add the onion and garlic and sauté for 7 to 8 minutes, or until the onion turns lightly golden. Add the parsley, mortadella, capers, parmigiano, bread crumbs, and mushroom stems. Season with salt and pepper. Cook for 1 to 2 minutes longer. Preheat the oven to 375 degrees.

Stuff each mushroom cap with the filling. Oil a baking dish lightly. Arrange the mushrooms in a single layer in the dish. Bake for 15 to 20 minutes, or until the mushrooms are lightly golden. Serve warm.

12 large mushrooms
¼ cup olive oil
1 small onion, finely chopped
2 garlic cloves, finely chopped
2 tablespoons chopped fresh parsley leaves
3 ounces mortadella or cooked ham, finely
*   chopped*
2 tablespoons rinsed and dried capers
¼ cup freshly grated parmigiano
⅓ cup unseasoned bread crumbs (prefera-
*   bly from day-old Italian or French*
*   bread)*
Salt and freshly ground black pepper

SERVES 4

Carpaccio

Carpaccio with Parmigiano, Capers, and Olive Oil

Carpaccio is the creation of Arrigo Cipriani, owner of the famous Harry's Bar in Venice. It seems that the original recipe for the sauce has been closely guarded by the Cipriani family. As a result, several interpretations of carpaccio are now found in Italian restaurants. This is the version of Ristorante Rodrigo in Bologna.

1 pound eye of round
¼ pound parmigiano, cut into small slivers
1 teaspoon Dijon mustard
Juice of 2 lemons
Salt and freshly ground black pepper
½ cup olive oil
3 to 4 tablespoons rinsed and dried capers

SERVES 6 TO 8

Put the meat in the freezer for about 1 hour to "firm" it a little, so that it can be sliced more easily.

Cut the meat by hand or by machine into very thin slices. If the slices are not very thin, pound them lightly until they are almost transparent.

Place 3 or 4 slices of meat on individual dishes. Sprinkle each slice generously with slivers of parmigiano. In a mixing bowl, combine the mustard, lemon juice, and salt and pepper and stir to dissolve mustard. Add the oil and capers and mix to incorporate. Taste and adjust the seasoning. Spoon the sauce over the meat and serve at room temperature.

If you object to raw meat, assemble the dish completely and leave it at room temperature for about 1 to 2 hours. The dressing will marinate and partially "cook" the very thin slices of beef.

Pasta

Technique for Making Basic Egg Pasta Dough by Hand

Put the flour on a pastry board and make a well in the center. Break the eggs into the well. Using a fork, blend the eggs in the well, drawing flour from the insides of the well to incorporate it into the egg. Add the flour a little at a time, always mixing with the fork. When you get to the point that a soft paste begins to stick heavily to the tines of the fork, switch to the dough scraper.

With the dough scraper, push all remaining flour to one side of the board and pick up any bits and pieces attached to the board. Add some flour to the paste and begin to mix the dough lightly with your hands, adding flour slowly as you go along, until eggs and flour are well combined. Do not add flour too hastily because you might not need to use all of it. At this point, the dough will be quite soft and sticky. Flour the board and your hands and knead the dough, continuing to add flour as you go along. The moment you have a soft, manageable dough, clean the board of the sticky pieces of dough with a pastry scraper. Wash and dry your hands.

Flour the cleaned board and your hands again and begin to knead the dough energetically, pushing the dough with the palms of your hands away from you and folding half the dough over toward you. Keep turning the dough as you knead it. Push, fold over, and turn. Knead 10 to 12 minutes, adding a bit of flour if the dough sticks to the board and to your hands.

Push a finger into the center of the dough.

If it comes out barely moist, the dough is ready to be rolled out. If the dough is sticky, knead it a little longer, adding a bit more flour. At the end of the kneading time, the dough should be compact, pliable, and as smooth as a baby's skin.

Dough made with soft white flour will be very smooth and pliable; dough made with hard wheat flour will be stiffer and coarser in texture and harder to knead.

Making Basic Egg Pasta Dough by Food Processor

Break the eggs into a food processor fitted with a metal blade and process briefly. Add the flour. Process on and off until the dough is all gathered loosely around the blade. At this point, the dough should be moist and slightly sticky. If the dough is too dry, beat an extra egg in a small bowl and add half of it to the dough. If the dough is too sticky, however, simply add a bit more flour.

Put the dough on a work surface. Dust your hands with flour and knead the dough for a few minutes by hand, adding a bit of flour if needed. Dough kneaded by a food processor won't be as elastic as dough kneaded by hand. However, it should still be smooth, pliable, and quite satisfactory.

Making Basic Egg Pasta Dough by Electric Mixer

Break the eggs into the bowl of an electric mixer fitted with a dough hook. Beat the eggs briefly at low speed. Add the flour, ½ cup at a time, beating well after each addition. Increase the speed and let the mixer knead the dough for 5 to 6 minutes. The dough should be smooth and pliable. If it is too soft, add a bit more flour; if it is too sticky, add a bit of water or half of a beaten egg.

Remove the dough from the bowl and put it on a work surface. Flour your hands lightly and knead the dough for a few minutes by hand.

Spinach Pasta

To make green pasta, add 1 to 2 tablespoons cooked, chopped, and squeezed spinach to the eggs. Beat well to incorporate the spinach into the eggs. Add the flour and proceed to make your dough by hand or by machine. Keep in mind that cooked spinach retains a certain amount of moisture; therefore, spinach pasta dough will need slightly more flour. The more spinach you use, the greener your dough is going to be.

Red Pasta

To make red pasta you need to incorporate into the eggs a bit of tomato paste or puréed cooked beets. As with spinach pasta, the more tomato paste or beets you add, the redder the pasta will be. Add the flour and proceed to make your dough by hand or by machine.

Turn leftover pasta into a frittata.

Leftover pasta that was dressed only with a vegetable sauce can become a pasta salad with the addition of oil, vinegar, some freshly chopped garlic, and fresh herbs.

Rolling Out Pasta by Hand

If you are rolling out the basic pasta dough by hand, the dough should be left to rest for 10 to 15 minutes before being rolled out, to allow the gluten to relax and, in turn, make the dough easier to roll out.

Put the dough in a bowl and cover the bowl with aluminum foil. After it has rested for 15 minutes, dust a large wooden board or working surface lightly with flour. Flatten the dough with your hands or with a rolling pin. Start rolling from the center of the dough forward, away from you, toward the edges. Rotate the dough slightly and roll out again from the center toward the edges. Continue to roll and rotate the dough to produce a circular sheet of dough, always rolling away from you, almost like stretching, and not down toward your body. If the dough sticks to the work surface, wrap it loosely around the rolling pin so that you can lift the dough and dust the work surface lightly with flour.

Now that you have a large circle of dough, you must roll it out into a larger, even thinner circle.

Wrap the far edges of the pasta sheet around the rolling pin. Roll about half of the pasta sheet lightly toward you. With the palms of your hands, gently press it against the center of the rolling pin. Your hands should never remain in the some position, but move from the center to the sides in a continuous motion. With this motion, the pasta will be stretched forward as well as sideways.

To retain a circular shape, wrap the far edge of the pasta sheet around the rolling pin to lift (dust the board lightly if necessary) and turn the circle slightly over the work surface. Continue stretching the dough by rolling the far edge of the pasta sheet around the pin. Dust the dough lightly if it is sticky. Keep rolling and stretching, until the pasta is very thin, almost transparent.

Now the dough is to be cut.

In Bologna, very experienced pasta makers drape part of the pasta sheet in front of themselves over the large wooden board; then they lean against it while they roll out the pasta forward and sideways.

Cutting Basic Dough by Hand

There are two methods of handling the dough here.

1. For stuffed pasta, the dough should be cut and stuffed immediately while it is still moist, so that the stuffed pasta can be sealed properly. See the individual recipes for detailed instructions.

2. For noodles of any kind, the pasta sheet should be allowed to dry a bit before it is cut into individual shapes, so that the noodles won't stick together.

When the pasta sheet is no longer sticky, after 15 to 25 minutes, depending on the temperature of your kitchen, fold the sheet of dough loosely into a flat roll not wider than 3 inches. With a flat, large, sharp knife, cut the pasta into the desired width, depending on the noodles you are making, by pressing down evenly with the knife. Unroll the noodles and place them in loose

bundles on a wooden surface or tablecloth, uncovered. The noodles can be cooked immediately or allowed to dry and cooked later.

Rolling Out Pasta by Machine

It is not necessary to let the dough rest before rolling by machine.

Set the rollers of the pasta machine at their widest opening. Cut off one small piece of dough, about the size of an egg, and flatten it with the palm of your hand. (Keep the rest of the dough in a bowl, covered with aluminum foil.) Dust the flattened piece of dough lightly with flour and run it once through the machine. Fold the dough in half, pressing it down with your fingertips. Run it through the machine again. Repeat this step four times, rubbing the dough lightly with flour, until the dough is smooth and not sticky. During these steps, the dough will acquire more "body" and consistency, since the machine at this point is really doing the kneading for you. Now that the dough is smooth and firm, it is ready to be stretched into a long, thin sheet of pasta.

Change the notch of the rollers to the next setting and run the dough through *once without folding it anymore*. Keep changing the setting and working the pasta sheet through the rollers once each time until it reaches the desired thinness. Gently pull the dough upward as you run it through the machine.

For stuffed pasta, the sheet of dough should be very thin, almost transparent. For noodles in general, it should be a bit thicker.

On all the pasta machines I have tried, I find that the last setting produces a sheet of dough that is much too thin, delicate, and breakable. Personally, I never use the last setting. If I want a very thin sheet of dough, I use the next-to-the-last roller setting and put the dough through two times.

Cutting Basic Dough by Machine

Here, just as in Cutting Basic Dough by Hand, for stuffed pasta the sheet of dough should be cut and stuffed immediately to ensure a tight seal. (See the individual recipes for detailed instructions.)

For noodles of any kind, the pasta sheets should dry before being cut to prevent the noodles from sticking together.

Roll out the pasta into thin sheets and allow to dry for 15 to 20 minutes, depending on the temperature of your kitchen. When the pasta is no longer sticky, put it through the cutting blades of the pasta machine, according to the width of the noodles you desire. Arrange the noodles in soft bundles on a board or the kitchen table. They can be cooked immediately or later on.

For fettuccine, the dough should be rolled out a little thicker than for other types of noodles.

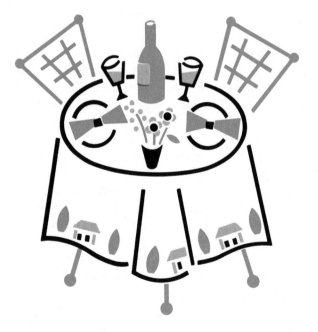

Capelli d'Angelo con Prosciutto, Panna e Limone

Angel's Hair with Prosciutto, Cream, and Lemon Sauce

I first had this dish a few years ago in Bologna at Notai's restaurant. I remember I had to be persuaded to try it. The idea of lemon on my pasta was not overly appealing. Well, I was proven wrong. The lemon on the noodles consists only of a bit of grated rind which is tossed together with butter, cream, prosciutto, parsley, and parmigiano. The result is a wonderfully delicate dish that has become one of my favorites.

Follow the instructions for preparing the Basic Egg Pasta Dough on page 63, using the proportions given here. Roll out the dough and cut into Capelli d'Angelo using the thinnest cutter on your pasta machine.

Bring a large pot of water to a boil. Add 1 tablespoon of salt and the pasta. Cook, uncovered, until pasta is tender but still firm to the bite; take care as these will cook very quickly.

While the pasta is cooking, prepare the sauce. Melt the butter in a large skillet. Add the cream, prosciutto, parsley, and lemon rind. Cook for about 1 minute. Season with salt and pepper. Drain the noodles and add them to skillet with the sauce. Add ⅓ cup of the parmigiano. Toss the pasta with the sauce over low heat until the pasta is coated. This step should be done fast or the sauce will dry out. Serve immediately with additional parmigiano.

One pound of imported factory-made pasta can be substituted for the homemade product.

If pasta sticks together as it cooks, it might be cooking in an insufficient quantity of water or it might be of a poor quality.

For the Capelli d'Angelo
2 cups all-purpose unbleached flour
3 large eggs

For the Prosciutto, Cream, and Lemon Sauce
1 tablespoon salt
4 tablespoons unsalted butter
1 cup heavy cream
¼ pound prosciutto, sliced and cut into short, thin julienne
1 tablespoon chopped fresh parsley leaves
Grated rind of 1 lemon
Salt and freshly ground black pepper
1 cup freshly grated parmigiano

SERVES 4

Ravioli Verdi di Branzino

Spinach Ravioli Stuffed with Sea Bass

Tender, delicate homemade pasta filled with a light fish stuffing is simply delicious and is becoming increasingly popular in Italy. If we spend the time to produce a superlative pasta and a stuffing that is sinfully good, it would be sheer folly to cover all this with a rich, overpowering sauce. A little melted butter, a bit of fresh herb that compliments the taste of the fish, and a sprinkling of parmigiano is all that is needed to fully enjoy such a dish.

For the Filling

2 slices white bread, crusts removed
¼ cup heavy cream
1½ pounds sea bass fillets
3 tablespoons unsalted butter
1 cup loosely packed fresh parsley leaves
2 large egg yolks
⅓ cup freshly grated parmigiano
Salt and freshly ground black pepper

For the Basic Spinach Pasta Dough

2 cups all-purpose unbleached flour
3 large eggs
1 tablespoon cooked fresh or frozen chopped
  spinach, squeezed of all moisture

To Complete the Dish

4 to 5 tablespoons unsalted butter
Salt
1 tablespoon fresh marjoram or chopped
  fresh parsley leaves
Freshly grated parmigiano

SERVES 4 TO 6

Prepare the filling: Break the bread into small pieces and put in a bowl with the cream. Squeeze bread into cream with your hands to blend them thoroughly. Set aside.

Cut the sea bass into small pieces. Melt the butter in a medium-size skillet. When the butter foams, add the fish pieces and sauté for a few minutes over medium heat.

Chop the marjoram in a food processor. Add the sea bass, soaked bread, egg yolks, and parmigiano. Season with salt and a bit of pepper. Process on and off until all ingredients are well incorporated and finely ground. Do not purée. Transfer the mixture to a bowl. Taste and adjust the seasoning. If the stuffing is too moist, add a bit more parmigiano. If it is too dry, add a bit of cream or an additional egg yolk. Cover the bowl tightly and refrigerate until ready to use.

Prepare the Basic Spinach Pasta Dough following the instructions on page 64, using the proportions given here. Cut off one small piece of dough, about the size of a large egg, and work through the pasta machine until you have a very thin sheet of pasta. Trim the sheet of pasta to a straight length 4 inches wide. Place heaping teaspoons of filling along the pasta sheet, about 2 inches apart. If the sheet of pasta is quite long, you might want to cut it into two or three parts for easier folding. Fold the pasta sheet in half over filling. Press the edges together firmly to seal them. If the dough is a bit dry, moisten it lightly with a bit of water. Use a scalloped pastry wheel to cut between the fillings in a straight line.

The ravioli can be cooked immediately or they can be kept in the refrigerator covered only with a kitchen towel for several hours. In this case, they should be turned over at least once to allow the bottom part to dry evenly. Remember that fresh pasta cooks very quickly; after the water comes back to a boil, cook the pasta about 1 minute and then test it. Chances are it will be just perfectly cooked.

Bring a large pot of water to a boil. Add 1 tablespoon of salt and the ravioli. Cook until tender but still firm to the bite. Meanwhile, melt the butter in a small saucepan and season it lightly with salt. Set aside.

Drain the pasta and put it in a warm large serving dish. Pour the melted butter over the ravioli, sprinkle with the fresh marjoram, and sprinkle generously with parmigiano. Mix gently and serve at once, accompanied by additional parmigiano.

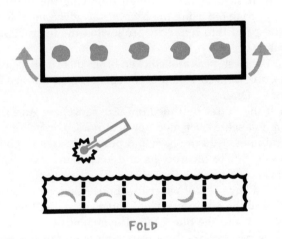

FOLD

Fettuccine alla Papalina

Fettuccine with Ham, Peas, and Egg Sauce

Once in San Francisco, I heard a well-known food expert saying categorically that in Italian cooking one should never combine egg pasta with egg sauce. Obviously, this expert had never had Fettuccine alla Papalina, a very delicious and very popular Roman dish.

Besides eggs, the sauce for this dish includes ham, onion, and peas. This is a relatively modern dish: It became popular in Rome after the Second World War. It is easy and quick to prepare, tasty and thoroughly satisfying. If you don't have time to prepare your own fettuccine, choose a good brand of imported Italian pasta. One pound of factory-made fettuccine will serve 4 generously.

For the Fettuccine

2 cups all-purpose unbleached flour
3 large eggs

For the Sauce

1 cup shelled fresh peas, or 1 cup frozen
  peas, thawed
1 cup chicken broth or water
4 tablespoons unsalted butter
1 onion, thinly sliced
¼ pound boiled or baked ham, cut into
  short, thin julienne
Salt to taste

To Complete the Dish

2 large eggs
1 cup freshly grated parmigiano
Salt and freshly ground black pepper

Serves 4

Prepare Basic Egg Pasta Dough following the instructions on page 63, using the proportions given here. Roll out the pasta into fettuccine, following the instructions on page 66.

Put the fresh peas and chicken broth in a small saucepan. Cook for 5 to 10 minutes depending on the size of the peas. Drain.

Melt the butter in a medium-size saucepan. Add the onion and sauté over medium heat until pale yellow, 5 to 7 minutes. Add the ham and peas and season lightly with salt. Stir to incorporate and keep warm over very low heat.

Bring a large pot of water to a boil. Add 1 tablespoon of salt and the fettuccine. Cook, uncovered, until tender but still firm to the bite. Do not overcook.

While pasta cooks, beat eggs with ¼ cup of the parmigiano in a large shallow dish. Season lightly with salt and several grindings of pepper.

Drain the fettuccine and add to the dish with the eggs. Toss quickly. Stir in prosciutto–peas mixture and toss well. Serve immediately with additional parmigiano.

For the freshest taste, the cheese that tops pasta should always be grated at the last moment; it will improve the overall taste of your dish.

Fettuccine al Gorgonzola

Fettuccine with Creamy Gorgonzola Sauce

Sweet, creamy gorgonzola paired with a bit of cream, becomes a heavenly easy-to-make sauce for fettuccine. There is no doubt that homemade fettuccine, if skillfully made, are unbeatable. In a pinch, however, a good brand of imported pasta will do. Since this sauce is very quick to prepare, I cook the pasta while I prepare the sauce. When you toss the pasta and sauce together, do it over very low heat and for a very brief time, or the sauce will thicken and dry out too much. If this should happen, just add a bit more cream. This sauce would also be excellent for Cavatelli with Butter and Cheese (page 205) or Green Potato Gnocchi with Pancetta and Fresh Sage (page 208).

Prepare the Basic Egg Pasta Dough following the instructions on page 63, using the proportions given here. Roll the dough out into fettuccine (page 66).

Melt the butter in a large skillet until it foams; then add cream. Cook for 1 minute over low heat. Add the gorgonzola and cook and stir until the gorgonzola is completely melted and the cream begins to thicken. Season lightly with salt and white pepper. Remove the skillet from the heat.

Bring a large pot of water to a boil. Add 1 tablespoon of salt and the fettuccine. Cook, uncovered, until the pasta is tender but still firm to the bite.

Put the skillet back over low heat. Drain the fettuccine and add it to the skillet with the sauce. Add ¼ cup of the parmigiano and toss quickly to incorporate. Serve with additional parmigiano, if desired.

For the Fettuccine
2½ cups all-purpose unbleached flour
3 large eggs

For the Sauce
4 tablespoons unsalted butter
1 cup heavy cream
¼ pound sweet, creamy gorgonzola
Salt and freshly ground white pepper
½ cup freshly grated parmigiano

SERVES 4

Linguine col Pesto, Patate, e Piselli

Linguine with Pesto, Potatoes, and Peas

This delicious springtime pasta is a variation of the classic Ligurian dish. The potatoes are part of the original dish, but the peas are not. Other additions could include asparagus tips or small string beans. The vegetables can be cooked separately and then tossed together with the pasta and the sauce at the last moment (be sure the vegetables are still warm) or they can be cooked together with the pasta.

Use the pesto sauce moderately. Too often this beautiful preparation is abused by an overabundance of thin, oil-saturated pesto sauce. If the pesto sauce is too thick and you don't want to use more oil, add a bit of the pasta cooking water to thin it out. If you are planning to use this dish as a first course, serve a small amount, because potatoes make it quite filling. Any broiled fish could follow beautifully. For a family meal, I generally make this a substantial one-dish course, to be followed only with some cheese and fruit.

For the Pesto Sauce

2 cups loosely packed fresh basil leaves
½ cup olive oil
¼ cup pine nuts
2 garlic cloves, peeled
1 teaspoon salt
½ cup freshly grated parmigiano
2 tablespoons freshly grated Pecorino Romano

To Complete the Dish

2 medium-size, or 4 small, potatoes
1 tablespoon salt
1 pound linguine
1 cup shelled fresh peas or thawed frozen peas
½ cup freshly grated parmigiano

SERVES 4 TO 6

To prepare the pesto sauce, put all the pesto ingredients, except the cheese, into a blender or food processor and process until smooth. Pour the sauce into a bowl. Add the parmigiano and pecorino and blend well. Taste and adjust the seasoning. This will make about ¾ cup of sauce.

Peel and cut potatoes into small slices, about 1 inch thick and 2 inches across. If the slices are too large, cut them into halves or quarters. Put potatoes in a saucepan of boiling water and boil just until tender. Drain and pat dry with paper towels.

Bring a large pot of water to a boil. Add the salt and linguine. Cook for 3 to 4 minutes. Add the fresh peas and cook for 4 to 5 minutes longer, or until the pasta is tender but still firm to the bite. If you are using frozen peas, add them to the pasta during the last minute of cooking.

Scoop out about 1 cup of the pasta cooking water and reserve it.

Drain the linguine and peas and put them in a warm serving dish or bowl. Add the pesto, hot potatoes, and a sprinkling of parmigiano. Add a few tablespoons of the reserved pasta cooking water if sauce looks too dry. Toss everything and serve at once.

Pesto sauce has been abused lately. A bit of this seductive sauce should lightly dress pasta or be used to brighten the taste of a dish, such as minestrone. Too much will be overwhelming.

Pesto sauce freezes very well. However, if you plan to freeze it, do not add the parmigiano to the sauce; it will have a fresher flavor and a more interesting texture if the cheese is added at the last moment.

Pasta con i Peperoni Arrosto e le Acciughe

Pasta with Roasted Peppers and Anchovies

This is my interpretation of a classic recipe of broiled red peppers combined with pasta. I simply love the result. Perhaps I didn't invent anything new, but I certainly added one more pasta dish to the list of my favorites.

Roast the peppers according to the instructions on page 59. Remove skin and seeds and lay the peppers on paper towels to dry thoroughly. Cut the peppers into 1- to 1½-inch-wide strips.

Bring a large pot of water to a boil. Add 1 tablespoon of salt and the pasta. Cook, uncovered, for 8 to 10 minutes, or until the pasta is tender but still firm to the bite.

While the pasta is cooking, heat the oil in a medium-size skillet. Add 2 tablespoons of the parsley, the basil, anchovies, and garlic. Sauté for about 1 minute over medium heat.

Add the pepper strips and season with salt and pepper. Stir to incorporate. Drain the pasta and add it to the skillet with the sauce. Add the remaining parsley and mix thoroughly. Serve immediately.

4 large sweet red or yellow peppers
1 pound penne, shells, or rigatoni
4 tablespoons olive oil, preferably virgin olive oil
3 tablespoons chopped fresh parsley leaves
¼ cup cut-up basil leaves, if available
3 anchovy fillets, finely chopped
2 garlic cloves, finely chopped
Salt and freshly ground black pepper

SERVES 4

This dish is also excellent served at room temperature.

Pennette 3 Vasselle

Pennette 3 Vasselle Style

The chef of Le 3 Vasselle restaurant in Torgiano prepared this wonderful and very unusual pasta dish for me, which he cooked with the same technique that he would have applied to preparing a risotto. Uncooked pennette (a smaller version of penne) are first sautéed in olive oil until they become thoroughly golden. A shot of good brandy is poured over the pasta and then the pasta is cooked with small additions of broth. Cream and mushrooms are also added. The cooking time of the pasta is approximately 10 to 12 minutes, and at that point no more broth should be left in the skillet. The end result is a pasta with an unusual texture and a creamy delicious consistency, as well as a dish with great eye appeal. Be sure to use a very large skillet that will accommodate all the pasta comfortably and stir the pasta as it cooks. The mushrooms can be sautéed a few hours ahead of time and added to the pasta during the last few minutes of cooking. Keep in mind that this is a deliciously rich dish, so don't go overboard with large portions.

For the Mushrooms
½ pound fresh small white cultivated
  mushrooms
3 tablespoons olive oil
2 garlic cloves, finely chopped
3 tablespoons chopped fresh parsley leaves
1 tablespoon chopped fresh basil, if available
Salt and freshly ground black pepper

To Complete the Dish
¼ cup olive oil
1 pound pennette or any small-size penne
¼ cup brandy
2 cups chicken broth (page 45), plus a bit
  more
1 cup heavy cream
⅓ cup freshly grated parmigiano

SERVES 4 TO 6

Clean the mushrooms thoroughly and cut them into thin slices.

Heat the 3 tablespoons of oil in a medium-size skillet. Add the mushrooms, garlic, 2 tablespoons of the parsley, and the basil, if using. Sauté over high heat until the mushrooms are lightly golden. Season with salt and pepper. Set aside.

In a large skillet, heat the ¼ cup of olive oil. Add the pennette. Sauté, stirring, over medium heat until the pasta becomes golden. Add the brandy. Stir and cook until the brandy has evaporated. Stir in 1 cup of the chicken broth. Cook over medium heat until the broth has been absorbed. Add 1 more cup broth and the cream. Cook and stir until the broth has evaporated.

Add the mushrooms and taste the pasta for doneness. If necessary, add a bit more broth and cook a few minutes longer.

Stir in the parmigiano and the remaining tablespoon of parsley and serve immediately with additional parmigiano, if desired.

Pasta con le Melanzane e Zucchine Grigliate

Pasta with Broiled Eggplants, Zucchini, and Crookneck Squash

Our mood and our state of mind definitely affect our performance. When my daughter Carla was accepted by the college of her choice, I was so exhilarated that when I played tennis that day I beat the daylights out of my opponent, and the food I cooked that night was spectacular. This is a dish I tossed together because I was happy, in high spirits, and also because I had tons of eggplants, zucchini, and crookneck squash in the house. I said to myself, "If I were Sicilian what would I do with all these vegetables?" This is the result. I loved it and hope you will like it too.

Preheat the broiler. Wash the eggplants, zucchini, and squash. Cut off both ends and cut them lengthwise into ¼-inch-thick slices. Brush the slices lightly with a bit of oil and place them on a broiling pan. Broil until the vegetables are golden on both sides.

Cut vegetables into juliennes not longer than the type of pasta you are cooking. Set aside.

Bring a large pot of water to a boil. Add 1 tablespoon of salt and the rigatoni. Cook, uncovered, for 8 to 10 minutes or until the pasta is tender but still firm to the bite.

While the pasta is cooking, complete the sauce. In a large skillet, heat the oil. Add anchovies, and sauté gently for about 1 minute. Add the parsley, oregano, garlic, sun-dried tomatoes, and hot chile pepper. Sauté for 1 to 2 minutes over low heat. Add the julienned vegetables and season with salt. Stir over low heat for a few minutes longer. If the sauce looks too dry, add a bit more oil or a few tablespoons of the pasta cooking water.

Drain the pasta and add it to the skillet with the vegetables. Raise the heat and toss the pasta and vegetables briefly. Taste and adjust the seasoning and serve hot.

4 small Japanese eggplants or 1 regular eggplant
3 small zucchini
2 crookneck yellow squash
Olive oil to baste
1 tablespoon salt
1 pound rigatoni or penne rigate
¼ cup olive oil, preferably virgin olive oil
2 anchovy fillets, finely chopped
2 tablespoons chopped fresh parsley leaves
¼ cup loosely packed fresh oregano or basil leaves or 1 tablespoon additional chopped parsley leaves
2 garlic cloves, finely chopped
4 sun-dried tomatoes, roughly chopped
1 small piece of a hot red chile pepper, finely chopped
Salt

SERVES 4

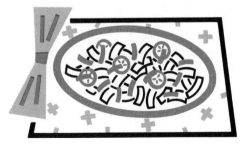

Spaghetti Integrali con il Cavolfiore e i Peperoni Rossi

Whole Wheat Spaghetti with Cauliflower and Red Pepper

Not too long ago, I was asked by the American Cancer Society of Sacramento to develop some dishes according to their nutrition and cancer guidelines. The guidelines were: Reduced calorie intake; more high-fiber foods and vegetables; and reduced intake of saturated and unsaturated fats. So I went into the kitchen and started to work. The following dish is one that received high praise. It is a simple, delicious dish that is typical of the Mediterranean diet which uses pasta, good olive oil, and plenty of vegetables. Besides being delicious, it is eye-pleasing and easy to prepare. What more can we ask of a dish that was created under strict dietary guidelines?

4 *large sweet red, yellow, or green peppers*
1 *small cauliflower*
4 *tablespoons olive oil, preferably virgin olive oil*
2 *garlic cloves, finely chopped*
1 *small piece hot red chile pepper, finely chopped*
4 *anchovy fillets, chopped*
2 *tablespoons chopped fresh parsley leaves*
2 *tablespoons rinsed and dried capers*
Salt to taste
1 *pound whole wheat spaghetti*

SERVES 4 TO 6

Roast the peppers according to the instructions on page 59. Then peel the peppers, cut them in half, and remove the seeds. Cut the peppers into small strips and set aside.

Wash the cauliflower. Remove the outer leaves and stem. Separate cauliflower into florets. If the florets are too large, cut them in half. Boil or steam the florets until tender but still firm to the touch.

In a large skillet heat the oil. Add the garlic, chile pepper, and anchovies, and sauté gently for 2 minutes. Add the parsley, capers, red peppers, and florets. Sauté for 1 to 2 minutes longer. Taste and adjust the seasoning. Keep warm over very low heat.

Bring a large pot of water to a boil. Add 1 tablespoon of salt and the spaghetti. Cook, uncovered, until tender but still firm to the bite (about 8 minutes). Drain the pasta and add to the skillet with the sauce. Raise the heat and toss the pasta with the vegetable mixture. Serve immediately, spooning vegetables over each serving of pasta.

If whole wheat pasta is not available, use a good brand of imported, 100 percent semolina flour pasta.

You can increase or decrease the amount of vegetables, substitute broccoli for cauliflower, or reduce the anchovies and increase the capers. This is a dish where ingredients can easily be readjusted to fit individual tastes.

Le Conchiglie con la Salsa di Funghi e Acciughe

Shells with Wild Mushrooms and Anchovy Sauce

The woodsy flavor of porcini and the distinctive taste of anchovies are combined into a fragrant, full-bodied sauce. This sauce can be prepared a few days ahead. It can also be frozen. Serve it over shells, penne, rigatoni, or gnocchi.

Soak the mushrooms in 1 cup of lukewarm water for 20 minutes. Strain the mushrooms and reserve the soaking water. Thoroughly rinse the mushrooms under cold running water to get rid of any sandy deposits. Line a strainer with paper towels and strain the mushroom soaking liquid several times until completely clear. Set aside.

Press the tomatoes through a food mill or a sieve to remove the seeds.

Heat the oil in a medium-size saucepan. Add the garlic and anchovies and sauté gently for 1 to 2 minutes. Add the mushrooms and sauté a few minutes longer. Stir in the strained mushroom soaking water. Cook over medium heat until the liquid is reduced by half. Add tomatoes and season with salt and several grindings of pepper. Cook, uncovered, over low heat for 15 to 20 minutes. During the last few minutes of cooking stir in the parsley. Taste and adjust the seasoning.

While the sauce is cooking, bring a large pot of water to a boil. Add 1 tablespoon of salt and the shells. Cook, uncovered, until the pasta is tender but still firm to the bite. Drain the pasta and put it into a warm bowl. Add the sauce and mix well to incorporate. Serve hot.

1 ounce dried wild mushrooms
1 28-ounce can imported Italian plum tomatoes with their juices
3 tablespoons olive oil
2 garlic cloves, finely chopped
2 anchovy fillets, finely chopped
Salt and freshly ground black pepper
1 tablespoon chopped fresh parsley leaves
1 pound pasta shells

SERVES 4

Bucatini alla Cipolle

Bucatini with Onion Sauce

When onions are cooked very slowly for 30 to 40 minutes, they become tender, sweet, and delicious. This is the base for a simple and tasty sauce. Strips of pancetta are added to the onions for additional flavor; then everything is tossed together with parsley. Bucatini, spaghetti, linguine, or perciatelli can be used for this dish.

2 pounds yellow onions
4 tablespoons olive oil
*¼ pound pancetta, sliced and cut into
    small strips*
Salt and freshly ground black pepper
2 tablespoons chopped fresh parsley leaves
1 pound bucatini or spaghetti
½ cup freshly grated parmigiano

SERVES 4

Peel and cut the onions into thin slices. Heat the oil in a large skillet. Add the onions and ⅓ cup of water. Cover the skillet and cook over very low heat for 30 to 40 minutes. Stir a few times during the cooking and add a bit more water if the sauce dries out too much. Add the pancetta and season with salt and several grindings of pepper.

Raise the heat and remove the lid. Cook, stirring, until the onion and bacon mixture takes on a light golden color. During the last few minutes of cooking, stir in the parsley.

Bring a large pot of water to a boil. Add 1 tablespoon of salt and the bucatini. Cook for 8 to 10 minutes, or until the pasta is tender but still firm to the bite. Before draining the pasta reserve 1 cup of the pasta cooking water. Drain the pasta and add it to the skillet with the sauce. Mix well. If the sauce is too dry, add a bit of the reserved pasta cooking water. Serve hot, accompanied by the parmigiano.

Spaghetti con i Calamari

Spaghetti with Squid

Looking at squid one would never think this odd-looking mollusc could be such a delicious treat.

To clean the squid, hold it in one hand and gently pull away the tentacles. Cut the head off just below the eyes and discard it. Remove the tentacles. Remove the squid "bone" from the body (this is actually a piece of cartilage that resembles a piece of clear plastic). Clean the inside of the sac under cold running water, pulling out any matter still inside. Wash and peel any skin from the body and tentacles.

Cut the squid body into 1-inch-wide rings; cut the tentacles into 1-inch pieces. Bring a small saucepan of water to a boil. Add the squid. Cook over medium heat for about 1 minute. Drain, rinse under cold water, and dry with paper towels.

Bring a large pot of water to a boil. Add 1 tablespoon of salt and the spaghetti. Cook, uncovered, until the pasta is tender but firm to the bite.

While the pasta is cooking, prepare the sauce. Heat the oil in a large skillet. Add the garlic, anchovies, and hot pepper. Sauté over medium heat for 1 to 2 minutes. Add the wine and cook over high heat until the wine has almost evaporated, about 2 minutes. Add the squid and parsley and season lightly with salt. Stir for a few seconds and taste for seasoning. Remove about ½ a cup of the pasta cooking water and reserve it.

Drain the pasta and add it to the skillet with the sauce. Add a few tablespoons of the pasta cooking water if the sauce is too dry. Toss everything together and serve immediately.

1 pound squid
1 tablespoon salt
1 pound spaghetti, preferably imported, such as De Cecco or Spiga d'Oro
4 tablespoons olive oil
2 garlic cloves, finely chopped
3 anchovy fillets, finely chopped
⅓ of a small dried hot red chile pepper, finely chopped
¾ cup dry white wine
2 tablespoons chopped fresh parsley leaves
Salt to taste

SERVES 4

There are two schools of thought on the proper cooking of squid. One is to blanch or fry it quickly for about 1 minute. The other is to simmer squid slowly in savory sauces or broth for about 1 hour. In fact, both methods work and will produce perfectly tender squid. The explanation lies in the fact that, after a few minutes of cooking, squid tends to become tough and needs long, slow moist cooking to become tender again.

Cleaning squid is a bit of a chore, but unless you are prepared to pay a higher price at the fishmarket for cleaned squid, I suggest you roll up your sleeves and learn how to do it.

Tagliatelle ai Porri

Noodles with Leeks

How can a plate of pasta be anything but good when ingredients as tasty as sweet leeks, savory pancetta, ham, and sweet peas are part of the sauce? The above ingredients, sautéed in butter and tied together with a bit of cream, are transformed into a divine, quick sauce. Tagliatelle are the classic egg noodles of Bologna.

1 large leek or 2 medium-size leeks
4 tablespoons unsalted butter
3 ounces pancetta, sliced and cut into small
*   strips*
3 ounces boiled ham, sliced and cut into
*   small strips*
½ cup cooked fresh or frozen peas
Salt and freshly ground black pepper
1 cup heavy cream
¾ pound tagliatelle, homemade or factory-
*   made*
½ cup freshly grated parmigiano

SERVES 4

Cut off the roots of the leeks and remove ⅓ of the green tops. Cut the leeks in half lengthwise and wash them thoroughly, making sure to remove all dirt that is trapped between the leaves. Slice the leeks very thinly.

Heat the butter in a large skillet. Add the leeks and sauté over medium heat about 15 minutes. The leeks should be completely cooked, soft, and wilted. Add the pancetta, ham, and peas. Season with salt and pepper. Cook for 2 to 3 minutes. Stir in the cream and simmer a few minutes longer.

Meanwhile bring a large pot of water to a boil. Add 1 tablespoon salt and the noodles. Cook, uncovered, until the noodles are tender but still firm to the bite. Drain the pasta and add to the leeks in the skillet. Sprinkle with the parmigiano and toss everything together over low heat very briefly. Serve at once.

Soups

Passato di Verdura Estiva

Cream of Summer Vegetables

Vegetables are very important to Italian cooking. Given a choice, an Italian would probably choose a pasta dish and a vegetable over meat most of the time. That explains why in Italy we have so many vegetable soups.

Summertime soups are lighter than their winter counterparts. Fresh peas and asparagus, small tender carrots, young zucchini, and fresh herbs replace the beans, cabbage, and potatoes that are used in winter. Pasta is usually added to winter vegetable soups and the soups are served piping hot. Warm-weather soups, on the other hand, often are puréed into creamy delicacies and served at room temperature or slightly chilled.

Wash the leeks very well, making sure to remove all the dirt that clings between the leaves. Chop the leeks very fine.

Heat the oil in a large saucepan. Add the leeks, 2 tablespoons of parsley, and garlic. Sauté over medium heat until the leeks are pale yellow, about 5 minutes.

Add all the vegetables, except the peas, to the saucepan. Cook for 2 to 3 minutes, stirring to mix the vegetables. Add the broth and tomato paste diluted in a bit of broth. Season with salt and pepper. Cover the pan and cook over low heat for 30 to 40 minutes.

Put the vegetable mixture into a blender or a food processor and process until smooth. Strain the puréed vegetables back into the saucepan.

Bring a small saucepan of water to a boil. Add the peas. Cook for 5 to 10 minutes, depending on the size of the peas. Drain the peas and add to the puréed vegetables. Stir in the heavy cream and simmer for a few minutes. Taste and adjust the seasoning. Cool to room temperature. Serve with a sprinkling of chopped parsley or chives and with a bit of parmigiano, if you wish.

Every time I cook this summer soup my husband and I have a small argument. I like my soup just the way I wrote this recipe. He would prefer to have it with chunky vegetables and without cream. Wouldn't it be nice if we could please someone all the time? In any event, here are the basic steps. This recipe can as easily produce a chunky soup if you simply do not purée the mixture.

2 medium-size leeks
¼ cup olive oil
2 tablespoons chopped fresh parsley leaves
2 garlic cloves, finely chopped
1 boiling potato, peeled and diced
2 carrots, diced
1 pound fresh asparagus, with the tough ends removed, cut into small pieces
½ pound small fresh white cultivated mushrooms, sliced
2 small zucchini, diced
10 cups homemade chicken broth (page 45), or 5 cups canned broth mixed with 5 cups water
1 tablespoon tomato paste
Salt and freshly ground black pepper
1 cup shelled fresh peas
¼ cup heavy cream
1 tablespoon chopped fresh parsley leaves or chopped fresh chives
1 cup freshly grated parmigiano (optional)

Serves 6 to 8

Minestrone Estivo al Pesto

Cold Vegetable Soup with Pesto

A summer minestrone that has the scent of freshly picked, sun-drenched vegetables, this soup should be eaten at room temperature to fully savor its flavor. For me, a cool vegetable soup eaten on a hot summer day is a terrific treat. As with all vegetable soups, even this summer minestrone tastes better the day after it is made. You might want to double the amount and freeze half. Bring the minestrone to room temperature and add the pesto just before serving.

1 cup shelled fresh peas
¼ pound fresh asparagus with tough ends
   removed
¼ pound small string beans
¼ pound fresh white cultivated mushrooms
2 carrots
2 celery stalks
2 potatoes
¼ cup olive oil
1 onion, diced
1 garlic clove, finely chopped
6 cups homemade meat broth (page 44), or
   3 cups canned meat broth mixed with 3
   cups water
Salt and freshly ground black pepper
1 tablespoon pesto sauce (page 77)
½ cup freshly grated parmigiano

SERVES 4 TO 6

Wash and dice all the vegetables.

Heat the oil in a large saucepan. Add the onion and garlic and sauté over medium heat until the onion is pale yellow. Add all vegetables, stir well, and cover the pan. Let vegetables stew for 4 to 5 minutes. Stir a few times so they won't stick to the pan. Add the broth and season with salt and pepper. Cover the saucepan and simmer for about 1 hour. Remove the saucepan from heat and cool minestrone to room temperature. Just before serving, stir in pesto sauce. Serve with a generous sprinkling of parmigiano.

Crema di Lattuga Primaverile

Chilled Springtime Lettuce Soup

In Sacramento, California, where I live, anything grows. Plant a seed one day and a week after you have a beautiful little plant. This warm climate is the ideal place to have a vegetable garden. My garden in the summer months is extremely prolific, and I generally have a surplus of vegetables and lettuce. I created this recipe because I had an abundance of deliciously crisp and tender lettuce.

I love to serve this soup slightly chilled. Sometimes I toast a few pieces of bread and brush them lightly with melted garlicky butter. Then I cut the bread into small pieces and add them to the soup.

Melt the butter in a large saucepan. Add the leeks, and sauté over medium heat until the leeks are thoroughly wilted, about 12 to 14 minutes.

Wash all lettuces well and discard any bruised outer leaves. Cut the lettuces roughly into small pieces. Add the lettuces to the leeks and stir to incorporate. Add broth, cover the saucepan, and cook over medium heat for 25 to 35 minutes.

Put the lettuce mixture through a food mill or a blender or food processor and process until smooth. Return to the saucepan and bring to a low simmer.

Beat egg yolks, cream, and parmigiano in a bowl. Season with salt. Slowly add 1 ladle of broth to egg mixture, beating with a whisk. Pour egg–cream mixture in a thin stream back into the simmering broth, whisking constantly. Remove the soup from the heat. Cool to room temperature; then cover and refrigerate.

Serve slightly chilled. Just before serving stir the soup to insure a smooth consistency and sprinkle some fresh chopped chives on each portion.

Any type of lettuce can be used here. If possible, try to use some sorrel also. Its acid flavor will give a particularly refreshing taste to the soup.

3 tablespoons unsalted butter

1 bunch leeks, white and green parts, carefully washed and finely chopped

1 head romaine lettuce

1 head Boston or butter lettuce

1 bunch sorrel, if available, or 1 bunch leaf lettuce

10 to 12 cups chicken broth (page 45)

2 large egg yolks

⅓ cup heavy cream

⅓ cup freshly grated parmigiano

Salt to taste

1 tablespoon chopped garlic chives (optional)

SERVES 8

Zuppa di Zucchine

Zucchini Soup

Italians prefer summer soups served at room temperature. I generally prepare this soup early in the morning and leave it on the stove, with the heat off, until dinner time. For a thicker soup I put half of the zucchini through a blender or food processor. Sometimes I omit the bread. Other times I add small pasta such as stars or rice to the soup. Occasionally, I purée everything, transforming this soup into a "Passato di Zucchini," a cream of zucchini soup. For an authentic Italian touch, add a drop of extra virgin olive oil to each serving and some freshly grated parmigiano.

6 medium-size zucchini
2 tablespoons olive oil
2 tablespoons unsalted butter
6 cups homemade chicken broth (page 45),
   or 3 cups canned broth mixed with 3
   cups water
Salt and freshly ground black pepper
2 large eggs
1 tablespoon chopped fresh parsley leaves
1 tablespoon chopped fresh basil leaves
½ cup freshly grated parmigiano
2 tablespoons heavy cream
8 slices Italian bread

SERVES 4

Wash the zucchini thoroughly and slice off their ends; dice into small pieces about the size of peas.

Heat the oil and butter in a large saucepan. Add the zucchini. Cook over medium heat for 3 to 5 minutes, stirring. Add the broth and season lightly with salt and pepper. Cover saucepan and cook 30 to 35 minutes. Remove from heat.

Beat the eggs in a small bowl. Add the parsley, basil, 2 tablespoons parmigiano, and cream. Beat to combine. Stir the eggs into the broth, beating well. Let the soup cool to room temperature.

Toast the bread under the broiler until golden on both sides. Place one or two slices of bread into individual soup dishes. Ladle the soup over the bread; sprinkle with parmigiano and serve.

Risotti

Risotto con la Mentuccia

Risotto with Mint

I confess that I am very partial to risotto: I could happily eat it every day with almost no desire for anything else. But then I say the same for pasta and for gnocchi and for polenta and . . .

The procedure for cooking this risotto is the classic one, which is to sauté the rice with the butter and onion and then to cook the rice with small additions of hot broth. For this risotto, however, we add some chopped mint, together with a bit of butter and parmigiano, during the last few minutes of cooking. The result is a sinfully delicious and delicate dish.

Heat the broth in a medium-size saucepan and keep warm over very low heat.

Melt 4 tablespoons of the butter in a large saucepan. When the butter foams, add the onion. Sauté over medium heat until the onion is pale yellow. Add the rice. Cook for 1 to 2 minutes, or just enough to coat the rice with the butter and onion. Stir in the wine. Cook, stirring constantly, until the wine has evaporated. Add a few ladles of broth, just enough to barely cover the rice. Cook over medium heat, until broth has been absorbed. Continue cooking and stirring the rice in this manner, adding broth a bit at a time, until the rice is done, 15 to 20 minutes. During the last 2 or 3 minutes of cooking, chop the mint very fine and add to the rice with the remaining tablespoon of butter and ⅓ cup of the parmigiano. Taste for seasoning and doneness. The rice should be tender but still firm to the bite. At this point, the rice should have a creamy, moist consistency. Serve immediately with the remaining parmigiano.

It is almost impossible to give the exact amount of liquid needed to cook a risotto because there are too many variables, so I always have some extra broth on hand, believing in the old saying that it is better to be safe than sorry.

---

6 cups homemade chicken broth (page 45), or 3 cups canned broth mixed with 3 cups water
5 tablespoons unsalted butter
1 onion, finely chopped
2 cups Italian Arborio rice
1 cup dry white wine
⅓ cup loosely packed fresh mint leaves
1 cup freshly grated parmigiano
Salt to taste

SERVES 4 TO 6

Risotto Delicato con l'Aragosta

Risotto with Lobster

Risotto is one of the most loved dishes of northern Italy. Even though risotto is a classic preparation and has to be cooked at the last moment, I see it as a very "modern" dish because it can be a meal all by itself, depending on how many ingredients go into the risotto.

The technique of cooking a risotto, which is to add broth at intervals, is essential to produce a perfectly cooked and creamy rice. "Timing" in cooking a risotto is essential to its success. Regardless of what ingredients one uses and at what stages they go into the rice, the risotto at the end of cooking should have a moist but not watery consistency, with creamy yet individually separated grains of rice.

There is only one way to achieve this perfect balance: practice. The more you do it the better you'll become. The fact that a risotto should be cooked at the last moment shouldn't bother you because with practice you will know exactly when to add that last ladle of broth and the last chunk of butter and when to remove the rice from the heat.

When you cook a risotto for the first time follow the recipe literally. Be on top of it. Stir and taste and try to remember the "look" and consistency that a well-made risotto has when it is done. Keep in mind that rice keeps cooking even after it is removed from the heat and tends to dry out fast. So make sure that your rice is slightly al dente and is moist and creamy when you serve it.

For the Fish Stock

2 to 3 pounds assorted pieces of fish for stock, including heads and tails
2 fresh or dry bay leaves
A few parsley sprigs
2 garlic cloves, crushed
1 small onion, sliced
1 carrot, diced
1 celery stalk, diced
1 cup dry white wine

Prepare the Fish Stock. Wash the fish pieces. Put them in a large saucepan together with the bay leaves, parsley, garlic, onion, carrot, celery, and wine. Add enough water to cover the fish by about 1 inch. Bring to a boil; then lower the heat and simmer gently for 30 to 40 minutes. Strain the broth through a fine sieve into another saucepan. Season lightly with salt. Keep the Fish Stock warm on a back burner while you prepare the Lobster Sauce.

Prepare the Lobster Sauce. Lay the lobster tail on its back and, with a sharp knife, cut through the tail along its length. Remove the meat. Cut the lobster meat into small pieces about the size of an olive.

Melt the butter in a small skillet. Add the garlic and parsley and sauté gently for 1 minute. Add the lobster pieces and sauté for 1 minute longer. Stir in the wine and cook for 1 to 2 minutes, or until the wine has almost evaporated. Season lightly with salt and set aside.

Prepare the Risotto. Melt 3 tablespoons of the butter in a large saucepan. When butter foams, add the onion and cook over medium heat, until the onion is pale yellow. Add the rice. Cook for 1 to 2 minutes, or just until the rice is coated with butter and onion.

Stir in the wine and cook and stir until the wine has evaporated. Add a few ladles of hot fish stock, just enough to barely cover the rice. Cook over medium heat until stock has been absorbed. Continue cooking the rice in this manner, adding the stock a little at a time, for about 15 minutes.

Add the Lobster Sauce. Stir and cook for 2 to 3 minutes longer. Stir in the remaining tablespoons of butter and sprinkle with the parsley. Taste for doneness and adjust the seasoning, if necessary. Serve at once.

Plain leftover risotto can be turned into sweet fritters with the addition of some sugar, raisins, and eggs.

For the Lobster Sauce
1 lobster tail, fresh or frozen
2 tablespoons unsalted butter
2 garlic cloves, finely chopped
2 tablespoons chopped fresh parsley leaves
½ cup dry white wine
Salt to taste

For the Risotto
4 tablespoons unsalted butter
1 onion, finely chopped
2 cups Italian Arborio rice
1 cup dry white wine
*1 tablespoon chopped fresh parsley leaves
or, if in season, a few basil leaves*

Serves 4 to 6

Risotto Verde

Green Risotto

1½ pounds fresh spinach, or 5 ounces frozen spinach
1 cup shelled fresh peas, or 1 cup frozen
  peas, thawed
6 cups homemade chicken broth (page 45),
  or 3 cups canned chicken broth mixed
  with 3 cups water
5 tablespoons unsalted butter
1 onion, finely chopped
¼ pound pancetta, sliced and diced
2 cups Italian Arborio rice
1 cup freshly grated parmigiano
Salt

SERVES 4 TO 6

Remove the stems from the spinach and wash it thoroughly under cold running water. Put the wet spinach in a large saucepan with a pinch of salt. Cook over medium heat until the spinach is tender. Drain well. Chop the spinach very fine. (A food processor can also be used.) Set aside.

In a medium-size saucepan, heat the broth and keep it warm over very low heat.

Melt 4 tablespoons of the butter in a large saucepan. When butter foams, add the onion. Sauté over medium heat for 3 to 4 minutes. Add the pancetta and cook until the pancetta and onion are light golden. Stir in the rice and cook until the rice is well coated with the butter, about 1 minute. Add the wine and cook, stirring constantly, until the wine has evaporated. Add just enough broth to barely cover the rice. Cook over medium heat until the broth has been absorbed. Continue cooking the rice in this manner, adding the broth a bit at a time, for about 4 to 5 minutes. Add the peas. Cook for 10 minutes longer. When the rice is almost ready, add the spinach. Cook for 1 to 2 minutes; then stir in the remaining tablespoon of butter and ⅓ cup of the parmigiano. If using frozen vegetables, add them to saucepan during the last few minutes of cooking. Mix thoroughly to blend.

At this point, the rice should have a moist, creamy consistency. Taste for seasoning and serve at once with the remaining parmigiano.

Risotto con i Carciofi

Risotto with Artichokes

Risotto is one of those dishes that cannot be prepared ahead of time because when reheated the rice will become sticky, dry, and overcooked. However, with a little bit of organization the cooking of risotto can be easy and fun. My method is to line up all my ingredients on a tray; I chop and sauté the onion in advance and keep the broth hot on a back burner. About 15 minutes before I want my guests or family to sit down for dinner, I start cooking the risotto. While the risotto is cooking, warm up the serving dishes, watch the news, or enjoy a glass of wine.

Prepare the artichokes. Have on hand a bowl of cold water with the juice of 1 lemon squeezed into it. Cut off the stems of the artichokes and trim away the outer green part, leaving just the white inner core. Cut the stems into small rounds and place them in the cold water. Remove all the outer tough leaves of the artichokes until you reach the white tenderer leaves. Slice off ½ inch from top of the artichokes. Cut the artichokes into quarters and, with a small knife, remove the fuzzy choke. Cut the quarters into slices ½ inch thick and add to the acidulated water.

To prepare the risotto, heat the broth in a medium-size saucepan and keep warm over low heat.

Melt 4 tablespoons of the butter in a large saucepan. When it foams, add the onion and parsley. Drain and dry the artichokes with paper towels. Add them to the onion. Sauté over medium heat for 4 to 5 minutes. Add ½ cup of the hot broth. Cook for 7 to 8 minutes, or until no more broth is left in the pan.

Add the rice to the saucepan. Cook for 1 to 2 minutes, just enough to coat the rice with the butter and onion. Stir in the wine. Cook, stirring constantly, until the wine has evaporated. Add a few ladles of broth, just enough to barely cover the rice. Cook over medium heat until the broth has been absorbed. Continue cooking and stirring the rice in this manner, adding broth a little at a time, until the rice is done, 15 to 20 minutes. The rice should be tender but still firm to the bite.

Stir in remaining tablespoon of butter and ½ cup of the parmigiano and cook for 1 minute longer. At this point, the rice should have a creamy, moist consistency. Taste for seasoning. Serve immediately with additional parmigiano.

My favorite part of the artichoke is the stem. Never discard the stem, because once you peel away the tough outer green layer, you will have a slightly tart but tender and very tasty morsel.

Juice of 1 lemon
2 medium-size artichokes
8 cups homemade chicken broth (page 45),
   or 4 cups canned chicken broth mixed
   with 4 cups water
5 tablespoons unsalted butter
1 onion, finely chopped
2 tablespoons chopped fresh parsley leaves
2 cups Italian Arborio rice
1 cup dry white wine
1 cup freshly grated parmigiano
Salt to taste

SERVES 4 TO 6

Risotto con i Piselli e Erba Cipollina

Risotto with Fresh Peas and Chives

When fresh, young, tender peas are abundant in the spring, I often prepare this risotto which both my husband and I love. In fact, we like it so much that it is not unusual for us to have seconds and clean out anything that is left in the pot. In winter, I use small frozen peas. Since this dish has to be watched and stirred almost throughout its cooking, I try to follow it with a second course that can be prepared ahead, such as Salad of Marinated Capon Breast (page 130) or Shrimp and Red Pepper Salad (page 132), which are perfect dishes to enjoy on a beautiful spring or summer day.

6 cups homemade chicken broth (page 45), or 3 cups canned broth mixed with 3 cups water
5 tablespoons unsalted butter
1 onion, finely chopped
2 cups Italian Arborio rice
1 cup dry white wine
1 cup shelled fresh peas, or 1 cup small frozen peas, thawed
1 tablespoon finely diced chives
1 cup freshly grated parmigiano
Salt to taste

SERVES 4 TO 6

In a medium-size saucepan, heat the broth and keep warm over very low heat.

Melt 4 tablespoons of the butter in a large saucepan. When the butter foams, add the onion. Sauté over medium heat for 5 to 7 minutes, or until the onion is pale yellow. Stir in the rice and cook until it is well coated with the butter and onion, about 1 minute. Add the wine. Cook, stirring constantly until it has evaporated. Add enough broth just to barely cover the rice. Cook, uncovered, over medium heat until the broth has been absorbed. Continue cooking the rice in this manner, adding the broth a bit at a time and stirring, for 4 to 5 minutes. Add the peas. Cook for 10 to 12 minutes longer, adding the broth slowly, until the rice is tender but still firm to the bite. If you are using frozen peas add them to the rice during the last few minutes of cooking. Taste and adjust the seasoning.

Stir in the remaining tablespoon of butter, ⅓ cup of the parmigiano, and the chives. Mix well to incorporate. At this point, the rice should have a moist, creamy consistency. Serve at once with the remaining parmigiano.

Risotto Primaverile

Springtime Risotto

I am always amused when I see a preparation "Primavera style" (spring style) that employs ingredients that have little or nothing to do with spring.

The risotto below is a small masterpiece. Why? Because it is made with a bounty of spring vegetables. Fresh asparagus, sweet peas, small tender carrots, red sweet peppers, and juicy, ripened tomatoes.

Boil or steam the asparagus, peas, and carrots until tender but still firm to the bite. Cut the asparagus into 1-inch pieces and dice the carrot and pepper into pea-size pieces.

Heat the broth in a medium-size saucepan. Add the tomatoes and cook for 10 to 20 seconds, or until the skin begins to split. Plunge the tomatoes into a bowl of cold water. Peel and seed the tomatoes and cut them into small chunks. Keep the hot broth over very low heat to cook the rice.

In a large saucepan heat 4 tablespoons of the butter. When the butter foams, add the onion. Sauté over medium heat until the onion is pale yellow, about 4 to 5 minutes. Add the rice and diced pepper and stir quickly to combine. Add the wine and cook, stirring until the wine has evaporated.

Add 1 ladle of hot broth or just enough to cover the rice. Cook over medium heat, stirring, until broth has been absorbed. Continue cooking and stirring the rice, adding broth a bit at a time for about 15 minutes.

Dilute the saffron in a ladle of broth and stir it into the rice. Add the asparagus, peas, carrots, and tomatoes. Cook for 2 to 3 minutes longer. Stir in the remaining tablespoon of butter and ¼ cup of the parmigiano. Mix thoroughly to blend. At this point the rice should be moist and creamy. Serve at once with the remaining parmigiano.

8 asparagus spears, peeled and trimmed
½ cup freshly shelled peas
1 small carrot, peeled
1 sweet red pepper, seeded
6 cups homemade chicken broth (page 45), or 3 cups canned chicken broth mixed with 3 cups water
2 medium-size ripe tomatoes
5 tablespoons unsalted butter
1 onion, finely chopped
2 cups Italian Arborio rice
1 cup dry white wine
Pinch of powdered saffron
1 cup freshly grated parmigiano

SERVES 4

Risotto con Zucchini e Fiori di Zucchini

Risotto with Zucchini and Zucchini Blossoms

This is, without a doubt, one of the loveliest preparations of Italian gastronomy. It is a dish that is as elegant as it is delicious. The more popular version of this dish uses only the blossoms of zucchini. However, when I am able to find the blossoms that are still attached to their tiny zucchini, I use the zucchini as well, because they are tender, delicate, and very tasty. If you have never made a risotto before and this is your first attempt, make sure to pay particular attention to the various steps. Stir the risotto often as it cooks. Add broth only a little at a time. Taste it a few times to make sure the rice is not overcooked. And remember that the end product should be moist and have a creamy consistency. The time needed to cook a risotto is 15 to 18 minutes.

10 zucchini blossoms

6 of the smallest zucchini that are attached to the blossoms

6 cups homemade chicken broth (page 45), or 3 cups canned chicken broth mixed with 3 cups water

5 tablespoons unsalted butter

1 onion, finely chopped

2 cups Italian Arborio rice

1 cup dry white wine

1 cup freshly grated parmigiano

Salt to taste

SERVES 4 TO 6

Detach blossoms from zucchini. Remove the stems and pistils from the blossoms. Wash the blossoms and zucchini and pat them dry with paper towels. Cut the zucchini into small rounds (you should have 1 to 1½ cups) and blossoms into medium-size pieces.

In a medium-size saucepan, heat the broth and keep it warm over very low heat.

Melt 4 tablespoons of the butter in a large saucepan. When the butter foams, add the onion. Sauté over medium heat for 5 to 7 minutes, or until the onion is pale yellow. Stir in the rice and cook until it is well coated with the butter and onion, about 1 minute. Add the wine. Cook, stirring constantly, until the wine has evaporated. Add a few ladles of broth, just enough to barely cover the rice. Cook, uncovered, over medium heat, until the broth has been absorbed. Add 1 more ladle of broth, the zucchini, and zucchini blossoms. Continue cooking and stirring the rice in this manner until it is tender but still firm to the bite.

Stir in remaining tablespoon of butter and ⅓ cup of the parmigiano. Mix thoroughly to blend. At this point, the rice should have a moist, creamy consistency. Taste and adjust the seasoning. Serve at once with the remaining parmigiano.

Zucchini blossoms are not routinely available at the market, but this still can be a wonderful, delicious dish. If zucchini blossoms are not to be found anywhere, make this risotto with only the smallest, youngest zucchini available.

Meat and Poultry

Coniglio Arrosto con Bacche di Ginepro

Roasted Rabbit with Juniper Berries

When my family and I moved to Sacramento from New York in 1970 I was somewhat dismayed at the lack of special ingredients that supermarkets and specialty stores had to offer. Often I had to go to San Francisco for milk-fed veal or special Italian ingredients. *A lot* has changed. Now in Sacramento I can find almost anything, imported ingredients from Italy, all kinds of herbs and spices, special vinegars and oil, cheeses from around the world, capons, duck, quail, milk-fed veal, and wonderfully plump rabbits.

Rabbit was a favorite of my mother. It was made available to us regularly from an aunt who had a small farm. We children did not like rabbit very much, so my mother would say: "Tonight we are having roasted chicken."

Rabbit meat is lean and solid. An average rabbit weighs between 3 and 4 pounds and should serve 4 to 6 people. Because of its low-fat content, rabbit tends to dry out a bit during cooking. So take care and baste it often as it cooks.

Wash and dry the rabbit pieces thoroughly. Coarsely chop the rosemary, sage, and garlic together. Crush the juniper berries and add them to the rosemary mixture. Rub rabbit pieces with rosemary–juniper mixture. Season with salt and pepper. Put the rabbit pieces into a large bowl and add the vinegar and oil. Let stand for a few hours at room temperature, turning a few times.

Transfer the rabbit and marinade to a large heavy casserole and bring to a boil. Lower the heat and cover casserole, leaving the cover slightly askew. Simmer for 40 to 50 minutes, stirring and basting a few times during the cooking.

Raise the heat to medium-high. Cook, uncovered, for 10 to 15 minutes, or until the rabbit is tender and only a few tablespoons of sauce remain in the casserole. Put the rabbit on a warm platter. Taste the sauce and adjust for seasoning; then spoon it over the rabbit and serve.

1 3- to 4-pound rabbit, cut into serving pieces
Leaves from a few rosemary sprigs, or 1 tablespoon dried rosemary
4 to 5 fresh sage leaves, or a pinch of dried sage
2 garlic cloves
10 juniper berries
Salt and freshly ground black pepper
4 to 5 tablespoons white wine vinegar
½ cup olive oil

SERVES 4 TO 6

This dish can be served in winter as well as summer.

Braciole di Maiale al Latte

Pork Chops Cooked in Milk

This is a very tasty way of cooking pork chops. The chops are first browned in butter and oil and then they are cooked slowly in milk. At the end of the cooking time, the milk will be reduced into a brown sauce that will give the chops additional flavor. Because the meat is cooked with moist heat, it will remain tender and succulent; but still take care not to overcook it.

2 tablespoons unsalted butter
2 tablespoons oil
4 1-inch-thick pork chops, cut from the loin
   or the ribs
2 garlic cloves, lightly crushed
4 to 5 fresh sage leaves (Do not use dried
   sage if fresh sage is not available.)
Salt and freshly ground white pepper
¾ cup milk

SERVES 4

In a large skillet, heat the butter and oil until the butter foams. Add the chops, garlic, and fresh sage. Sauté the chops over medium heat until brown on both sides, about 5 to 6 minutes. Season lightly with salt and pepper. Add the milk. Stir to pick up the bits and pieces attached to the bottom of the skillet. Lower the heat and cover the skillet. Simmer for 12 to 14 minutes, turning the chops once during the cooking. If the milk evaporates completely during cooking, add a bit more.

Transfer the chops to a plate. Raise the heat and cook the sauce down until only a few tablespoons of thickened curds are left in the skillet. Off the heat, remove as much fat as possible. Return the chops to the skillet and return to the heat again. Cook briefly until the chops are well coated with the thick, browned milky sauce. Serve at once.

Gli Arrosti Misti

Mixed Roasted Meats

Imagine a large tray that displays several kinds of perfectly cooked, gloriously succulent roasted meats. A skillful waiter cuts a thin slice from each one and serves it with a bit of the roast's natural juices. Sheer delight!

Several of Bologna's best restaurants serve Arrosti Misti. These roasts generally include milk-fed veal, pork, baby lamb, roast beef, and roasted rabbit. Occasionally, one finds capon and suckling pig as well. Because preparing Arrosti Misti for the average family is quite expensive, the Bolognesi prefer eating these in restaurants. I find, however, that mixed roasted meats are perfect for a summer party; they can be prepared several hours ahead and can be eaten at room temperature.

Two or three meats can be cooked together in a large roasting pan and removed from the oven as they are ready. At the moment of serving, the pan juices could be reheated and spooned over the roasts.

Add to such a buffet grilled vegetables, such as zucchini, eggplants, peppers, tomatoes, and onions, which are perfect accompaniments to the roasts, a fresh summer salad, and a large bowl of ripe fresh fruit or a fruit salad. This is all you need to make a summer party an event to be remembered.

In this recipe I have used three kinds of meat—veal, pork, and turkey—but add or substitute anything else you prefer.

Preheat the oven to 375 degrees at least 15 minutes in advance. Choose a large heavy roasting pan that can accommodate all the meats. Combine the garlic, rosemary, 2 tablespoons of the oil, and salt and pepper in a small bowl. Rub this mixture over the meats.

Put the remaining oil in the roasting pan. Put the meats in the pan and roast for 2 to 2½ hours, basting the meats several times with the pan juices and a bit of dry white wine. Test the individual meats for doneness with a meat thermometer and remove the roasts as they are cooked. Put the meats on a cutting board and leave them, covered only with a kitchen towel, until ready to serve. Set aside the pan with its collected juices.

Before serving, skim off the fat from the pan juices. Put the roasting pan over medium heat (or transfer pan juices to a saucepan) and bring to a boil. Add the remaining white wine to the roasting pan and stir to pick up bits and pieces attached to the bottom of the pan. Cook until the sauce is reduced and has a medium-thick consistency. Slice the meats and serve with the sauce.

3 garlic cloves, finely chopped
Several rosemary sprigs, or 3 tablespoons dried rosemary
¼ cup olive oil
Salt and freshly ground black pepper
1 3-pound boneless veal roast from the shoulder or breast, firmly tied
1 3-pound boneless center-cut pork loin roast, firmly tied
1 whole 5- to 6-pound turkey breast
1 cup dry white wine

SERVES 12 TO 14

A thicker sauce can be produced by reduction or by thickening: Cook the sauce over high heat until it is reduced to whatever amount and consistency you wish to produce a highly flavorful concentrated sauce. Or thicken by adding 1 tablespoon of butter incorporated into a bit of flour and whisked bit by bit into the pan juices.

Broiled or boiled meats can make tasty salads when tossed together with boiled potatoes, capers, and onions.

Arrosto di Manzo Freddo con Capperi e Acciughe

Cold Roast Beef with Capers and Anchovies

Roast beef is hardly an Italian dish. Yet this typical English preparation has become quite popular in Italy. Italians, however, seem to prefer roast beef when it is cold and especially if it is dressed lightly with oil, lemon, and, perhaps, some capers. When roast beef is treated as it is in this recipe, it almost resembles carpaccio, except that carpaccio, of course, is raw.

After the beef is roasted, I let it rest and cool completely; then I cut it into thin slices, dress it, and refrigerate it until ready to serve. I find this a great summer dish because it tastes good, looks good, and it can be prepared completely ahead of time.

8 slices cold, thinly cut roast beef

For the Dressing
Juice of 1 lemon
Salt and freshly ground black pepper
⅓ cup olive oil
2 anchovy fillets, finely chopped
2 tablespoons rinsed and dried capers
1 tablespoon chopped fresh parsley leaves
¼ cup thin slivers of parmigiano (optional)

SERVES 4

In a small bowl, combine all the dressing ingredients, except the parmigiano. Taste and adjust the seasoning. Arrange the roast beef slices on a large serving dish. Spoon the dressing over the meat. Cover the dish and refrigerate for 15 to 20 minutes. Serve slightly chilled, sprinkled with slivers of parmigiano, if you wish.

I generally use bottom round beef, even though other cuts, such as rump roast, can also be used. I cook my roast only with a bit of oil and salt and pepper in a very hot oven (450 degrees) for about 10 to 15 minutes to sear in the juices; then I lower the oven temperature to 350 degrees and cook until done to my liking. Any favored method of roasting the meat is fine.

Filetto alla Griglia con Salsa Balsamica

Broiled Filet of Beef with Balsamic Vinegar

Some of the best food I had during my last trip to Italy, while I was doing research for this book, was at Le 3 Vasselle Restaurant in Torgiano. Torgiano is a very small town nestled in the Umbrian hills not far from Perugia. The cooking at Le 3 Vasselle reflects the traditions of Umbria, which is prevalently a farming region. However, a staff of young, talented chefs also take pride in updating and modernizing some of the region's best dishes.

Here is an example of the straightforward approach of Umbrian cooking as interpreted by Le 3 Vasselle Restaurant. A filet of beef is steeped in a flavorful marinade of balsamic vinegar, fresh herbs, and good red wine; then it is broiled to perfection. The marinade is reduced over high heat to a thick consistency and spooned over the sliced beef. Nothing could be simpler or more outstanding.

Trim the beef of part of its fat (leave some fat on for added moisture). Tie the filet securely to keep its shape and place in a bowl.

Combine the ingredients for the marinade and pour over the filet. Leave at room temperature for about 1 hour. Baste and turn the filet a few times.

Preheat the broiler at least 15 minutes ahead of time. Put the filet in a broiling pan and broil until golden on all sides.

Transfer the filet to the center of the oven. Lower the oven temperature to 400 degrees and bake for 10 to 15 minutes longer. Test for doneness by pressing the meat lightly with a finger. If the meat is firm, yet springy, it is rare. If the meat is firm and unyielding, it is well-done. (For rare, a meat thermometer should register 120 degrees.)

Transfer the filet to a cutting board, remove the string, and let the meat rest for 5 minutes.

Meanwhile, pour the marinade into a skillet and bring to a boil. Cook and stir until the sauce is reduced by half.

Slice the meat and arrange it on warm serving dishes. Spoon the sauce over the meat. Sprinkle each serving with a few red peppercorns, if you wish. Serve at once.

1 3-pound filet of beef

For the Marinade
2 tablespoons balsamic vinegar (see note page 37)
4 tablespoons olive oil
Juice of ½ lemon
1 cup good, full-bodied red wine
A few rosemary sprigs or a pinch of dry rosemary
¼ cup loosely packed fresh oregano leaves, or a pinch of dry oregano
Salt to taste
2 tablespoons rinsed and dried red peppercorns (optional)

SERVES 6

To increase the thickness of the sauce, incorporate 1 tablespoon of butter into a bit of flour and whisk into the sauce bit by bit. Cook rapidly while whisking, until the sauce reaches the desired consistency.

Il Maiale Tonnato della Carla

Cold Pork in Tuna–Pickled Vegetable Sauce

Vitello Tonnato is a classic Italian dish. Because milk-fed veal is very expensive, even in Italy, other cuts of meat are now used for this dish. My sister Carla prepared it with center-cut pork loin. She cooked the pork exactly as she would have cooked the veal. However, to the tuna sauce she added other ingredients, such as pickled onions and roasted peppers, which made the sauce livelier and thoroughly delicious. This is an example of a good cook's creativity.

This dish can be prepared 1 or 2 days ahead of time, which makes it great for informal entertaining or for a good, easy family meal. Follow with a salad of fresh mixed spring vegetables, such as small string beans, zucchini, etc. Dress the salad only with olive oil and lemon juice. These are the joys of summer—good food with very little fuss.

For the pork

1 3-pound center-cut pork roast, boned,
    trimmed, and tied
1 carrot, cut into pieces
1 celery stalk, cut into pieces
1 onion, sliced
2 to 3 cups dry white wine

Tuna–Pickled Vegetable Sauce

1 7-ounce can white tuna in olive oil
3 anchovy fillets
3 tablespoons rinsed and dried capers
4 to 5 small pickled onions, rinsed
4 to 5 small pickles (gherkins)
2 to 3 slices canned roasted pepper
Juice of 1 lemon
½ cup olive oil
½ cup of the broth in which the meat has
    cooked

Mayonnaise

2 egg yolks at room temperature
Salt to taste
1 cup olive oil
Juice of ½ lemon

Bring a large saucepan half full of water to a boil. Add the meat, carrots, celery, onions, and wine. Be sure the liquid covers the meat completely; if not, add boiling water to the pan. Cover the pan, lower the heat, and simmer for 2 to 2½ hours. Keep the liquid at a low simmer or the meat will become tough.

When cooked, transfer the meat and broth to a large bowl and cool completely. Discard the vegetables. The meat can be cooked 1 or 2 days ahead and kept in its own broth, tightly covered in the refrigerator.

To prepare the Tuna–Pickled Vegetable Sauce, put all the ingredients in a blender or food processor and process until smooth. Add ½ cup of the broth in which the meat was cooked, and continue to process until the sauce is a medium-thick consistency. Transfer to a bowl, cover, and refrigerate until ready to use.

Prepare the mayonnaise. Put the egg yolks and a pinch of salt in a bowl. Beat with a wire whisk until the yolks are pale yellow. Slowly beat in a few drops of olive oil. Keep adding oil, a few drops at a time, beating constantly. Do not add the oil too fast or the sauce will not emulsify. Beat in the lemon juice. Taste and adjust the seasoning. Refrigerate the mayonnaise until ready to use.

Cut the pork into thin slices. Cover the bottom of a

large serving dish with a thin coating of the sauce. Arrange the meat over the sauce; then cover the meat with additional sauce. Cover platter and refrigerate for several hours or overnight. When ready to serve, sprinkle with the capers and, if you wish, some chopped parsley or chopped chives.

Garnish
Rinsed and dried capers
Chopped fresh parsley (optional)
Chopped fresh chives (optional)

SERVES 8

Cooling and storing the pork in its cooking liquid keeps it tender and juicy.

Make an easy Vitello Tonnato with leftover roasted veal or an equally easy Maiale Tonnato with leftover roasted pork. Follow the directions for Maiale Tonnato. Slice the leftover roast meat and leave it in the sauce for several hours before serving as described in the basic recipe.

Costolette di Vitello alla Salvia

Veal Chops Sautéed with Butter and Sage

Whenever milk-fed veal is available in Sacramento, I invariably prepare this dish. The preparation is totally effortless and the ingredients few, which is why good-quality veal becomes very important; I would not consider doing this dish without the best milk-fed veal.

In a large skillet, heat the butter and oil. When butter foams, add the sage and veal. Cook over medium heat for 3 to 4 minutes on each side. The veal should have a nice golden color outside and be slightly pink inside. Season with salt and pepper. Serve immediately with the lemon slices.

4 ¾-inch-thick veal chops cut from the loin
2 tablespoons unsalted butter
2 tablespoons olive oil
8 fresh sage leaves, or 4 dried sage leaves, crumbled
Salt and freshly ground black pepper
Lemon slices

SERVES 4

Mamma Lea's Roasted Potatoes (page 260) and String Bean Salad with Lemon (page 139) would be perfect accompaniments to this lovely veal dish.

Scaloppe di Maiale alle Ciliege

Pork Tenderloin with Cherries

Cooking with fruit is nothing new. In many dishes from the Renaissance, we find that fruit appears often in conjunction with meats or fowls. Ancient Romans loved to eat figs with liver; and modern Italians love figs and melon with sweet Parma prosciutto. *La Nuova Cucina Italiana*, in its pursuit of newer and exciting food combinations, has rediscovered fruit and uses it liberally. Here and abroad we have available, today, in most markets, tropical fruit that was once impossible to obtain. And, thanks to refrigeration, we can freeze the summer bounty and use it throughout the year. At Christmastime I love to stuff my turkey with prunes, dates, and figs, and the Sicilian salad of oranges and fennel is one I adore. For me, the only way to eat game is paired with fruit as a foil to the gamy taste. With a little imagination and some adventuresomeness, one can try innumerable combinations. The following is an adaptation of a marvelous dish I had in Milano.

Melt the butter in a large skillet. When butter foams, add the pork slices, and sauté over medium heat until light golden on both sides, about 2 minutes. Season with salt and pepper. Then add the wine and stir and cook until the wine has evaporated. Transfer the meat to a plate.

Add the cherries, Marsala, and brandy to the skillet. Cover and cook until the cherries are tender, about 15 minutes. Add the cherry preserve and sugar and stir. Return the pork slices to the skillet. Cook, uncovered, over medium heat for 7 to 8 minutes.

Transfer the meat to a warm serving platter and keep it warm in a very low oven. Adjust the consistency of the sauce: If it is too thin, boil it down until it is medium-thick and somewhat syrupy. Spoon over the meat and serve.

3 tablespoons unsalted butter
1½ pounds boneless pork tenderloin, cut into ½-inch-thick slices
Salt and freshly ground black pepper
1 cup good-quality red wine
2 cups pitted fresh or frozen cherries
½ cup dry Marsala wine, preferably Florio brand
¼ cup brandy
2 tablespoons cherry preserve
1 tablespoon sugar

SERVES 4

If you are using frozen cherries, cut the cooking time. After the meat has been sautéed and transferred to a plate, add the frozen cherries along with the Marsala, brandy, cherry preserve, and sugar to the skillet. Cook over high heat until the sauce is medium-thick before returning the pork to the skillet for the final cooking.

Scaloppine di Vitello al Vino Bianco

Veal Scaloppine with White Wine Sauce

Scaloppine still remain, uncontestably, the best of all fast Italian dishes. Good scaloppine can be prepared virtually in a matter of minutes. For perfect scaloppine follow these simple steps:

- Start with good milk-fed veal and have scaloppine cut from the top round.
- Scaloppine should be neither thicker nor thinner than ¼ inch. Slices that are much thinner than ¼ inch will dry out during cooking.
- Scaloppine should be cooked very fast over high heat. The meat should be golden outside and still pink and juicy inside.
- Do not crowd the skillet. If necessary, cook the scaloppine a few at a time and keep them on a plate until you are ready to put them back into the skillet to be mixed with the sauce.
- Scaloppine should never be prepared ahead of time because in reheating the meat will become tough and dry.

I know that a lot of people become apprehensive when cooking has to be done at the last moment. My suggestions are: Practice with the dish a few times before you make it for company, and do not make scaloppine for more than 4 to 6 people, unless you are very skillful at the stove and can handle a couple of skillets at the same time. Finally, have all your ingredients premeasured on a tray. If you follow this advice, I have no doubt that you will be making the best scaloppine in town.

Put the scaloppine between two pieces of wax paper and pound lightly. Then put the scaloppine on a piece of aluminum foil and sprinkle lightly with the flour. Season with salt and pepper.

Heat 3 tablespoons of the butter and the oil in a large heavy skillet. When the butter foams, add the scaloppine. Cook over high heat until the veal is lightly golden on both sides, about 2 minutes. Transfer the veal to a plate.

Add the remaining tablespoon of butter to the skillet. Then add the wine. Deglaze by stirring to dissolve the meat juices attached to the bottom of the skillet. When the wine is reduced by half, add the parsley and stir to incorporate.

Return the veal to the skillet and mix gently and very briefly with the sauce. Transfer the meat to a warm serving platter, spoon the sauce over the veal, and serve.

1½ pounds veal scaloppine from the top round, cut ¼ inch thick
½ cup all-purpose unbleached flour
Salt and freshly ground black pepper
4 tablespoons unsalted butter
1 tablespoon oil
1 cup good dry white wine, such as a Chardonnay
1 tablespoon chopped fresh parsley leaves

SERVES 4 TO 6

Spezzatino Primaverile

Springtime Veal Stew

This stew is lighter than its winter counterpart. The meat is browned without the addition of flour. The tomatoes are fresh and so are the zucchini and the peas. The vegetables are cooked only long enough to be tender. The result is a dish that blends, and yet retains individual flavors.

4 tablespoons olive oil
1 garlic clove, finely chopped
1 onion, finely chopped
2½ pounds veal shoulder, cut into 2-inch cubes
1 cup dry white wine
½ cup homemade or canned chicken broth
Salt and freshly ground black pepper
4 ripe tomatoes, peeled and seeded (page 55)
3 small zucchini
1 cup shelled fresh peas
2 tablespoons chopped fresh parsley leaves, or ⅓ cup shredded small fresh basil leaves

SERVES 4 TO 6

Heat the oil in a large skillet or casserole. Add the garlic and onion and sauté over medium heat for 1 to 2 minutes. Raise the heat and add the veal. Cook and stir until the meat is lightly golden. Add the wine and cook until it has evaporated. Stir in the broth and season lightly with salt and pepper. Cover the skillet, leaving the cover slightly askew, and cook over low heat for 25 to 30 minutes.

Meanwhile, chop the tomatoes roughly. Cut the zucchini into medium-thick slices (about ¼ inch). Add the tomatoes, zucchini, and peas to the skillet. Cover and cook for 8 to 10 minutes. Taste the vegetables for doneness and the sauce for seasoning. Stir in the parsley and cook for 1 to 2 minutes longer; then serve.

Arrosto di Vitello Ripieno

Stuffed Veal Roast

This roast is very popular in my region of Emilia-Romagna. My mother would prepare it for special occasions accompanied by fluffy mashed potatoes and seasonal vegetables. The day after, we would eat, cold, whatever roast was left, next to a mixed green salad. Classic, honest food will never go out of style.

This wonderfully versatile dish can be served warm with its own sauce at a formal sit-down dinner, or at room temperature at an informal gathering, buffet, or luncheon.

Beat the eggs in a small bowl. Add the parmigiano, chive, basil, or parsley and season with salt and pepper. Beat to combine.

Heat the oil in a 10-inch nonstick skillet. Add the egg mixture. Cook over medium heat for 4 to 5 minutes or until the bottom of the frittata is lightly browned. Put a large plate on top of the skillet and turn the frittata onto the plate. Slide the frittata back into skillet, uncooked side down. Cook for 2 to 3 minutes longer, then slide it onto another plate.

Place the veal on a work surface. Season it lightly with salt and pepper. Cover meat with the slices of pancetta, leaving about a 3-inch free border around the veal. Put the frittata in the center over the pancetta. Roll up the veal, jelly-roll fashion, and tie securely with string.

Heat the butter and oil in a large, heavy casserole. When the butter foams add the veal. Brown the meat on all sides over medium heat. Add the wine and stir to pick up bits and pieces attached to the bottom of the casserole. Cook until the wine is reduced by half. Cover the casserole, leaving the lid slightly askew. Add more wine if the sauce dries out too much. Cook for 1½ to 2 hours or until meat thermometer inserted into the veal reads 150 degrees. Turn the veal a few times throughout cooking. During the last 5 minutes of cooking, cook the veal, uncovered, over high heat, stirring and turning the veal until the sauce reaches a thick, syrupy consistency and coats the veal thoroughly.

Transfer the veal to a cutting board and let it rest for 5 to 10 minutes. Remove string and slice the meat. Arrange the veal on a serving platter or on individual dishes. Strain the sauce; spoon a bit over each slice and serve.

To increase the amount of sauce, after the veal has been transferred to a cutting board, add 1 cup dry white wine or dry Marsala wine to the casserole, together with a few tablespoons of heavy cream. Simmer the sauce, uncovered, until it is reduced approximately by half and it is thick and velvety.

For the Frittata

3 large eggs
2 tablespoons freshly grated parmigiano
3 tablespoons chopped chives, fresh basil leaves, or fresh parsley leaves
Salt and freshly ground black pepper
2 tablespoons olive oil

For the Roast

1 6- to 7-pound veal breast, boned and trimmed of all excess fat
Salt and freshly ground black pepper
¼ pound pancetta, sliced
2 tablespoons unsalted butter
3 tablespoons olive oil
1 cup dry white wine

SERVES 10

Pollo alle Erbe

Chicken with Herbs

Sometimes it takes more time, effort, and money to go out for a pizza than to cook a simple, delicious dish. The chicken for this dish was on sale—less than $3.00 for a 3-pound bird. The herbs were picked from my garden. It took me 10 minutes to chop the herbs, wash the chicken, and start the dish. Then, with the exception of an occasional stir, the chicken didn't need any of my attention. It was ready, start to finish, in 35 minutes, and it was enough for my family of 4. But the best part was that it was so good that we soaked up every little bit of sauce that was left on the plates and in the casserole. A crusty loaf of Italian bread and a mixed green salad is all you need to make this a complete meal.

1 cup canned imported Italian plum tomatoes with their juices

1 3- to 3½-pound frying chicken, cut into serving pieces

4 tablespoons olive oil

2 or 3 rosemary sprigs, or 1 tablespoon dried rosemary, chopped

4 fresh sage leaves, chopped, or ½ teaspoon dried sage, crumbled

2 garlic cloves, finely chopped

¼ cup good red wine vinegar

½ cup homemade or canned chicken broth

1 tablespoon fresh chopped parsley leaves

SERVES 4

Press the tomatoes through a food mill or sieve to remove the seeds. Wash and dry the chicken pieces thoroughly.

Heat the oil in a large skillet. Add the rosemary, sage, and garlic. Stir for a few seconds and then add the chicken pieces. Sauté over medium heat until the chicken is browned on all sides. Add the vinegar and stir and cook until the vinegar has evaporated. Add the chicken broth and tomatoes. Season with salt and pepper. Cover the skillet, leaving the cover slightly askew. Cook over low heat for 30 to 40 minutes, or until the chicken is tender. Transfer the chicken to a warm serving platter and keep warm in oven, if necessary.

Skim as much fat as possible from the pan juices in the skillet. Return to the heat and add the parsley. Cook, stirring for 1 to 2 minutes, or until the sauce has a nice thick consistency. Spoon the sauce over the chicken and serve hot.

Petti di Pollo Marinati

Sautéed Marinated Chicken Breast

Chinese and Italian cooking have several similarities. Both use pasta and rice and many dishes are cooked briefly over high heat. The chicken in this dish is marinated in oil, lemon juice, and fresh herbs; then it is sautéed quickly in its own marinade. The marinade and the short cooking time produce a very tender chicken. Besides being fast, it is also economical and very easy to prepare. I generally serve this chicken with Broiled Eggplant with Garlic and Fresh Oregano (page 140) or with Roasted Red Peppers and Yellow Tomato Salad (page 136).

Skin, bone, and split the chicken breasts. Put the breasts in a large bowl. Add the oil, 2 tablespoons of lemon juice, garlic, and basil. Season with salt and several grindings of pepper. Mix well. Cover the bowl and marinate at room temperature for about 1 hour.

Put a large skillet over medium-high heat. Add the chicken and all of its marinade. Cook for 7 to 8 minutes, turning the chicken once during the cooking. The chicken should have a light golden color.

Stir in the additional lemon juice and cook and stir until the juice has evaporated. Serve hot.

2 large chicken breasts
5 tablespoons olive oil
2 tablespoons fresh lemon juice
2 garlic cloves, finely chopped
¼ cup roughly chopped fresh basil leaves, or 2 tablespoons finely chopped fresh parsley leaves
Salt and freshly ground black pepper
Juice of 1 large lemon

SERVES 4

The marinated chicken can also be broiled or grilled.

Costolette di Vitello alla Pizzaiola

Veal Chops with Tomato–Onion Sauce

Even though I love to eat grilled food when the weather gets hot, occasionally I feel the urge for something with a sauce—one that I can soak up with some good bread. These chops are wonderfully light and are perfect for a summer meal even with the addition of a fresh tomato sauce.

4 tablespoons olive oil
4 ¾-inch-thick veal chops from the loin
Salt and freshly ground black pepper
1 small onion, finely chopped
1 garlic clove, finely chopped
½ cup dry white wine
4 juicy ripe tomatoes, peeled and seeded (page 55) and cut roughly into pieces, or 1 cup canned imported Italian plum tomatoes, roughly chopped, with their juices
¼ cup loosely packed fresh oregano leaves, or
1 tablespoon chopped fresh parsley leaves

SERVES 4

Heat the oil in a large skillet. Add the veal chops and cook over medium heat for 3 to 4 minutes on each side, or until the veal has a nice golden color outside and is still medium-pink inside. Season lightly with salt and pepper. Transfer the veal to a large serving platter and keep warm in the oven while you finish the sauce.

Add the onion and garlic to the skillet. Cook over medium heat until the onion is lightly golden, 5 to 7 minutes. Raise the heat and add the wine. Cook and stir to pick up the bits and pieces attached to the bottom of the skillet. When the wine has evaporated, add the tomatoes and season with salt and pepper. Cook over high heat for 4 to 5 minutes. Stir in the oregano. Spoon some of the sauce over each chop and serve.

Filetti di Tacchino con Le Mele

Fillet of Turkey Breast with Apples

Turkey is as popular with Italians as it is with Americans and today we have the convenience of being able to buy turkey parts as well as the whole bird. The breast is especially good for preparations, such as roasts or scaloppine, while the darker meat is generally cooked with various sauces. When milk-fed veal is not available, sliced turkey breast—scaloppine—is a good, as well as economical, substitute.

This Fillet of Turkey Breast with Apples is simple to prepare and delicious. Leftover roasted turkey (I use leftover Christmas turkey) can also be paired with buttered apples for a lovely family meal. The only important thing to keep in mind in cooking turkey is not to overcook it or it will become dry and stringy.

Peel, core, and slice the apples. Put the apple slices, wine, and butter in a medium-size skillet. Bring to a boil; then lower the heat and simmer the apples for 3 to 5 minutes, depending on the thickness of the slices. The apples should still be a little firm to the touch. Tilt the skillet and remove most of the liquid left in the skillet with a tablespoon. Add the 3 tablespoons of butter and the sugar to the pan and sauté briefly. Keep warm over very low heat.

Sprinkle the turkey slices very lightly with flour. Season with salt and pepper.

Heat the 3 tablespoons of butter in a large skillet. When the butter foams, sauté the turkey slices for 1 to 2 minutes on each side, or until they are lightly golden. Transfer the meat to a platter and keep it warm in the oven. Add the wine to the skillet and stir to pick up any bits and pieces attached to the bottom of the skillet. When the wine is reduced by half, add the chicken bouillon cube and apple juice. Cook over high heat for 2 to 3 minutes, or until the liquid is again reduced by half. Lower the heat and add the cream. Simmer for a few minutes, or until the sauce has a medium-thick consistency. Taste and adjust the seasoning.

Place a few slices of turkey on 4 warm individual serving dishes. Spoon a bit of sauce over each serving. Arrange some apple slices over each dish and serve.

One of my favorite family traditions is to serve leftover Christmas turkey with apples as prepared here.

For the Apples

3 Golden Delicious apples
1 cup dry white wine
3 tablespoons unsalted butter
¼ cup sugar

For the Turkey

1½ pounds turkey breast, cut into ¼-inch-thick scaloppine
½ cup all-purpose unbleached flour
Salt and freshly ground black pepper
3 tablespoons unsalted butter
1 cup dry white wine
1 chicken bouillon cube, crushed
½ cup apple juice
⅓ cup heavy cream

SERVES 4

Spiedini in Salsa

Chicken Skewers with Wine and Worcestershire Sauce

These are spiedini with a twist: They are sautéed in butter and oil instead of being broiled or grilled. The wine, Worcestershire sauce, and fresh rosemary produce a nice sauce and give the meat a lovely flavor. Because sausage takes a bit longer to cook than chicken, I parboil it briefly before I thread it onto the skewers. I also fold over the thinner part of the breast of chicken when I put it on the skewers, so it will cook evenly. The skewers used in this recipe are the short (6-inch) bamboo skewers that are easily available in the Oriental food section of most supermarkets.

1 pound Italian mild sausage
2 chicken breasts, skinned, boned, and split
¼ pound pancetta, cut into ⅛-inch-thick slices
⅓ cup all-purpose unbleached flour
2 tablespoons unsalted butter
2 tablespoons olive oil
1 rosemary sprig, or 1 teaspoon dried rosemary
1 cup dry white wine
2 tablespoons Worcestershire sauce
Salt and freshly ground black pepper

SERVES 4

Cut the sausages into 2-inch-long pieces. Bring a small saucepan of water to a boil. Add the sausage pieces and cook for 1 to 2 minutes. Drain and pat dry with paper towels.

Cut the chicken into 2-inch cubes and pancetta into 2-inch pieces. Thread the chicken on the skewers, alternating the sausages and pancetta. Sprinkle the spiedini lightly with the flour.

Heat the butter and oil in a large skillet. When the butter foams, add the spiedini and rosemary. Cook, uncovered, over medium heat, until golden on all sides, about 7 to 8 minutes.

Add the wine, Worcestershire sauce, and salt and pepper. Cook over high heat, turning the spiedini, until the wine has evaporated and only a few tablespoons of thick sauce are left in skillet. Place two spiedini on each plate, dribble some of the sauce over them, and serve immediately.

Seafood

Branzino al Pomodoro Fresco

Sea Bass Poached with Fresh Tomatoes

When juicy fresh tomatoes are in season, prepare a simple sauce seasoned with olives, anchovies, and capers. Braise a nice fish fillet in the sauce for a short time and then sit back and enjoy the best product of land and sea in a flavorful, succulent combination. The amount of tomatoes needed to braise this fish should be only enough to keep the fish moist. If your fillet is an inch thick, you need only half an inch of liquid, in this case tomatoes, in the skillet. Remember that the sauce should simmer, not boil, or the fish will break up. Swordfish and shark are also excellent when cooked in this way.

Chop the olives and anchovies roughly. Bring a large saucepan two-thirds full of water to a boil. Add the tomatoes. Cook for 30 to 40 seconds, or until the skins begin to split. With a slotted spoon, transfer the tomatoes to a bowl of cold water. Peel and seed the tomatoes and then cut them into chunks. Put them through a food mill together with the olives and anchovies.

In a large skillet, heat the oil. Add the tomato mixture and season with salt and pepper. Cook, uncovered, over medium heat for 10 to 12 minutes. Add the sea bass, cover, and simmer for about 10 minutes. During the last few minutes of cooking add the capers and parsley.

Transfer the fish to individual warm dishes. Spoon the sauce all around the fish and serve at once.

8 pitted black olives

3 anchovy fillets

2 pounds juicy ripe tomatoes, or 4 cups canned imported Italian plum tomatoes with their juices, puréed in a food mill

3 tablespoons olive oil

Salt and freshly ground black pepper

4 sea bass fillets, about 1 inch thick (1½ to 2 pounds total weight)

2 tablespoons rinsed and dried capers

1 tablespoon chopped fresh parsley leaves

SERVES 4

Pesce Spada con Salsa Verde di Acetosa e Peperoni

Broiled Swordfish with Green Sorrel and Pepper Sauce

Salsa Verde is a classic green sauce made with parsley, capers, anchovies, garlic, and olive oil. This sauce is widely used in northern Italy as an accompaniment to mixed boiled meats. The sauce in this recipe follows the same principle, except its main ingredient is sorrel (*acetosa*), a spinach-like vegetable that has a slightly tart lemon flavor. Sweet red or yellow peppers are added here for additional taste and a bit of crunchiness. The result is a sauce that is delicate and appetizing and so good that you'll find yourself eating it with a spoon. The sauce can be kept in the refrigerator for several days; serve it at room temperature to fully appreciate its fine flavor. Use Italian parsley if sorrel is not available.

For the Sauce

¼ pound sorrel or 2 cups loosely packed
    fresh parsley leaves
½ cup olive oil
Juice of 1 large lemon
2 garlic cloves
2 tablespoons rinsed and dried capers
1 large sweet yellow or red pepper
Salt and freshly ground black pepper

For the Swordfish

2 pounds 1-inch-thick swordfish steaks cut
    into 4 serving pieces
Olive oil

SERVES 4

Prepare the sauce. Wash the sorrel and pat it dry with paper towels. Tear the leaves away from their stalks. Discard the stalks and cut the leaves into rough pieces. Put the leaves in a food processor or a blender and add the oil, lemon juice, garlic, and capers; process until smooth.

Wash and dry the pepper. Cut it in half and remove the seeds. Cut the pepper into rough pieces and add them to the food processor. Process, turning the machine on and off until the pepper is cut into very small pieces, but do not purée it. Season lightly with salt and pepper. Taste and adjust the seasoning. Pour the sauce into a bowl, cover tightly, and refrigerate until ready to use.

Preheat the broiler or prepare a barbecue so that the coals are ready when you are ready to grill the fish. Brush the swordfish steaks lightly with oil. Place under the broiler or on the grill over the hot coals about 4 inches from the heat source and cook for 3 to 4 minutes on each side. The fish is done when the top is lightly golden and the inside is opaque—take care not to overcook it.

Serve the fish accompanied by 2 tablespoons of the sorrel–pepper sauce.

Vongole alla Marinara

Clams with Savory Tomato Sauce

Whenever I find small littleneck clams at my local market, I let myself be carried away and always buy more than I really need. Those clams then become a succulent feast for the evening meal, cooked simply with onion, garlic, parsley, wine, and tomatoes, in the true, straightforward Italian way. Cook the clams briefly until they open. Some, like people, are stubborn and will require a little longer cooking before opening. However, if they fail to open, simply discard them.

Soak the clams in cool salted water for 20 minutes; then wash them, scrubbing as necessary in cool running water. Put the clams in a large saucepan. Add the wine, oil, and 1 cup of water. Cover the saucepan and cook over high heat until the clams open; remove them with a slotted spoon as they do. When all the clams have been removed, bring the cooking liquid back to a boil and cook until it is reduced to about 1 cup. Strain the liquid through paper towels to remove the sandy deposits. Set aside.

Put the tomatoes through a food mill or strainer to remove the seeds. Wipe the saucepan in which the clams were cooked and pour in the oil. Add the onion and sauté over medium heat until it is pale golden. Add the garlic and almost all the parsley and cook for about 1 minute without letting the garlic turn brown. Add the wine and reduce by half; add the reserved clam juice and tomatoes. Season with salt and several grindings of pepper. Cook, uncovered, over medium heat, for 10 to 12 minutes. The sauce should be thick; add a bit more wine if necessary to thin it.

Add the clams and sprinkle with the remaining parsley. Cook for about 1 minute, stirring to coat the clams with the sauce. Serve with slices of crusty Italian bread.

For the Clams

4 pounds littleneck clams, the smallest possible
1 cup dry white wine
1 tablespoon olive oil

For the Sauce

2 cups canned imported Italian plum tomatoes with their juices
4 tablespoons olive oil
⅓ cup finely chopped onion
2 garlic cloves, finely chopped
2 tablespoons chopped fresh parsley leaves
1 cup dry white wine
Salt and freshly ground black pepper

SERVES 4 AS A MAIN COURSE

Trota alla Griglia

Broiled Trout

Nothing could be simpler, better, and healthier than fresh fish broiled with only a few drops of good olive oil. Italians and other Mediterranean people have known this for centuries, and Americans are now beginning to adopt this simple style of cooking. Broiled fish goes hand in hand with broiled vegetables.

4 trout, about ¾ pound each
4 tablespoons chopped fresh parsley leaves
3 garlic cloves, finely chopped
⅓ cup olive oil, preferably virgin olive oil, plus extra oil to sprinkle on the cooked fish
Salt and freshly ground black pepper
Lemon slices

SERVES 4

Scale, wash, and dry the trout. Cut off their heads and tails, if you wish. With a sharp knife make a few shallow slashes in the skin of each trout.

In a small bowl, combine the parsley, garlic, some of the olive oil, and salt and pepper. Press this mixture into the slashes in the trout and into the cavities. Brush the trout with the remaining oil.

Preheat the broiler or start a barbecue so that the coals are ready when you are ready to grill the fish. Oil the barbecue grill, if using, or the broiler pan. Put the fish 4 to 5 inches from the heat source. Cook for 4 to 5 minutes on each side. The fish is done when the interior of the flesh is just opaque. Serve with the lemon slices and a few drops of good olive oil.

Serve this dish with Warm Roasted Eggplant, Pepper, and Tomato Salad (page 123) or with a refreshing String Bean Salad with Lemon (page 139). If you wish to start your meal with an appetizer, consider serving Crostini with Spicy Scallops (page 58) or Crostini with Fresh and Sun-Dried Tomatoes (page 56).

Involtini di Pesce Spada

Stuffed Swordfish Bundles

In this recipe, a savory stuffing is spread over thin slices of swordfish steak; then the fish is rolled up into tight bundles and broiled. As swordfish tends to become dry, especially when broiled or barbecued, it should be basted often during cooking. Salmoriglio is a classic Sicilian sauce that almost invariably accompanies broiled fish. I generally prepare my swordfish bundles early in the day, brush them with salmoriglio, and refrigerate them until they are to be cooked. While I preheat the broiler, I bring the fish back to room temperature, set the table, and prepare the salad.

Combine the ingredients for the sauce in a small bowl and beat to incorporate.

Cut 1 slice of swordfish into small pieces.

Heat the oil in a medium-size skillet. Add the onion and sauté over medium heat until it begins to color, 4 to 5 minutes. Add the cut-up fish, parsley, and garlic. Stir and cook a few minutes longer. Add the bread crumbs and mix briefly with the other ingredients. Put the mixture in a blender or in a food mill and process until smooth. Transfer the mixture to a bowl and add the diced cheese and eggs. Season with salt and pepper. Mix until the ingredients are well combined.

With a meat pounder, lightly flatten the fish slices. Spread some of the onion–egg mixture over each slice. Roll each slice up into a bundle and secure with 1 or 2 wooden toothpicks. Brush the bundles with some of the sauce. The dish can be prepared to this point several hours ahead of time and then refrigerated.

Preheat the broiler or prepare barbecue so that the coals are ready when you are ready to grill the fish. Again, brush each bundle with some of the sauce. Put the bundles on an oiled broiling pan and place under broiler about 4 inches from the heat source. Or put them on the grill over the hot coals. Cook for 3 to 4 minutes, or until lightly browned. Gently turn the bundles, brush again with the sauce, and broil 3 to 4 minutes longer. Serve hot, accompanied by the remaining Salmoriglio sauce.

A tomato salad or Broiled Eggplant with Garlic and Fresh Oregano (page 140) could accompany these savory bundles.

For the Salmoriglio Sauce
Juice of 1 lemon
Salt and freshly ground black pepper
½ cup olive oil
1 tablespoon chopped fresh parsley leaves

For the Swordfish Bundles
9 thin slices swordfish steaks, about ¼ inch thick, with skin removed
3 tablespoons olive oil
1 onion, sliced
2 tablespoons chopped fresh parsley leaves
1 garlic clove, finely chopped
¼ cup unseasoned bread crumbs
⅓ cup finely diced Provolone or parmigiano
2 large eggs
Salt and freshly ground black pepper

SERVES 4

Il Rombo di Pierino

Turbot with Vinegar–Mint Sauce

Pierino is the owner and chef of the remarkable Gambero Rosso restaurant of Cesenatico, a beautiful resort town on the Adriatic coast. A Neapolitan by birth, Pierino cooks fish probably better than anybody I know. This is one of his delicious dishes made with turbot, a flat fish with a delicate and delicious flavor that is caught on the Atlantic coast of Europe and the Mediterranean. Occasionally, we can find here fresh or frozen Greenland turbot; flounder or halibut are good substitutes.

2 *pounds turbot, flounder, or halibut fillets, cut into 4 serving pieces*
2 *tablespoons olive oil*
1 *garlic clove, finely chopped*
1 *cup dry white wine*
2 *tablespoons good white wine vinegar*
1 *tablespoon chopped fresh mint, parsley, or basil leaves or chives*
Salt and freshly ground black pepper

SERVES 4

Preheat the broiler. Place the broiler pan 4 inches from the heat source at least 10 minutes ahead of the cooking time. Brush the fish lightly with oil on both sides and put it on the hot broiling pan. Cook for 10 minutes for each inch of thickness. The fish is done when the top is lightly golden and the inside still is opaque.

Meanwhile, prepare the sauce. Heat the oil in a small saucepan. Add the garlic and sauté very lightly, but do not let it turn brown. Add the wine and vinegar and cook over medium heat, uncovered, until reduced by half. Add the mint and season with salt and pepper; cook for 20 to 30 seconds longer.

Transfer the fish to individual warm serving plates, spoon a bit of the vinegar–mint sauce over each fillet and serve immediately.

Grigliata di Pesce Misto

Skewers of Mixed Broiled Fish

Italians love grilled and broiled food. "La bistecca ai ferri," "la carne ai ferri," "il pesce ai ferri" are favorite items on restaurant menus. This is a love that was born with the ancient tradition of cooking meat, fish, and fowl on a spit. Grilling or broiling heightens and highlights the flavor of food. If done expertly, food cooked in this manner can achieve a rarely surpassed succulence. What could be better for the hurried life-style that most of us have today than cooking fast, tasty grilled dishes.

My sister-in-law in Bologna works long hours for a small local fashion company. On her way home from work she shops for what she wants to cook that particular night. Three out of five nights she prepares grilled or broiled food. If a fish is broiled, she might prepare a simple Salsa Verde to accompany it. Tomatoes, eggplants, or onions might go alongside the fish on the broiler pan; potatoes will roast with fresh rosemary and garlic. And everything will be absolutely delicious.

The fish in this recipe is marinated in parsley, garlic, bread crumbs, anchovies, oil, and lemon for a few hours and then threaded onto metal skewers and coated with an additional marinade mixture to protect the delicate flesh from scorching while adding a delicious flavor.

Any firm-fleshed fish, such as tuna, shark, and cod, can be used in this dish. Don't be limited by my recipe. Just go ahead and explore new possibilities.

In a large bowl, combine all the marinade ingredients. The mixture should be fairly moist. Add a bit more oil, if necessary.

Shell and devein the prawns. Wash under cool running water and pat dry with paper towels. Add the prawns to the bowl with the marinade and mix to coat them. Cut the halibut and swordfish into 2-inch cubes. Add to bowl and mix to coat. Let stand at room temperature for about 1 hour, or cover the bowl tightly with aluminum foil and refrigerate for several hours.

Preheat the broiler. Thread equal amounts of the fish onto 4 metal skewers. Put the skewers on a broiler pan under the broiler 4 to 5 inches from the heat source. Broil for 2 to 3 minutes, or until the fish becomes lightly golden. Turn the skewers and broil a few minutes longer. Serve hot with lemon wedges.

Of course, these fish skewers are equally, if not even more, delicious grilled over charcoal.

For the Marinade
⅓ cup chopped fresh parsley leaves
3 garlic cloves, finely chopped
2 anchovy fillets, finely chopped
A few basil sprigs if available, leaves chopped
½ cup dry unseasoned bread crumbs
½ cup olive oil
Juice of 1 lemon
Salt and freshly ground black pepper

For the Fish
8 large prawns or jumbo shrimp
1 pound boneless and skinless halibut
1 pound boneless and skinless swordfish
Lemon wedges

SERVES 4

Scampi col Pomodoro Fresco

Shrimp with Fresh Tomatoes

In 1983, television station KCRA of Sacramento sent me to Italy with a reporter and a cameraman to film some of Italy's best restaurants. One of our stops was Venice, where we featured the superlative food of the Cipriani hotel. The dishes that were served to us were, in the true Italian tradition, all quite simple. What made them so spectacular was the freshness of the ingredients and the accurate, elegant presentation.

Fresh shrimp and juicy tomatoes are all you need to successfully execute this specialty of the Hotel Cipriani.

5 juicy ripe tomatoes
3 tablespoons virgin olive oil or regular
   olive oil
Salt and freshly ground black pepper
1½ pounds medium-size shrimp
3 tablespoons unsalted butter
2 garlic cloves, finely chopped
1 cup dry white wine
1 to 2 tablespoons chopped fresh parsley
   leaves

SERVES 4

Bring a large saucepan of water to a boil. Add the tomatoes. Cook for 30 to 40 seconds, or until the tomato skins begin to split. Put the tomatoes in a bowl of cold water. Peel and seed the tomatoes and then cut them into chunks.

Heat 2 tablespoons of the oil in a small saucepan. Add the tomatoes and season with salt and pepper. Cook over high heat, uncovered, for 4 to 5 minutes, or until the tomatoes give up their excess liquid. At the end of the cooking time, the tomatoes should still be a bit chunky.

Meanwhile, shell and devein the shrimp. Wash them under cool running water and then pat dry with paper towels.

In a large skillet, heat the butter with the remaining 1 tablespoon of oil. When the butter foams, add the garlic and shrimp and sauté over medium heat until the shrimp are lightly colored, 1 to 2 minutes. Raise the heat and add the wine. When the wine is reduced by half, add the tomatoes. Sprinkle with the parsley and mix well. Taste and adjust the seasoning. Transfer the shrimp to a warm serving dish. Serve hot, accompanied by boiled or steamed rice, if you wish.

Cape Sante Appetitose

Scallops with Parsley, Garlic, and Wine Sauce

Everything here is cooked over high heat, so stir the scallops constantly and shake the skillet to prevent them from scorching. In spite of the stirring, some of the bread crumbs will stick to the skillet, but don't worry. Add the wine and stir vigorously to pick up everything attached to the bottom of the skillet. The bread crumbs will thicken the sauce. Try to select scallops that are uniform in size for even cooking.

I cooked this dish on my regular local television segment in Sacramento and the station received several hundred requests for the recipe!

In a large bowl, combine the ingredients for the marinade. Wash the scallops and pat them dry with paper towels. Add the scallops to the marinade and mix well to coat them. Cover the bowl with aluminum foil and let stand for 1 hour.

Heat the 2 tablespoons of oil in a large skillet. Add the scallops and the marinade and cook over high heat for 1 to 2 minutes. Add the wine and stir quickly. Cook for 1 to 2 minutes longer. At this point the wine will be almost completely evaporated and the sauce will have a nice thick consistency. Taste and adjust the seasoning. Serve with some boiled or steamed rice as the main course, or with broiled slices of Italian bread as an appetizer.

For the Marinade
⅓ cup chopped fresh parsley leaves
3 garlic cloves, finely chopped
A few oregano sprigs, if available
½ cup dry unseasoned bread crumbs
⅓ cup olive oil
Salt and freshly ground black pepper

For the Scallops
1½ pounds sea scallops
2 tablespoons olive oil
1 cup dry white wine

Serves 4

Aragosta alla Griglia

Broiled Lobster Tails

I could call this dish "Lobster the Italian Way," because of the passion that Italians have for grilled fish. Perhaps it is because grilling is simple and straightforward that grilled fish retains all of its individual flavor and taste.

This recipe is for broiling but an outdoor grill also can be used. In this recipe, I use lobster tails because they are easily available, meaty, and delicate. Some bread crumbs are added over the fish before broiling to protect the skin from scorching.

4 lobster tails (about ¾ pound each)
Juice of 1 lemon
½ cup olive oil
1 tablespoon chopped fresh parsley leaves
Salt
½ cup fresh bread crumbs
Lemon wedges

SERVES 4

Lay each lobster tail on its back and, with a sharp knife or scissors, cut through the tail along its length. Remove the meat. Slice the meat in half lengthwise and put the pieces in a deep dish. Add the oil, lemon juice, and parsley and season with salt. Marinate for about 1 hour.

Preheat the broiler. Put the lobster pieces on a broiling pan about 4 to 5 inches from the heat source. Sprinkle the fish with the bread crumbs. Broil for 2 to 3 minutes. Turn and broil for 2 to 3 minutes longer. Serve with the lemon wedges.

Salads

Insalata di Tacchino, Patate, e Piselli

Roasted Turkey, Potato, and Peas Salad

I like to roast a whole turkey breast, serve it one night, and prepare this wonderful salad with the leftovers for the next day. Roasted or boiled chicken can also be used and can be just as good as the turkey. Don't worry too much about the exact proportion of ingredients for this salad. Simply do with what you have.

Cut the turkey into 1-inch pieces and put them in a large salad bowl.

Boil the potatoes until tender. Drain and pat dry with paper towels. When they are cool enough to handle, cut them into 1-inch cubes. If you are using new potatoes, don't peel them; if you are using regular potatoes, they should be peeled. Put the potato cubes in the bowl with the turkey.

Cook the peas until tender. Drain and pat dry with paper towels. Add the peas, onion, capers, and parsley to the salad bowl. Cover and refrigerate the salad for 1 hour.

In a small bowl, combine anchovies, mustard, vinegar, and salt and pepper and mix well. Add the olive oil and stir to incorporate. Taste and adjust the seasoning. Pour the dressing over the salad and mix to incorporate. The salad can be prepared completely several hours ahead of time and kept tightly covered in the refrigerator. Serve slightly chilled.

Add roasted red or yellow peppers for a splash of extra color and taste.

For the Salad
1 pound roasted turkey breast
8 to 10 small red new potatoes, or 4 regular potatoes
1 cup fresh or frozen small peas, thawed
1 small red onion, thinly sliced
2 tablespoons rinsed and dried capers
1 tablespoon chopped fresh parsley leaves

For the Dressing
2 anchovy fillets, finely chopped
1 teaspoon Dijon mustard
3 tablespoons red wine vinegar
Salt and freshly ground black pepper
½ cup olive oil

SERVES 4

Insalata Appetitosa

Mushroom, Ham, and Cheese Salad

I am the only one in our family who is quite fond of salads. Occasionally, however, I come up with a salad that is positively appetizing. So, I make a double batch, thinking it can become our evening meal, especially on a day when the temperature outside has gone over the 100-degree mark. Nevertheless, after a few helpings my husband pats his stomach and says: "This was very appetizing . . . is the pasta ready yet?"

For the Salad
½ pound fresh white cultivated mushrooms
*¼ pound Swiss cheese, sliced and then cut
  into small strips*
⅓ cup parmigiano cut into small slivers
¼ pound smoked ham, cut into thin strips

For the Dressing
Juice of 1 lemon
1 teaspoon Dijon mustard
⅓ cup olive oil
1 tablespoon chopped fresh parsley leaves
Salt and freshly ground black pepper

SERVES 4

Clean the mushrooms and cut them into small slices. Put them in a salad bowl with the Swiss cheese, parmigiano, and smoked ham.

In a small bowl, combine all the ingredients for the dressing. Add to the mushrooms and mix to combine. Taste and adjust the seasoning. Cover and refrigerate. Serve slightly chilled.

Insalata Calda di Melanzane, Peperoni, e Pomodori Arrosto

Warm Roasted Eggplant, Pepper, and Tomato Salad

This beautiful medley of roasted vegetables was, and still is, very popular in Sicily where this dish originates. Select the smallest firm eggplants and the most beautiful sweet peppers. Shop for ripe meaty tomatoes and buy the best virgin olive oil; then you will have a small masterpiece, a perfect accompaniment to any roasted meat.

Wash and dry the eggplants. Cut them into ¼-inch-thick slices. Sprinkle the slices with salt and put them in a colander or on paper towels to drain for 1 hour.

Roast the peppers according to the instructions on page 59. Peel the peppers and remove the seeds. Cut the peppers into small strips and place in a salad bowl.

Cut each tomato in half horizontally and remove the seeds. Put the tomatoes on a baking sheet, cut side up.

Pat the eggplant slices dry with paper towels. Brush the slices on both sides with oil and place alongside the tomatoes on the baking sheet. Broil until the eggplant slices are lightly golden on both sides and tomatoes' skins begin to wrinkle and their tops begin to brown.

Cut the eggplants into small strips and the tomatoes into medium-size chunks. Add to the roasted peppers. Dress the vegetables with the salt and pepper, olive oil, and vinegar. Sprinkle with the parsley, if desired, and serve either warm or at room temperature.

2 small firm eggplants
4 sweet red, yellow, or green bell peppers
4 ripe tomatoes
Salt and freshly ground black pepper
⅓ cup virgin olive oil
1 to 2 tablespoons red wine vinegar
1 tablespoon chopped fresh parsley leaves or chives (optional)

SERVES 6 TO 8

If you omit the vinegar and add good crusty bread, this makes an excellent appetizer.

Insalata di Riso alla Siciliana

Rice Salad the Sicilian Way

Rice salads are very popular in Italy. The glorious delicatessens Peck of Milano and Tamburini of Bologna, as well as scores of gourmet specialty shops, have incredible displays of rice salads. Even though rice is the main ingredient, shellfish, ham, cheese, or vegetables are generally added. Rice salads are perfect summer food. They must be prepared ahead of time, because they should be served at room temperature or slightly chilled. They have great eye appeal and, most important, they taste good. Rice salads can be served as a luncheon or as a light supper. They can also be served as an appetizer.

2 cups rice, preferably Italian Arborio
Salt
5 tablespoons olive oil
3 ripe tomatoes
1 onion, finely chopped
2 tablespoons white wine vinegar
½ cup dry white wine
Juice of 2 lemons
1 teaspoon Dijon mustard
2 anchovy fillets, chopped
Pinch of chopped fresh marjoram or dried marjoram
1 cup pitted black olives, cut into quarters
Freshly ground black pepper

SERVES 4 TO 6

Bring a large saucepan of water to a boil. Add the rice and 1 tablespoon of salt. Cook, uncovered, over medium heat for 15 to 20 minutes, or until the rice is tender but still firm to the bite; do not overcook or the texture of the salad will be mushy. Drain the rice and put it in a large salad bowl. Add 2 tablespoons of the oil, mix, and set aside to cool.

Bring a medium-size saucepan of water to a boil. Add the tomatoes. When the tomato skins begin to break, transfer the tomatoes to a bowl of cold water. Peel, seed, and cut the tomatoes into chunks. Set aside.

In a medium-size skillet, heat the remaining 3 table-spoons of oil. Add the onion and sauté until it is lightly golden, about 5 minutes. Stir in the vinegar. Cook until the vinegar has evaporated. Stir in the wine, lemon juice, mustard, and anchovies. Cook for 1 to 2 minutes longer. Add the reserved tomatoes, marjoram, and olives. Season with salt and several grindings of pepper. Toss everything briefly over high heat; then add to the rice. Mix well and taste and adjust the seasoning. Cool to room temperature and serve.

This salad can be prepared a day ahead, covered, and refrigerated. Serve at room temperature or slightly chilled.

Conchiglie con i Broccoli in Insalata

Shells Salad with Broccoli, Anchovies, and Capers

In the past, if you asked most Italians about pasta salads they would look at you with disbelief. Pasta was a sacred cow in Italy and no one was supposed to serve it cold or, for that matter, in a salad. However, times have changed. What was totally unthinkable yesterday is up for experimentation today. I confess I am not particularly fond of pasta salads. However, when the mercury goes up and we perspire if we only turn sideways, the thought of a cold pasta dish becomes a bit more appealing.

The recipe below is a classic one and was meant to be served hot. But on a particularly hot day in Sacramento, when the temperature reached 108 degrees, I added a few tablespoons of red wine vinegar to the pasta, chilled it, and conveniently forgot about tradition.

Bring a large pot of water to a boil. Add 1 tablespoon of salt and the pasta. Cook, uncovered, over high heat until the pasta is tender but still firm to the bite, 8 to 10 minutes. Drain the pasta and put it in a large salad bowl. Add 2 tablespoons of the oil and mix well. Set aside to cool.

Remove the florets from the broccoli stalks and reserve the stalks for another use, such as a vegetable soup. Wash the florets in cool water.

Bring a saucepan of water to a boil. Add 1 teaspoon of salt and the broccoli florets. Cook over medium heat for 4 to 5 minutes, or until the florets are tender but still firm to the touch. Drain and set aside.

Heat the remaining 5 tablespoons of oil in a medium-size skillet. Add the garlic and anchovies, and sauté gently for about 1 minute. Add the broccoli florets, parsley, and capers and season lightly, if at all, with salt and plenty of pepper. Stir in the vinegar. Pour the sauce over the pasta and mix thoroughly. Taste and adjust the seasoning.

This salad can be prepared completely several hours ahead of time and refrigerated. Serve it at room temperature.

1 pound pasta shells
Salt
7 tablespoons olive oil
2 bunches fresh broccoli (about 2½ pounds total weight)
3 garlic cloves, finely chopped
4 anchovy fillets, chopped
1 tablespoon chopped fresh parsley leaves
2 tablespoons rinsed and dried capers
Freshly ground black pepper
1 to 2 tablespoons red wine vinegar

SERVES 6

To serve this dish hot, prepare the sauce as directed above. Cook the pasta, drain, and add it to the sauce in the skillet. Mix and serve at once.

Insalata di Pesce

Mixed Seafood Salad

Imagine you are eating in a little trattoria facing the sea, with the blue sky above and the gentle breeze that carries the scent of the sea to your nostrils. Around you there are happy sounds, laughs, joyous conversations, and the waiter scurries around with carafes of local wine and with food that smells absolutely tantalizing. If next to you there is your loved one and all your senses are keener than ever, chances are that you'll never forget that moment and that food.

That moment is mine to cherish. That food is something to be shared. There are so many interpretations of seafood salads. This one is from Trattoria Nora in Vasto, a beautiful seaside town in Abruzzo.

For the Fish

2 pounds mussels
2 pounds clams, the smallest possible
2 cups dry white wine
1 pound bay scallops
1 pound squid
1 pound medium-size shrimp

For the Dressing

½ cup olive oil
Juice of 2 lemons
2 tablespoons chopped fresh parsley leaves
2 garlic cloves, finely chopped
Pinch of chopped fresh marjoram leaves

SERVES 6 AS A MAIN COURSE OR 10 TO 12 AS AN APPETIZER

Soak the mussels and clams in cool salted water for 20 minutes to draw out their sand. Scrub them with a brush and rinse thoroughly under cool running water. Put the shellfish in a large saucepan together with 1 cup of water and 1 cup of the wine. Cover and bring to a boil. Remove the mussels and clams with a slotted spoon as they open. Some might take a little longer than others to open; however, if they fail to open, discard them. Remove the meat from shells and pat it dry with paper towels. Put the meat in a salad bowl. Discard or remove the cooking liquid for another use, such as a seafood risotto.

Wash the scallops in cool water. In a medium-size saucepan, bring 4 cups of water and the remaining cup of wine to a boil. Lower the heat and add the scallops. Simmer for 2 to 3 minutes. (When done, the scallops should be chalky white all the way through.) Remove the scallops with a slotted spoon and dry them on paper towels. Add the scallops to the salad bowl. Keep the scallop cooking liquid at a low simmer while you clean the squid, following the instructions on page 79.

Shell and devein the shrimp. Add the shrimp to the simmering liquid and cook for 2 to 3 minutes, or just until they are opaque all the way through. Drain and pat dry with paper towels. Add the shrimp to the salad

bowl. Cover with aluminum foil and refrigerate for at least 1 hour.

Prepare the salad dressing. In a small bowl, combine all the dressing ingredients thoroughly. Taste and adjust the seasoning. Pour the dressing over the seafood and toss well. Serve slightly chilled.

Don't be put off by the many steps involved in this preparation; it is really quite simple to put the salad together and it can be prepared and dressed several hours ahead of time. Leave it at room temperature for a while before serving as it should be slightly chilled and not cold. Serve it as an antipasto or as a main course.

Insalata del Lunedì

Salad of Roasted Meat and Red Onions

Insalata del Lunedì means "Monday Salad." Years ago, when the Sunday meal was a serious occasion, families in Italy would cook up a storm, because relatives or friends were often invited. The day after, one would have enough leftovers to feed an army. My mother utilized these leftovers in several ways. Roasted meats would become a stuffing for pasta or tiny meat balls, but sometimes they were transformed into appetizing salads.

For the Salad
¾ pound leftover roast pork, veal or
   chicken
1 small red onion, thinly sliced
3 tablespoons rinsed and dried capers
1 garlic clove, finely chopped
5 to 6 cornichons, cut into small rounds
⅓ cup finely shredded fresh basil leaves, or
   2 tablespoons chopped fresh parsley
   leaves

For the Dressing
3 tablespoons red wine vinegar
1 teaspoon Dijon mustard
⅓ cup olive oil
Salt to taste

SERVES 4

Cut the meat into small cubes or strips. Put the meat in a salad bowl and add the onion, capers, garlic, cornichons, and basil. Mix well.

In a small bowl, combine the vinegar, mustard, oil, and salt. Add to the salad and toss well. Cover and refrigerate for 30 minutes. Serve with slices of Italian bread.

Insalata di Riso e Frutti di Mare

Rice and Shellfish Salad

One of the most beautiful sights of the Italian Riviera or, for that matter of all the seaside resort towns in Italy in summertime, is the incredible display of cold dishes as interpreted by local restaurants. Platters laden with everything that land and sea have to offer, from marinated grilled vegetables to spectacular seafood salads, are placed strategically in full view of patrons. The choice is unbelievable. One of my favorite summer dishes is this Rice and Shellfish Salad. It looks great and tastes even better and it can be prepared ahead of time. The dressing, however, should be added at the last moment or the rice will become soggy.

Bring a large pot of salted water to a boil. Add the rice and cook, uncovered, over medium heat for 15 to 20 minutes, or until the rice is tender but still firm to the bite. Stir several times during the cooking. Remove the rice when it is still a bit undercooked, or the salad will have a "mushy" texture. Drain the rice and rinse under cold running water. Pat dry with paper towels. Brush a large bowl with oil. Add the rice and 2 additional tablespoons of oil. Mix and cool to room temperature.

Cut the olives into quarters. Slice the pickles into small rounds. Cut the anchovies into pieces. Wash the red pepper and remove the seeds. Cut into very small thin julienne. Add all ingredients, including the capers, to the rice and mix to blend.

Soak the clams and mussels in cool salted water for about 1 hour to draw out the sand. Scrub them with a brush and rinse thoroughly. Put the mussels and clams in a large saucepan with 1 cup of water and bring to a boil. Remove the clams and mussels as they open. Some might take a little longer to open. However, if they fail to open, discard them. Remove the meat from the shells and add it to the rice salad with the shrimp. Cover bowl with aluminum foil and refrigerate until ready to serve.

In a small bowl, combine all the ingredients for the dressing and stir to blend well. Pour over the rice and mix thoroughly. Taste for seasoning. Serve slightly chilled.

Keep in mind that recipes should be used as general guidelines. If you want 25 mussels and 25 clams, instead of 20 as the recipe suggests, do so. The real purpose of a recipe should be to guide you into the "flavor" of the dish, rather than dictate an exact course of action.

For the Shellfish Salad
2 cups rice, preferably Italian Arborio
2 tablespoons olive oil
1 cup black pitted olives
4 to 5 small pickles
3 anchovy fillets
1 red sweet pepper
3 tablespoons rinsed and dried capers
20 mussels, the smallest possible
20 clams, the smallest possible
½ pound small shrimp, cooked, shelled, and deveined

For the Salad Dressing
Juice of 2 lemons
1 teaspoon Dijon mustard
Salt and freshly ground black pepper
½ cup olive oil
1 tablespoon chopped fresh parsley leaves
2 garlic cloves, finely chopped

SERVES 6 TO 8

Petto di Cappone in Insalata

Salad of Marinated Capon Breast

During my last trip to Italy, I had the good fortune to dine at Il Cigno in Mantua. This restaurant is consistently rated as one of the best in Italy. One of the dishes I thought was superlative was a delicate salad of poached capon breast (which had first been soaked in a sweet and sour marinade for several hours) served over a bed of mixed chicory. This sounds like a very contemporary dish, but, in fact, it dates from the sixteenth century; the recipe is a well-guarded secret, but I was able to obtain enough information from our waiter to successfully duplicate it.

For the Capon

2 cups dry Marsala

A few marjoram sprigs or a pinch of dried marjoram

A few fresh laurel leaves or 2 to 3 bay leaves

1 tablespoon whole black peppercorns

1 onion, cut into pieces

1 celery stalk, cut into chunks

1 carrot, sliced

Salt to taste

1 capon, approximately 6 to 7 pounds

For the Marinade

Juice of 2 lemons

1 teaspoon good balsamic vinegar (see Note)

1 tablespoon sugar

½ cup olive oil

Salt and freshly ground black pepper

To Complete the Dish

3 Belgian endives

Several small radicchio and rucola leaves (optional)

SERVES 4

To prepare the capon, bring a large pot half full of water to a boil. Add all the ingredients, except the capon. Boil gently for 20 to 30 minutes. Add the capon to the flavored broth, making sure it is covered with liquid. Cover the pot and cook over very low heat (barely a simmer) for about 1 hour. Remove from the heat and let the capon cool in the broth for a few hours or overnight. Transfer the capon to a cutting board and let it cool completely. Separate the breast from the rest of the bird (see Note).

Meanwhile, prepare the marinade. Combine all the ingredients for the marinade in a bowl. Taste and correct the seasoning.

Slice the capon breast into medium-size (2- to 3-inch-long) strips and place in a large bowl or deep dish. Cover the meat with the marinade. Cover the bowl and refrigerate for several hours or overnight. Baste the meat a few times while it is marinating. Bring it to room temperature before serving.

Slice the endives horizontally into small strips and put them in a bowl with the radicchio and rucola leaves, if using. Dress with a few tablespoons of marinade and arrange on individual plates. Place a few strips of capon over the lettuces, spoon a bit more marinade over the capon and lettuce, and serve. If you wish a touch of color, roast a few sweet bell peppers (page 59), cut them into strips, and arrange around the capon.

Good balsamic vinegar is quite important to this dish. As balsamic vinegar varies in strength depending on its age, the amount needed should be adjusted accordingly.

Capons are neutered male chickens that have been specially fattened. Their meat is flavorful and quite tender. Their weight averages between 6 and 9 pounds. Because capons are not always easy to obtain, a whole plump chicken or chicken breasts may be used instead. In poaching the poultry, make sure you keep the liquid at a very low simmer or the meat will dry out. I generally undercook my poultry and then turn the heat off and leave the bird in its flavorful broth for a few hours or overnight. The result is a deliciously tender meat. Skim the fat from the broth; then strain the broth and use it for soups. The darker meat can also be used in a simple salad, such as the Roasted Turkey, Potato, and Peas Salad (page 121).

Insalata di Gamberetti e Peperoni Rossi

Shrimp and Red Pepper Salad

Seafood salads are extremely popular in the summertime in Italy, especially in seacoast towns. Indeed, nothing is more magnificent than a beautiful platter of fresh seafood tossed in an olive oil, lemon, and herb dressing. It is a feast for the eye and a temptation for the palate.

In this dish, fresh shrimp, sweet broiled peppers, and fresh oregano are combined into one of the loveliest summer salads. Assemble the salad completely and leave it to steep in its own dressing for about 1 hour at room temperature. This salad can also be prepared completely several hours ahead of time and refrigerated. However, it should be served at room temperature, as an appetizer or a luncheon or a light supper dish accompanied by crusty Italian bread.

For Cooking the Shrimp
1 small onion, sliced
1 carrot, cut into chunks
1 celery stalk, cut into chunks
A few parsley sprigs
1 cup dry white wine
1½ pounds unshelled medium-size shrimp

For the Salad Dressing
3 large sweet red or yellow peppers
*¼ cup fresh oregano leaves, or 1 table-
  spoon chopped fresh parsley leaves*
1 garlic clove, finely chopped
⅓ cup olive oil
Juice of 1 large lemon
Salt and freshly ground black pepper

8 slices of Italian bread, toasted

SERVES 4 AS A MAIN COURSE OR 8 AS AN
  APPETIZER

Fill a medium-size saucepan halfway with water. Add the onion, carrot, celery, parsley, and wine. Bring to a boil, lower the heat, and simmer for 15 to 20 minutes. Add the shrimp and simmer for about 2 minutes. Drain and shell the shrimp as soon as you can handle them. Put the shrimp in a bowl and set aside.

Roast the peppers according to the instructions on page 59. Peel and seed the peppers; then cut them into thin small strips. Add the peppers and the remaining dressing ingredients to the shrimp. Mix well; then taste and adjust the seasoning. Cover the bowl and leave at room temperature for about 1 hour.

When ready to serve, transfer the salad to a shallow serving platter. Serve with slices of toasted Italian bread.

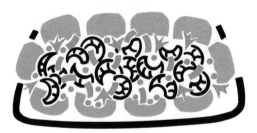

Frittatas

A frittata is a flat omelet. Italians adore them and make them with almost anything under the sun. Fresh vegetables, herbs, cheeses, hams, and leftover meats can go into a frittata. Even pasta finds its way into a frittata. For a perfect frittata follow these basic rules:

- Use a nonstick pan or a skillet with a heavy bottom.
- Cook the frittata over medium heat, never too high, to avoid sticking and burning the eggs.
- Make sure that the bottom of the frittata is completely cooked and top is beginning to solidify before inverting the frittata onto a plate.

Another way to cook a frittata is to place it briefly under the broiler to cook the top once the bottom is done. Personally, I like to turn frittata onto a plate, because it is more challenging and the frittata stays moister. If the first attempt is not successful, don't despair. Try again. Remember that practice makes perfect.

Frittata con Menta e Prezzemolo

Frittata with Mint and Parsley

If you are in a hurry, cook a frittata. If you are on a tight budget, cook a frittata. And if you want something light and tasty to eat on a warm summer night, cook one more frittata.

In a medium-size bowl, beat the eggs, cheese, salt and pepper, parsley, and mint together.

Heat the oil in a heavy 8- or 10-inch skillet. Add the egg mixture and cook over medium heat for 7 to 8 minutes, or until the bottom of the frittata is lightly browned and the top begins to solidify.

Place a large plate over the skillet and turn the frittata onto plate. Slide the frittata back into the skillet to cook the other side. Cook for 4 to 5 minutes longer. Slide frittata onto a serving dish, cut into wedges, and serve.

The Salad of Roasted Red Peppers and Yellow Tomatoes (page 136) or String Bean, Potato, and Pancetta Salad (page 137) would be a good accompaniment to this frittata.

6 large eggs
½ cup freshly grated parmigiano
¼ cup freshly grated Pecorino Romano
Salt and freshly ground black pepper
2 tablespoons chopped fresh parsley leaves
¼ cup loosely packed shredded fresh mint leaves
3 tablespoons olive oil

SERVES 4

Frittata con Pomodori e Acciughe

Frittata with Tomatoes and Anchovies

In an informal gathering, frittata is often served at room temperature as an appetizer. This frittata combines a hint of anchovy with the freshness of basil and tomatoes.

2 ripe tomatoes, peeled and seeded (page 55)

3 tablespoons olive oil

1 garlic clove, finely chopped

2 anchovy fillets, finely chopped

6 large eggs

½ cup freshly grated parmigiano

½ cup loosely packed shredded fresh basil leaves, or 2 tablespoons chopped fresh parsley leaves

Salt and freshly ground black pepper

SERVES 4

Roughly dice the peeled and seeded tomatoes. Put the tomatoes in a strainer and put the strainer over a bowl to drain off the excess juices. Reserve the juices for soups or sauces if you wish.

Heat the oil in a heavy 8- or 10-inch skillet. Add the garlic and anchovies, and sauté over medium heat for 1 to 2 minutes. Before the garlic turns brown, add the tomatoes. Raise the heat and cook for 4 to 5 minutes, or until the tomato juices have completely evaporated.

In a medium-size bowl, beat the eggs, cheese, basil, and salt and pepper together. Pour the tomato mixture in the bowl into the egg mixture and stir quickly to incorporate.

Add a bit more oil to the skillet, if necessary. When the oil is hot, pour the egg mixture into the skillet. Cook over medium heat for 7 to 8 minutes, or until the bottom of the frittata is lightly browned and the top begins to solidify.

Place a large plate over the skillet and turn the frittata onto the plate. Slide the frittata back into the skillet to cook the other side. Cook for 4 to 5 minutes longer. Slide the frittata onto a serving dish, cut into wedges, and serve.

Vegetables and Simple Salads

Carciofi con Piselli e Prosciutto

Artichokes with Peas and Prosciutto

When artichokes are plentiful and their price is reasonable, generally March through May, try this delicious vegetable dish. The white tender part of the artichokes and sweet tender peas are cooked separately; then they are combined with prosciutto into a lovely, fresh preparation. Select tight, compact artichokes with a bright green color. In buying fresh peas, select pods that are well filled with no discolorations. Serve this dish as an accompaniment to any roasted meat or fowl.

Cut off the artichoke stems. Peel off the tough outer part of the stems and slice them into 1-inch pieces. Put the pieces in a medium-size saucepan. Cover with water and add the lemon juice. Remove all the outer leaves of the artichokes until you reach the soft white cone. Slice off 1 inch from the top of the cone. Cut each artichoke into four parts lengthwise. Remove the fuzzy choke with a small sharp knife. Cut each quarter into thinner slices and put them in the saucepan with the acidulated water. Add 1 tablespoon of the oil and bring to a boil. Lower the heat and cook gently until the slices are tender but still firm to the touch. Drain and set aside.

Put the peas in a small saucepan and add the broth. Cook for 5 to 10 minutes, depending on the size of the peas. Drain.

In a medium-size saucepan, heat the butter with the remaining 2 tablespoons of oil. Add the prosciutto and cook for 1 to 2 minutes. Stir in artichokes and peas and season with salt and pepper. Sauté for 1 to 2 minutes and serve.

4 medium-size artichokes
Juice of 1 lemon
3 tablespoons olive oil
1 cup shelled peas (about 1 pound)
1 cup canned chicken broth or water
2 tablespoons unsalted butter
¼ pound prosciutto, sliced and then cut into small strips
Salt and freshly ground black pepper

SERVES 4

This preparation can easily become a tasty, light pasta dish. Simply toss the finished dish with 1 pound of short pasta, such as penne or fusilli.

Insalata di Peperoni Rossi e Pomodori Gialli

Salad of Roasted Red Peppers and Yellow Tomatoes

Bright red peppers, golden yellow tomatoes, and green fresh basil are the colors of summer. This breathtaking summer salad doesn't only look good, it also *tastes* good. Sure, you could substitute green peppers for the red ones and red tomatoes for the yellow, but it would not be the same. If we want something special, we must be willing to go the extra mile. Red peppers are now easily available. Yellow tomatoes will have to be sought out. If you really can't find them, use unripened red tomatoes that are still quite green in color (green tomatoes are popular in Italian salads). Fresh basil, oregano, chives, mint, or, if all else fails, parsley, will complete and complement this salad.

4 red or yellow peppers
3 yellow or unripened red tomatoes
⅓ cup finely shredded fresh basil leaves, or
* 1 tablespoon chopped fresh parsley*
* leaves*
Salt and freshly ground black pepper
Olive oil, preferably virgin olive oil

Serves 4

Roast the peppers according to the instructions on page 59. Peel and seed the roasted peppers and cut them into large strips. Put the peppers on a plate to cool. (The peppers can be prepared several hours or a day ahead and kept tightly covered in the refrigerator.)

Wash and dry the tomatoes and cut them into slices. When ready to serve, place a few strips of peppers and some tomato slices on individual salad dishes. Sprinkle with the basil. Season lightly with salt and pepper and dribble some olive oil over all.

In Italy, we generally don't add any vinegar to a roasted pepper salad. However, if you like a drop of vinegar, feel free to add it.

Insalata di Fagiolini, Patate, e Pancetta

String Bean, Potato, and Pancetta Salad

In this dish potatoes, string beans, and pancetta are combined to produce a tasty salad. Choose the smallest beans, with deep green color. As I love small red new potatoes, I use them whenever they are available. I boil or steam them unpeeled. If small new potatoes are unavailable, regular boiling potatoes will do. The dressing consists only of a good olive oil, a touch of mustard, wine vinegar, and salt and pepper. Serve this salad alongside a veal cutlet or a frittata or anything you like.

Snap off both ends of the beans and wash the beans under cool running water. Bring a large saucepan of water to a boil; then add the salt and beans. Cook, uncovered, for 5 to 10 minutes, depending on the size of the beans. Drain the beans and pat them dry with paper towels. Put them in a large salad bowl.

Bring another saucepan of water to a boil. Add the potatoes and cook until tender but still a bit firm. Transfer the potatoes to a bowl to cool. If you are using boiling potatoes, peel and cut them into 1-inch pieces. If you are using the red new potatoes, cut them in halves or quarters. Put the potatoes in the bowl with the string beans.

Heat the oil in a small saucepan. Add the pancetta and cook over medium heat until the pancetta is lightly crisp and golden in color. Transfer the pancetta to paper towels and pat dry to remove the excess fat. Add the pancetta to the beans. Cover the bowl and refrigerate until ready to use.

In a small bowl, combine all the dressing ingredients. Pour over the salad and toss to coat. Taste and adjust the seasoning. Serve at room temperature.

It is almost impossible to give the "exact" proportion for the salad dressing. Use mine as a guideline and then adjust it to suit your own individual taste.

For the Salad
1½ pounds small string beans
1 teaspoon salt
7 or 8 unpeeled small red new potatoes, or 2 to 3 boiling potatoes, unpeeled
2 tablespoons olive oil
¼ pound pancetta, sliced and then cut into small, short julienne

For the Dressing
⅓ cup olive oil
2 tablespoons good red wine vinegar
1 tablespoon Dijon mustard
Salt and freshly ground black pepper

SERVES 6

Stufato di Fave

Fava Beans with Bacon and Tomatoes

My mother was particularly fond of fava beans. She would buy them by the pound and munch on them secretly while she scurried around the kitchen. At the end of a meal, all of us would shell the beans at the table and dip them in a bit of oil and salt. It was almost like a contest to see who could eat more beans.

The beans are good raw, but they are delicious when cooked with tomatoes and herbs. They can be served as a side dish to Fried Sausage with Broccoli and Hot Pepper or to Roasted Leg of Lamb the Tuscan Way (page 232).

2½ to 3 pounds unshelled fava beans
3 tablespoons olive oil
1 small onion, finely sliced
¼ pound pancetta, sliced and then cut into thin strips
1 tablespoon chopped fresh parsley leaves
Pinch of chopped fresh marjoram or dried marjoram
3 tablespoons tomato paste diluted with 1 cup chicken broth (page 45)
Salt and freshly ground black pepper

SERVES 4

Shell the fava beans and set aside.

In a medium-size saucepan, heat the oil. Add the onion and sauté over low heat for 4 to 5 minutes. Add the pancetta, parsley, and marjoram and cook for 2 to 3 minutes, stirring. Add the tomato paste and broth. Cook, uncovered, over medium heat for 8 to 10 minutes. Add the beans and cook for 8 to 10 minutes longer, depending on the freshness and size of the beans. If the sauce thickens too much during the cooking, add a bit more broth. Season with salt and several grindings of pepper. Serve hot.

Fresh fava beans are usually available in the spring and early summer. When not in season, use dry fava beans. Soak the beans in cold water to cover for several hours or overnight and cook them in plenty of water before adding them to the sauce.

Carote al Marsala

Carrots with Marsala

Tender, young carrots become very sweet when they are cooked in Marsala. Serve them next to a roasted veal, pork, turkey, or chicken.

Peel the carrots and trim the ends. Cut the carrots into rounds or small julienne.

Melt the butter in a medium-size skillet. When the butter foams, add the carrots and sauté over high heat for 2 to 3 minutes, or until the carrots are lightly browned. Add the Marsala and cook over medium heat, stirring, until the carrots are tender and wine is completely reduced. If too much wine is left in the skillet, remove the carrots with a slotted spoon to a warm dish or bowl and reduce the Marsala over high heat. Only a few tablespoons of thick, syrupy wine sauce should be left in the skillet. Spoon the sauce over the carrots or return the carrots to the skillet and mix with the sauce and then serve.

1 pound small, tender carrots
4 tablespoons unsalted butter
1 cup dry Marsala, preferably Florio

SERVES 4

Fagiolini al Limone

String Bean Salad with Lemon

Lemon, not vinegar, is used for this salad dressing, which makes it delightfully refreshing. Serve this salad with any broiled or barbecued fish.

Snap off both ends of the beans and wash the beans under cool running water. Bring a large saucepan of water to a boil. Add the salt and green beans and cook, uncovered, for 5 to 10 minutes, depending on the size of the beans. Drain the beans and pat them dry with paper towels. Put the beans in a large bowl, cover, and refrigerate until ready to use.

Bring the beans to room temperature. In a small bowl, combine all the dressing ingredients and pour over the beans. Taste and adjust the seasoning and serve.

For the Beans
1½ pounds small string beans
1 teaspoon salt

For the Dressing
Juice of 1 lemon
⅓ cup olive oil
Salt and freshly ground black pepper

SERVES 4 TO 6

To retain the green color of vegetables when they are going to be boiled, add some salt to the water. Cook them uncovered and rinse them with cold water immediately after draining.

Melanzane alla Griglia con Aglio e Oregano

Broiled Eggplant with Garlic and Fresh Oregano

Rustic and peasant cooking has always featured an abundance of vegetables. In Italy even the poorest farmer or fisherman has a small strip of land in which to grow his vegetables. Grilled vegetables are part of the southern Italian tradition with food, wonderful simple food that becomes even more tantalizing by the addition of delicious olive oil.

This dish was originally from Puglia, a sunny region basking in the glow of the Adriatic sea. Today, because of its simplicity, grilled vegetables have become a staple in innumerable Italian kitchens. Don't limit yourself to eggplants—peppers, tomatoes, zucchini, corn, and onions can all be cooked and prepared this way.

2 small firm eggplants
Salt
½ cup olive oil
2 garlic cloves, finely chopped
¼ cup loosely packed fresh oregano leaves
   or finely chopped fresh parsley leaves
Salt and freshly ground black pepper
1 tablespoon red wine vinegar

SERVES 6 TO 8

Cut off the ends of the eggplants and cut the eggplants lengthwise into ½-inch-thick slices. Sprinkle the eggplant slices with salt and place in a large dish. Let stand for about 30 minutes. The salt will draw out the bitter juices.

Preheat the broiler or prepare a barbecue so that the coals are ready when you are ready to grill the vegetables.

In a small bowl, combine the oil, garlic, oregano, and salt and several grindings of pepper. Brush the mixture over both sides of the eggplant slices. Broil or barbecue the slices until lightly golden on both sides. Place on a serving dish and sprinkle lightly with vinegar. Serve warm or at room temperature.

Bietole in Padella

Sautéed Swiss Chard with Oil and Lemon

Swiss chard is very popular in Italy. The stems and the leaves are never cooked together. The leaves are steamed or gently boiled and used in salads, or they are cooked with garlic or grated parmigiano and a touch of heavy cream. The stalks are boiled separately and generally baked with parmigiano.

In this preparation, the sweetness of the leaves blends beautifully with the pungency of the lemon.

Remove the Swiss chard leaves from the stems and reserve the stems for another use. Wash the leaves thoroughly in several changes of cool water. Put them in a saucepan with only the water that clings to the leaves. Season with salt, cover, and cook for 10 to 12 minutes, or until tender. Drain and press the leaves lightly with a large spoon to remove as much water as possible.

In a small skillet, heat the oil. Add the garlic and sauté until the garlic is lightly golden. Remove the garlic and add the Swiss chard. Season with salt and pepper and stir and cook for 1 to 2 minutes. Add the lemon juice and cook until the juice has evaporated. Serve hot.

2 bunches Swiss chard
Salt
4 tablespoons olive oil
2 garlic cloves
Salt and freshly ground black pepper
Juice of 1 lemon

SERVES 4

To make a nice salad, cook the leaves through the first step above. Cool in a salad bowl and then dress with oil, lemon juice, salt and pepper.

Asparagi con le Uove Fritte

Asparagus with Fried Eggs

Spring is announced by the warmer sun and the appearance in the market of the first asparagus. Most of us like asparagus to some degree, but my father was absolutely crazy about it. My mother, to make him happy, would cook asparagus as often as possible in a variety of ways. Quite often asparagus and eggs would become a light supper. The asparagus was boiled and then topped with parmigiano and a bit of melted butter. Eggs were fried and placed over the asparagus. Today, this dish is still popular, especially at lunchtime, as the big noon meal is slowly disappearing in Italy.

2 pounds asparagus
5 tablespoons unsalted butter
Salt
½ cup freshly grated parmigiano
8 large eggs

SERVES 4

Cut off the tough asparagus ends and peel the outer skin with a potato peeler or a knife. Wash the asparagus in cool water. Boil or steam the asparagus until tender, 5 to 10 minutes, depending on the size. Drain and pat the asparagus dry with paper towels. Put the asparagus on a plate and keep it warm in the oven.

In a large skillet, melt 3 tablespoons of the butter. Fry the eggs sunny-side up and season lightly with salt.

Put the asparagus on individual dishes and sprinkle liberally with the parmigiano. Melt the remaining 2 tablespoons of butter in a small saucepan and spoon equal amounts over the asparagus. Lay 2 eggs over each serving and serve.

Le Patate con la Salvia

Potatoes with Fresh Sage and Garlic

I must have been twelve or thirteen years old when I spent my first vacation away from home. I had been invited by a friend to stay at her family's summer home in Cesenatico, a small but lovely resort town on the Adriatic about sixty miles from Bologna. As a normal teenager I was not at all interested in food other than eating everything in sight when I was hungry. There was a dish, however, and more precisely a vegetable dish, that my friend's mother had prepared several times, which I absolutely loved and gorged on whenever possible. Potatoes with fresh sage. Mrs. Ferioli would boil the potatoes but leave them slightly undercooked. She would then sauté them in butter with freshly picked fragrant sage from her garden and a touch of garlic. When the potatoes turned barely golden, she would season them with salt and serve them piping hot. So easy, so simple, and so absolutely delicious.

Peel and cut the potatoes into medium-thick slices. Put 2 inches of water in a large skillet and bring the water to a boil. Add the potatoes and boil for 2 to 3 minutes. Drain the potatoes and pat them dry with paper towels.

Dry the skillet and put it back on the heat with the butter and oil. When the butter foams, add the potatoes, sage, and garlic. Cook, uncovered, over medium heat, until the potatoes turn lightly golden. Transfer the potatoes to paper towels to remove the excess fat. Put the potatoes on a serving dish, sprinkle with salt, and serve piping hot.

4 large boiling potatoes
3 tablespoons unsalted butter
1 tablespoon oil
5 or 6 fresh sage leaves
2 garlic cloves, lightly crushed and peeled
Salt to taste

SERVES 4

Fresh fragrant sage is the dominant ingredient in this simple dish. Even though some dry sage could be used, I personally would not bother to make this dish without fresh sage.

Piselli con i Porri Saltati

Sautéed Peas with Leeks

Fresh tender peas and milk-sweet leeks are quickly tossed together in a bit of olive oil. The result is a simple, delicious vegetable dish that makes a wonderful accompaniment to any roasted meats. Two and a half pounds of unshelled peas yields approximately 2½ cups of shelled peas.

Shell the fresh peas. Bring a small saucepan of water to a boil. Add the peas and cook for 5 to 10 minutes, depending on the size. Drain the peas and set aside.

Remove the green part of the leeks and reserve for another use. Cut off the roots of the leeks and wash the white parts thoroughly under cool running water. Cut the white parts into thin rings.

Heat the oil in a medium-size saucepan. Add the leeks and sauté over medium heat until they are pale yellow and tender. Stir in the peas and season with salt and pepper. Cook for 1 to 2 minutes longer and serve.

2½ pounds fresh unshelled peas, or 2 10-ounce packages frozen small peas, thawed
2 large leeks
4 tablespoons olive oil
Salt and freshly ground black pepper

SERVES 4

Verdure Primaverili Glassate

Glazed Spring Vegetables

With this lovely dish we salute spring. For this reason, only the freshest and smallest vegetables should be used. We all know that by steaming vegetables they retain most of their nutritional qualities and, when tender and fresh, these vegetables will be done in no time at all.

The sautéing of this dish is done over medium heat, very briefly, to give vegetables a shiny coat. Serve this medley of spring vegetables with any broiled, grilled, or barbecued meats.

¼ pound string beans, the smallest possible
¼ pound baby carrots
1 pound fresh asparagus
1 pound fresh peas
½ pound very small red new potatoes
3 tablespoons unsalted butter
2 tablespoons sugar
Salt to taste

SERVES 4 TO 6

Trim off the ends of the string beans and wash the beans under cool running water. Wash the carrots and asparagus. Cut off the tough white ends of the asparagus. Peel the outer skin of the asparagus. Shell the peas and wash the potatoes. Boil or steam the vegetables until they are tender but still firm to the touch. Set aside.

In a large skillet, melt the butter. When butter foams, add the sugar and stir to melt. Add the vegetables and season lightly with salt. Sauté gently until the vegetables are coated with the butter and sugar and are shiny and glazed, about 1 minute. Serve hot.

Whenever you have some extra time at hand, boil or steam a variety of vegetables, such as zucchini, string beans, carrots, potatoes, etc. They can be used during the week for quick mixed cooked vegetable salads or sautéed.

Desserts

Granita di Caffè

Espresso Granita

Granita! The mere word evokes a typical Italian scene of people sitting at an outdoor café, slowly savoring this refreshing icy treat.

Granita is a dessert, made of fruit juices that are frozen into granular crystals. Granita di Caffè is undoubtedly the most popular granita in Italy.

The slightly bitter taste of espresso granita, together with its granular consistency, blends beautifully with a smooth dollop of whipped cream. It is a totally simple and refreshing dessert, perfect for hot, balmy summer nights.

Put the coffee and sugar in a flat metal container or ice-cube tray without the dividers. Add the sugar and stir well. Let the coffee cool completely.

Place the tray in the freezer for 30 minutes. Remove the tray and stir the mixture with a fork, scraping the edges of the tray which will freeze first. Return the tray to the freezer and freeze 1 hour longer. Again remove the tray and mix the contents energetically. Return to the freezer for 1 more hour.

Ten to 15 minutes before serving, transfer the tray to the refrigerator. Then transfer the mixture to a bowl and chop or whisk into a fine icy granulation. Spoon the granita into chilled glasses, top with the whipped cream, and serve at once.

2 cups freshly made espresso coffee
⅓ cup sugar
1 cup whipping cream, beaten to a thick consistency with 3 tablespoons of sugar

SERVES 4

Crostata di Fragole e Arancie

Strawberry and Orange Tart

It was an "in between" season. The calendar said it was spring, but it was chilly and it was too early for the rich variety of fruit that spring brings. I had a class to teach and I knew my students were looking forward to a fresh fruit tart dessert, so I decided to improvise and do with what was available.

This fruit tart is made with oranges and strawberries. A classic pastry cream is spread into the precooked shell. The oranges and strawberries are laid over the cream and then the top of the fruit is glazed with a syrup made with jam and liqueur.

The pastry shell can be baked a day ahead and stored in a cool place. The basic pastry cream can also be prepared a day ahead. However, the tart should be assembled at the last moment or it will become soggy.

For the Sweet Pie Pastry

1⅓ cup all-purpose unbleached flour

6 tablespoons unsalted butter (at room temperature for hand mixing or cold and in small pieces for the food processor)

1 large egg

1 tablespoon sugar

2 to 3 tablespoons chilled dry white wine

1 large egg white, beaten

For the Basic Pastry Cream (Crema Pasticcera)

2 cups milk

6 large egg yolks

⅓ cup granulated sugar

A few drops of vanilla extract

⅓ cup all-purpose unbleached flour

To Complete the Dish

2 large oranges

2 cups strawberries

1 16-ounce jar orange marmalade

¼ cup Grand Marnier

SERVES 8

In a medium-size bowl or in the bowl of a food processor fitted with a metal blade, mix the flour and butter until crumbly. Add the egg, sugar, and wine. Mix until the dough is gathered all around the blade, before it forms into a bowl. Put the dough on a working surface and quickly work into a ball. Wrap in aluminum foil and refrigerate for 1 hour.

Preheat the oven to 400 degrees. On a lightly floured surface, roll out the dough to a 12-inch circle. Place dough carefully into a 10-inch tart pan with a removable bottom. Trim edges of the dough by gently rolling the rolling pin over the top of the pan. Prick the bottom of the pastry shell in several places with a fork. Line pastry shell with aluminum foil. Fill the foil with uncooked rice or beans to prevent the pastry from shrinking while baking. Bake for 15 minutes. Remove the foil and rice or beans. Brush the dough with the beaten egg white and bake for 10 minutes longer, or until the pastry is lightly golden in color.

Prepare basic pastry cream. In a medium-size saucepan bring the milk to a boil. In a large bowl, beat the egg yolks, sugar, and vanilla until the mixture is pale yellow and thick. Slowly beat in the flour. Pour the hot milk slowly into the egg mixture, stirring constantly. Strain the cream back into the saucepan and cook over medium heat, beating constantly for 4 to 5 minutes. Pour the cream into a bowl and cool to room temperature. The pastry cream can be kept tightly covered in the refrigerator until ready to use.

Prepare fruit and glaze. Cut off the ends of the oranges. Remove the orange peel, making sure to remove all white membranes. Cut the oranges into medium-thick rounds. Put the rounds on paper towels and pat dry with more paper towels.

Wash and hull the strawberries. Pat dry with paper towels. In a small saucepan, combine the orange jam and Grand Marnier. Cook over medium heat for 4 to 5 minutes. Strain the glaze into a bowl, pressing the mixture with a spoon. Return the glaze to the saucepan and cook until thick and syrupy.

To assemble the tart, spread the pastry cream evenly over the bottom of baked tart shell. Arrange the orange slices, overlapping, over the cream in a wide circle. Fill the center of the tart with strawberries. Brush the orange slices and strawberries with the orange glaze. Transfer the tart to a serving plate. Serve it within the hour, or the juices of the fresh fruit will make the tart soggy.

Until not so long ago in Italy these lovely desserts were made mostly by pastry chefs for their own "pasticcerie." Today, thanks to the food processor and the many cookbooks available, Italian women can prepare their own professional-looking desserts.

Strudel di Mele

Apple Roll with Raisins, Pine Nuts, and Jam

An Italian dessert with a foreign name, strudel is a typical dessert of Trentino–Alto Adige, a beautiful alpine part of Italy which borders with Austria. Trentino–Alto Adige was the South Tyrol of Austria before the First World War.

This lovely dessert used to be time-consuming to prepare since it had to be done completely by hand. Today, thanks to the modern processor, we can make a wonderful pastry dough by machine in no time at all. We can chop and grate at the speed of sound and, with a bit of organization, we can prepare this stunning dessert with a minimal amount of energy and hassle.

The recipe has many steps but it is fairly simple to prepare. Get organized. Prepare your pastry dough, blanch, peel, and chop almonds several hours or a day ahead, if you wish. Then prepare the apple filling, roll out the dough, stuff it, and bake it. The strudel can also be baked and kept in the refrigerator for several days. Serve it, however, at room temperature.

For the Pie Crust

2 cups all-purpose unbleached flour
4 ounces (1 stick) butter (at room temperature for hand mixing or cold and cut into small pieces for the food processor)
1 large egg
2 tablespoons sugar
3 to 4 tablespoons chilled white wine

For the Filling

1 cup golden raisins
½ cup unblanched whole almonds
6 large Golden Delicious apples
½ cup sugar
⅓ cup pine nuts
Grated rind of 1 orange
1 cup orange, plum, or apricot jam
¼ cup rum
2 tablespoons unsalted butter
½ cup unseasoned bread crumbs

Prepare the pie crust. In a medium-size bowl or in the bowl of a food processor fitted with a metal blade, mix the flour and butter until crumbly. Add the egg, sugar, and wine. Mix until the dough can be gathered loosely. Put the dough on a work surface and work lightly into a ball. Wrap in aluminum foil and refrigerate for 1 hour.

Prepare the filling. Soak the raisins in lukewarm water for 20 minutes. Drain and pat dry with paper towels. Set aside. Bring a small saucepan of water to the boil. Add the almonds and boil 30 to 40 seconds. Drain and rinse the almonds under cool running water. Place almonds in a kitchen towel and rub them against each other to remove the skins. Chop the almonds into very fine pieces and place in a large bowl.

Peel and core the apples. Cut them into thin slices and add them to the bowl with the almonds. Add the sugar, raisins, pine nuts, orange rind, jam, and rum.

Melt the 2 tablespoons of butter in a small saucepan. Add the bread crumbs and cook over medium heat, stirring, until the crumbs are lightly golden. Set aside to cool. (Do not prepare the filling too far in advance. See Note.)

Preheat the oven to 375 degrees. Lightly butter a 15-

by 12-inch baking sheet. On a lightly floured surface, roll out the dough very thinly into a rectangle. (The length of the rectangle should be approximately 20 inches. The other side should not exceed the length of your baking sheet.)

With a fluted pastry wheel or a sharp knife, trim the edges of the pastry into straight lines. Flip the far side of pastry over the rolling pin loosely and lift. Slide a kitchen towel under the pastry that has been lifted. Unroll the pastry back over the towel. Now flip the side of the pastry near you over the rolling pin. Place another towel under the pastry. Unroll the pastry again over the towel.

Spread the bread crumbs over the pastry, leaving about a 2-inch border free on all sides and a 4-inch border on the side near you. Spread the apple–jam mixture evenly over the bread crumbs. Fold the empty 4-inch border over the apple filling; then pick up the edges of the towel and roll the pastry over, loosely, jelly roll fashion until you have rolled up all the pastry.

Very carefully place the strudel on the buttered baking sheet with the seam facing up. If necessary, trim the roll to fit the sheet.

Brush the top and sides of the strudel with the beaten egg. Bake for 40 to 50 minutes, or until the pastry is golden brown.

Remove from the oven and cool to room temperature. Carefully transfer the strudel to a large serving platter, dust with confectioners' sugar, if you wish, and serve.

The apple filling will become too juicy if it is left to sit. If this does happen, drain the filling in a strainer: then spread it over the pastry.

To Complete the Dish
Butter for the baking sheet
1 large egg, lightly beaten for glazing the strudel
Confectioners' sugar (optional)

SERVES 10 TO 12

Fragole all'Aceto Balsamico

Strawberries with Balsamic Vinegar

If you've had the good fortune to eat very small, wild strawberries with a few drops of precious old balsamic vinegar, you probably had one of the finest culinary experiences in the world. Balsamic vinegar is finally available in this country, though most of it is mass produced; it is even possible to find a more precious, older vinegar in specialized stores. Balsamic vinegar varies in strength. The older the vinegar, the more concentrated and aromatic it becomes (see page 37).

3 cups fresh strawberries
⅓ cup sugar
Balsamic vinegar

SERVES 4 TO 6

Wash the strawberries under cool running water. Remove the stems and dry the strawberries with paper towels. If the strawberries are large, cut them into halves or thirds; if they are small, leave them whole.

Put the strawberries in a large bowl. Add the sugar and a few drops of balsamic vinegar. Toss gently to blend. A bit more sugar or vinegar might be needed. Taste and adjust to your liking. Refrigerate for 1 hour. When ready to serve, spoon the strawberries into chilled glasses.

Spumone di Pesche

Peach Mousse

In Italy there is a whole category of *Dolci al Cucchiaio*. Desserts that are eaten with a spoon. *Zuppa Inglese, Zabaglione* custards, and mousses fall into this category. Many of these dishes are extremely easy to prepare. This *spumone* (literally meaning "large foam") employs ripe, tasty peaches that are combined with rum, sugar, a bit of gelatin, and whipped cream into a soft, fluffy mixture. Each spoonful is sinfully delicious.

The summer bounty provides us with a great variety of fruit that can be transformed into *spume* or *spumoni*.

Peel the peaches, remove the pits, and cut the peaches into chunks. Put the chunks into a food processor or a blender with the sugar, lemon juice, and rum. Process until smooth; then transfer the pureé to a large bowl.

In a small bowl, combine the gelatin and water. Mix well to dissolve and incorporate.

Beat the cream until thick and fold into the peaches. Transfer the mixture to a large glass bowl, cover, and refrigerate for several hours or overnight. Just before serving, decorate the top of the spumone with whipped cream, candied cherries, or fresh strawberries.

2½ pounds ripe peaches
¾ cup sugar
Juice of 1 lemon
¼ cup rum
2 envelopes unflavored gelatin
⅓ cup lukewarm water
1 cup whipping cream
Candied cherries (optional)
Ripe strawberries (optional)

SERVES 6 TO 8

La Torta allo Yougurt e Uvetta Sultanina della Carla

Carla's Yogurt and Raisin Cake

This is the type of cake that my sister Carla likes to have around the house. A little slice with a cup of espresso will satisfy the desire for something a bit sweet. It is a simple, unassuming cake that can be put together in minutes. It has a firm, compact consistency and a not too sweet taste. The quantity of raisins can be increased or decreased to your liking. Make sure the batter is very loose and soft, or the cake will become too heavy and compact.

Soak the raisins in the Marsala for 20 minutes. Drain the raisins and pat dry with paper towels.

Preheat the oven to 375 degrees. Butter and flour an 8-inch springform pan.

In a large bowl, beat the eggs and sugar until pale yellow and thick. Beat in the grated lemon rind, yogurt, and melted butter. Beat in the dry yeast and flour. Fold in the raisins thoroughly with a spatula. At this point the batter should have a loose consistency that should fall off a spoon easily. If it is too thick, add a bit more yogurt or another egg.

Pour the batter into the prepared pan and smooth the top with a spatula. Shake the pan to allow the batter to settle evenly. Bake for 40 to 50 minutes. The cake is done when the top is lightly golden and it begins to pull away from the side of pan. Cool in pan; then transfer to a platter. Cool completely. Before serving sprinkle the top with confectioners' sugar.

1 cup golden raisins
Dry marsala or sherry
3 large eggs
½ cup sugar
Grated rind of 1 lemon
2 cups plain yogurt
5 tablespoons unsalted butter, melted and cooled
1 envelope active dry yeast
3 cups all-purpose unbleached flour
Confectioners' sugar

SERVES 8

Food That I Crave in Spring and Summer   **151**

Brutti ma Buoni

Ugly but Good Hazelnut Cookies

Brutti ma Buoni are delicious little hazelnut cookies that are a specialty of Piemonte. Their appearance leaves a lot to be desired—thus the name—but just put a plate of these cookies on the table, and they will disappear before you can even say hello.

12 ounces shelled hazelnuts
6 large egg whites at room temperature
1½ cups sugar
A few drops of vanilla extract

MAKES 15 TO 20 COOKIES

Preheat the broiler. Put the hazelnuts on a baking sheet and put the sheet under the broiler, about 5 inches from the heat source. Remove the nuts when they are golden brown on all sides and put them in a large kitchen towel. Rub the hazelnuts energetically against each other, inside the towel, to remove the skins. Put the nuts in a food processor or a blender and process to a very fine powder.

In a large bowl, beat the egg whites until frothy. Add sugar and vanilla a little at a time and keep beating until stiff peaks form. Fold the hazelnuts into the egg whites. Transfer the hazelnut mixture to a medium-size saucepan. Cook over very low heat for 8 to 10 minutes, stirring until the mixture turns dark brown in color and comes away clean from the side of the pan. Remove from the heat and let the mixture stand for 5 to 10 minutes.

Preheat the oven to 275 degrees. Butter a baking sheet. Place tablespoons of the hazelnut mixture on the buttered cookie sheet, spacing them well apart. Bake for 25 to 35 minutes. Remove from the oven and allow to cool before removing from the baking sheet.

Ugly but Good Hazelnut Cookies are great either warm or at room temperature. They can be kept for several days in an airtight container.

Il Fior di Latte della Roberta

Roberta's Molded Custard with Caramel Glaze

In 1982, I was teaching in Bologna at the prestigious cooking school of Marcella Hazan, which was located in the premises of the Hotel Milano. There I became acquainted with Roberta, the young wife of the maître d'hotel of the hotel restaurant. Roberta was also involved in the restaurant. Once a week she would prepare all the sausage for the restaurant, as well as most of the restaurant's lovely desserts. My favorite was a light and delicate caramel custard which I simply couldn't resist. This is Roberta's Caramel Custard.

8 cups milk
1¼ cups sugar
Grated rind of 1 lemon
1 long vanilla bean
3 large eggs
4 large egg yolks

SERVES 4 TO 6

In a large saucepan, heat the milk with ½ cup of the sugar, the lemon rind, and vanilla bean. Simmer for 30 to 40 minutes, or until the milk is reduced to a little more than half of its original amount (5 to 6 cups). The milk should have a pale, yellow color. Set aside to cool.

Prepare the caramel. Put the remaining sugar and ⅓ cup of water in a small heavy pan and cook over medium heat until the mixture is light brown and has a thick syrupy consistency. Pour the syrup into a warm, dry mold or a 9- by 5-inch loaf pan. (These molds can be warmed up by filling them with hot water and then drying them well.) Holding the mold or loaf pan with a kitchen towel, tilt to coat sides and bottom completely with the syrup. This step has to be done quickly to ensure an even distribution of syrup before it cools and sets. Cool the mold for about 15 minutes.

Preheat the oven to 350 degrees.

In a large bowl, beat eggs and egg yolks lightly. Pour the cooled milk into the eggs slowly, stirring constantly. Strain the mixture into the cooled caramelized mold. Place the mold in a deep baking dish and pour some hot water into the baking dish. The water should come about three quarters of the way up the sides of the mold. Place the baking dish in the oven. Bake for 1 hour and 15 minutes to 1½ hours. The custard is done when a thin knife inserted into the cream comes out clean.

Cool the custard. Run a thin knife around the mold to free the custard. Place a flat serving dish over the mold and invert to unmold. Pat gently and lift up the mold. The custard will have a glaze of caramel over the top and sides. Serve at room temperature.

Bomba Gelata ai Tre Colori

Three-Flavor Ice Cream Bombe

Ice cream, or *gelato* to Italians, was, until a few years ago, something we would indulge at the local *gelaterie* or at an outdoor café. Now this delicious treat can be made at home thanks to wonderfully efficient and easy-to-use ice cream machines.

With the basic ice cream, we can also create myriads of tempting new desserts, like this bombe with three flavors, which features vanilla, chocolate, and strawberry ice cream.

It is a somewhat lengthy, even though easy, dessert to prepare. The good features are that it must be prepared several hours or a day ahead of time, and, when unmolded, it is simply glorious. As I see it the only problem with this dessert is that it keeps disappearing as fast as it is made, scoop, after scoop, after scoop . . .

For the Vanilla and Chocolate Ice Cream
3 ounces semisweet chocolate squares
2 cups heavy cream
2 cups milk
4 large egg yolks
¾ cup sugar
2 to 3 drops of vanilla extract

For the Strawberry Ice Cream
1 pint strawberries
Juice of ½ lemon
⅓ cup sugar
½ cup whipping cream, beaten to a medium-thick consistency

SERVES 8

Cut the chocolate into small chunks and place in an ovenproof bowl. Place the bowl in a preheated 200-degree oven until the chocolate has melted, about 7 to 8 minutes.

While the chocolate is melting, prepare the basic custard cream. In a medium-size saucepan, heat the cream and milk just short of a boil. Set aside.

In a large bowl or in the top part of a double boiler, beat the egg yolks and sugar until pale yellow and thick. Set the bowl or the top part of the double boiler over simmering water. Do not let the water boil. Add cream–milk mixture to the eggs very slowly, mixing constantly with a wire whisk. Cook for 5 to 6 minutes, or until the mixture coats the back of a spoon and has thickened slightly. Strain equal amounts of the cream into two clean bowls.

Pour a few drops of vanilla extract into one bowl and

mix to blend. Pour the melted chocolate slowly into other bowl, whisking to keep the mixture smooth and to blend the chocolate thoroughly with the cream. (These creams can be prepared a few days ahead of time and kept tightly covered in the refrigerator.)

While the chocolate and vanilla creams cool, prepare the strawberry ice cream. Wash and hull the strawberries. Put them in a food processor with the lemon juice and sugar. Process until smooth. Pour the mixture through a strainer and into the cool bowl of the ice cream machine. Run the machine for 10 to 15 minutes. Add the whipped cream and run for 10 minutes longer.

Chill an ice cream bombe mold. Put the strawberry ice cream into the chilled mold and smooth the tip with a spatula. (The strawberry ice cream should fill only one third of the mold.) Cover and freeze for 1 hour. Clean the bowl of the ice cream machine.

While the strawberry ice cream freezes, put the vanilla cream in the bowl of the ice cream machine and run for 20 to 25 minutes, or until the ice cream is fluffy and solid.

Remove the mold from the freezer. Place 1 layer of vanilla ice cream over the strawberry ice cream to fill two thirds of the mold. Cover and freeze for 1 hour. Clean the bowl of the ice cream machine.

Now, put the chocolate cream in the bowl of the ice cream machine. Run the machine for 25 minutes.

Remove the mold from the freezer and place a final layer of chocolate ice cream in the mold to fill it to the rim. Cover the mold tightly and freeze overnight.

When ready to serve, transfer the mold from the freezer to the refrigerator for 15 to 20 minutes. Dip the mold quickly into hot water. Dry the outside of the mold and invert it onto a chilled serving dish. Serve at once.

Cassata Gelata

Stuffed Ice Cream Bombe

Cassata is probably the most popular of the Sicilian desserts. It was originally made with sponge cake and a mixture of ricotta, chocolate, and candied fruit. Cassata Gelata follows the same idea of the Sicilian cassata, except it is made with ice cream. The ice cream is pressed into a bombe mold and stuffed with a mixture of whipped cream, chocolate, and candied fruit. In Italy, these eye-catching desserts are generally bought in pastry shops and ice cream shops. Lately, however, with the popularity of the home ice cream machines, they are made more and more frequently at home.

For the Vanilla Ice Cream

3 cups milk
4 large egg yolks
1 teaspoon vanilla extract
¾ cup sugar
1 cup whipping cream, beaten to a medium-thick consistency

For the Ice Cream Filling

¾ cup mixed candied fruit
⅓ cup Grand Marnier or any other liqueur of your choice
3 1-ounce squares semisweet chocolate
1 cup whipping cream, beaten to a medium-thick consistency together with 1 tablespoon sugar

Serves 6 to 8

To prepare the vanilla ice cream, heat the milk in a medium-size saucepan. In a large bowl or the top part of a double boiler, beat the eggs, vanilla, and sugar until pale yellow and thick. Add the hot milk very slowly, a little at a time, beating constantly. Set the bowl or the top part of the double boiler over 2 inches of simmering water (the water should be simmering, not boiling, or it will curdle the eggs). Cook for 4 to 5 minutes, stirring constantly, until the custard coats the back of a spoon and has thickened slightly.

Strain the custard into a clean bowl and cool to room temperature. The custard can be prepared up to this point a few days ahead and kept tightly covered in the refrigerator.

Put the custard mixture in the bowl of the ice cream machine and run for about 15 minutes; then add the whipped cream. Run the machine for 5 to 10 minutes longer, or until ice cream is ready.

Chill the ice cream mold. Line the mold with ice cream. Smooth the ice cream over the sides and bottom of mold, leaving a hollow cavity in the center. Cover the mold and place in the freezer for 30 minutes.

To prepare the filling, chop the candied fruit into small pieces about the size of small peas. Place in a bowl and add the Grand Marnier. Soak for 15 to 20 minutes.

Chop the chocolate into small chunks. Drain the candied fruit and pat it dry with paper towels. Fold the candied fruit and chocolate into the whipped cream.

Remove the mold from the freezer. Fill the cavity with the cream–candied fruit mixture, pressing it lightly and smoothing the top with a spatula. Put a lid on the mold or cover it tightly with aluminum foil. Freeze for several hours or overnight. When ready to serve, put the mold in the refrigerator for 15 to 20 minutes.

Fill the kitchen sink with hot water and dip the mold into the water quickly. Dry the mold and remove the lid or foil. Invert the mold onto a chilled serving plate. Slice into the desired portions and serve immediately.

Be sure that the mold is filled to the rim with ice cream and filling or it might break when inverted onto the platter.

Pesche al Vino Rosso

Peaches Marinated in Red Wine

Fruit is standard at the end of a family meal in Italy. When fruit is treated in a special way, it becomes more important and can be served as the conclusion of a formal or informal dinner. We all know of berries with cream or with zabaglione. In Italy we have another favorite: fruit in wine. Peaches or strawberries in wine are a delightful summer treat. Choose ripe, but not overripe, peaches and marinate them in wine, lemon juice, and sugar for several hours. A good Chianti, a young Zinfandel, or a Pinot Noir can be used. Keep an eye on the children when they eat this preparation since they might like it a little too much. The last time I prepared peaches in wine, my twelve-year-old daughter Paola had several servings; then she began to giggle, and giggle, and giggle.

Peel the peaches and remove the pits. Cut the peaches into medium-thin slices. Put the slices in a large glass bowl. Add the lemon juice and sugar and cover the peaches with wine. Cover the bowl and refrigerate for several hours. Spoon the peaches and wine into individual bowls or glasses and serve quite chilled.

8 medium-size ripe peaches
Juice of 1 lemon
½ cup sugar
Enough wine to cover the peaches, preferably a young Chianti

SERVES 4

Crostata di Fichi

Fig Tart

Sweet, ripe figs are a delicacy and Italians take advantage of them whenever they are in season—figs and prosciutto are a time-honored combination and a favorite appetizer, figs and cheese can end a meal on an elegant note, and succulent figs alone can easily replace a sweet dessert. However, when you are in the mood for something sinfully delicious, try this fig tart. Bake the shell a day ahead, if you wish, but assemble the tart not more than 1 or 2 hours before you are ready to serve it, or the juices of the figs will make the crust soggy.

For the Sweet Pie Pastry

1⅓ cups all-purpose unbleached flour
6 tablespoons unsalted butter (at room temperature for hand mixing or cold and in small pieces for the food processor)
1 large egg
1 tablespoon sugar
2 to 3 tablespoons chilled white wine
1 large egg white, lightly beaten

To Assemble the Dish

2 baskets ripe black or green figs
1 12-ounce jar fig jam or marmalade
⅓ cup rum

SERVES 8

Prepare the sweet pie pastry. In a medium-size bowl or in the bowl of a food processor fitted with a metal blade, mix the flour with butter until crumbly. Add the egg, sugar, and wine. Mix until the dough can be gathered into a ball. Put the dough on a work surface and work into a ball. Wrap in aluminum foil and refrigerate for 1 hour.

Preheat the oven to 400 degrees. On a lightly floured surface, roll out the dough to a 12-inch circle. Place the dough carefully into a 10-inch pan with a removable bottom. Trim the edges of the dough by gently rolling the rolling pin over the top of the dough. Prick the bottom of the pastry shell in several places with a fork. Line the pastry shell with aluminum foil. Fill the foil with uncooked rice or beans. This will prevent the pastry from shrinking while baking. Bake for 15 minutes. Remove the foil and rice or beans. Brush the dough with the beaten egg white and bake for 10 minutes longer, or until the pastry is golden in color.

Peel the figs and cut them in half lengthwise.

In a small saucepan, combine the jam and rum. Cook over medium heat for 4 to 5 minutes, stirring. Strain the jam into a bowl, pressing the mixture with a spoon. Return to the saucepan and cook until thick and syrupy. Brush the syrup over the bottom of the tart shell.

Place the figs, cut side up, into the shell, arranging them close together. Brush the syrup over the figs and dribble any remaining syrup over all. Transfer the tart to a serving dish and refrigerate until ready to use. Serve at room temperature.

Fritelle di Mele con Salsa di Lamponi

Apple Fritters with Raspberry Sauce

Take a simple homey dessert like apple fritters and serve them with a few tablespoons of raspberry sauce—sheer heaven! The raspberry sauce can be prepared a few days ahead. The batter for the apples can also be prepared a few hours ahead. At the last moment, the only thing to do is the frying. Serve these apple fritters while they are still hot and crunchy. The raspberry sauce can be served hot or at room temperature.

Beat the egg yolks in a medium-size bowl. Add the milk and beat to blend. Gradually add the flour, mixing to prevent lumps. Let stand at room temperature for about 1 hour. The batter should be the consistency of home-made mayonnaise.

Prepare the raspberry sauce. If using frozen raspberries, thaw them to room temperature and drain off the excess juices. Put the fresh or frozen raspberries in a blender or food processor fitted with a metal blade. Add the sugar and raspberry brandy. Blend to a smooth sauce. Press the mixture through a sieve into a bowl to remove the seeds. (This step can be done well ahead of time and the pureé refrigerated.) Put the sauce into a saucepan and bring to a gentle boil. Cook, uncovered, until the sauce is reduced by half. Taste and, if necessary, add a bit more sugar or liqueur. Keep warm over very low heat.

In a medium-size bowl, beat the egg whites and a pinch of salt until stiff. Fold the whites into the fritter batter.

Core and peel the apples. Cut the apples into ¼-inch-thick rounds. Pour 2 inches of oil into a large saucepan or skillet. Heat the oil. Test the oil with a bit of the batter: If the batter turns golden almost immediately, the oil is ready for frying. When the oil is hot enough, hold the apples with two forks and dip them into the batter. Let the excess batter drip off. Drop the coated apples into the hot oil. When brown on both sides, remove the fritters with a slotted spoon to paper towels.

Arrange the fritters on a serving dish, sprinkle with sugar, and serve immediately with warm raspberry sauce.

For the Batter

2 large eggs separated and at room temperature
1½ cups sugar
1 cup all-purpose unbleached flour
Pinch of salt

For the Raspberry Sauce

2 cups fresh or frozen raspberries
½ cup sugar
⅓ cup raspberry brandy or any other liqueur of your liking

To Complete the Dish

5 apples, preferably Golden Delicious
Oil for frying
⅓ cup sugar

SERVES 6 TO 8

Semifreddo con Salsa di Lamponi

Frozen Zabaglione Mousse with Raspberry Sauce

Semifreddo literally means "half cold." There are innumerable semifreddi in Italy. They are not ice creams and they are not cakes. They are "in between." In spite of the many steps to this recipe, this dessert is really quite simple to prepare. An added bonus is that it must be prepared ahead of time. When unmolded, semifreddo is truly an eye-catching dessert. The raspberry sauce adds flavor as well as color to this preparation.

For the Zabaglione

7 large egg yolks
¾ cup sugar
⅓ cup dry Marsala, preferably Florio
¼ cup raspberry brandy
½ pint whipping cream
5 large egg whites at room temperature
½ cup sugar

For the Raspberry Sauce

2 cups fresh or frozen raspberries (thawed if frozen)
½ cup sugar
⅓ cup raspberry brandy

Chocolate Whipped Cream for Decorations

½ pint whipping cream
2 tablespoons sugar
3 tablespoons unsweetened cocoa powder

SERVES 8

Prepare the zabaglione. Put the eggs and sugar in the top of a double boiler. Beat until the mixture is pale yellow and thick. (This can be done with an electric beater.) Place the pan on the lower part of the double boiler containing about 2 inches of simmering water. Add the Marsala and raspberry brandy slowly and beat with a large wire whisk until the mixture swells into a large, soft mass and doubles in volume. Remove from the heat and set the pan containing zabaglione over a bowl of ice water. Stir with a whisk until the zabaglione is completely cool.

Beat the cream until stiff and fold into the zabaglione. Beat the egg whites until foamy. Add the sugar a little at a time and beat until the whites are shining and soft peaks form. Fold the beaten egg whites into the zabaglione.

Butter the sides and bottom of an 8½- by 4½-inch loaf pan. Line the bottom and sides of the pan with a sheet of plastic wrap, leaving about 5 inches overhanging on each side. Pour the zabaglione mixture into the pan and smooth the top with a spatula. Fold up the overhanging wrap to cover the mold tightly. Freeze for at least 10 to 12 hours. Semifreddo can be prepared up to this point several days ahead.

Prepare the raspberry sauce. In a blender or food processor, combine the raspberries, sugar, and brandy. Process until smooth. Put the sauce through a sieve and refrigerate until ready to use. (This will yield approximately 2 cups of sauce.)

Prepare the chocolate whipped cream. Beat the cream

until thick. Add the sugar and cocoa powder. Beat a bit more until very thick. Refrigerate until ready to use.

One hour before serving, remove the semifreddo from the freezer. Put a few inches of hot water into the sink. Dip the pan briefly into the hot water (2 to 3 seconds). Dry the outside of the pan. Using a serving dish that can be put safely into the freezer, place the dish over the loaf pan. Invert the pan over the dish. Gently remove the pan and peel off the plastic wrap. Clean the dish of any runny semifreddo.

Put the chocolate cream into a pastry bag fitted with a medium-size tip and decorate all around and on top of the cake. Return to the freezer without covering it until ready to serve.

Cut the semifreddo into slices and place the slices on individual chilled serving dishes. Spoon a bit of the raspberry sauce over each slice and serve at once.

Wonderful Autumn and Winter Fare

When winter's snow, rain, and freezing temperature drive us indoors for much of the time, my inclination turns to homemade pasta and bread, hearty soups, rich stews, and golden polenta. This is real, reassuring, and uncomplicated food; like a soft, warm blanket, it envelops you with immediate comfort.

When we were children, my brother, sister, and I would roast chestnuts on the big wooden stove in the kitchen. We lived in an old, medieval building in the center of Bologna; it had high ceilings but no heat. The large kitchen, the warmest spot in the house, *was* truly the center of every family activity.

I did my homework on the table on the "dining room side" of the kitchen, while my mother worked on the kitchen side. On those cold, rainy days when we came home from school, she would greet us at the door. Then she would help us change our wet socks and rub our cold hands until they became warm again. We would then sit at the table and indulge in hot soup or hot chocolate, freshly baked apple cake or pastry ring.

Memories of love and good food stay with you throughout the years, and every winter I feel the urge to re-create that wonderful spell.

Today, we have so much kitchen equipment at our disposal that cooking is easier and fun. There is nothing wrong in letting a food processor knead your bread, and there is nothing wrong with a pasta machine that stretches our homemade dough, or with a machine that chops and slices at the speed of sound. However, I will go a mile out of my way to obtain that special ingredient, because I feel that good ingredients are vital to good cooking.

When the parmigiano is dried out and the pancetta has an unpleasant taste, when the fish is old and the lettuce is wilted, there is no genius that can transform them into great dishes. However, take a slice from a loaf of fresh bread and rub it with garlic. Add a few chunks of perfectly ripened tomatoes and dribble it with good olive oil and then you will understand how extraordinary even the most humble food can be when good, fresh ingredients are used.

Even though in winter we tend to eat richer and more satisfying food, it is important not to go overboard. Friends and acquaintances are always amazed that with all my Italian cooking I don't weigh two hundred pounds. Perhaps the secret is that even though I eat a little of everything I cook, I don't gorge on it. Those heaped-up plates are not only unappealing and quite distasteful to me, but also totally unnecessary for today's sedentary life-style. Moderation is the key word and nobody can teach us moderation but ourselves.

It would be unrealistic for most of us to give up totally some dishes we love because they are too rich, too sweet, or too spicy. We all love and crave "forbidden" foods from time to time. If we are selective with the food we cook and moderate with the amount we eat, there is no reason why we should not indulge in a special treat once in a while.

During the long, cold, and often tedious winter days our body demands more satisfying food. We all know we eat differently in different seasons. When the thick fog envelops the Sacramento valley or the pounding rain prevents me from jogging or playing tennis, I go to the kitchen and cook up a storm. I cook dishes that I can freeze and that will give me extra time later. Very often dishes that take a long time to cook require very little of our time and attention, because they cook gently all by themselves. A large roast can be braised slowly for hours, asking only to be turned and basted once in a while, and, as an added bonus, these dishes will reward us for they are economical and taste even better a few days after they are made.

Food is, for most of us today, something we approach with a new awareness. We want good food without repetitive actions and without fuss. What we seek is a renewal of the pleasures of the table with the freedom to adapt the food we love to fit our own needs.

I have tried to do so throughout this section and this book, and I have discovered something that is not a discovery at all: Regardless of how one cooks, good food simply doesn't go out of style.

Appetizers

Bocconcini di Melanzane

Eggplants Stuffed with Fontina and Sun-Dried Tomatoes

Bocconcini means "little bites" or "little morsels." In this dish, eggplant slices are sandwiched with Italian fontina and sun-dried tomatoes. They are dipped in eggs and coated with a mixture of bread crumbs and parmigiano and then fried until golden. The eggplants can be stuffed and coated several hours ahead of time, ready to fry at the last moment. To fry properly, make sure the oil is very hot—this will give the eggplants a crunchy texture without an extra "oily" taste.

Wash and dry the eggplant. Trim off the ends but leave the skin on. Slice the eggplant into 10 to 12 rounds, ¼ inch thick. Put the slices on a large platter or baking sheet, sprinkle with salt, and let stand for about 1 hour. Pat the slices dry with paper towels.

Put 1 slice of fontina and half of a sun-dried tomato on each eggplant slice. Top with another eggplant slice. Repeat to use all of the ingredients.

Beat the eggs and salt and pepper in a shallow dish. Dip the bocconcini into the eggs and then coat with the bread crumb–parmigiano mixture on both sides. Press the mixture gently onto the eggplants with the palm of your hand. Let stand 15 to 20 minutes.

Heat the oil in a large skillet. Lower the stuffed eggplant into oil a few at a time, to avoid splattering. Do not crowd them in the skillet. Fry until golden on both sides.

Transfer the eggplants to paper towels and pat them dry to remove the excess oil. Transfer to a warm serving dish. Continue frying until all eggplants are done. Sprinkly lightly with salt and serve hot.

1 firm medium-size eggplant (about 1 pound)
Salt
4 ounces Italian fontina, roughly cut into slices
10 sun-dried tomatoes, packed in oil
2 large eggs
Salt and freshly ground black pepper
1½ cups unseasoned bread crumbs
½ cup freshly grated parmigiano
Oil for frying

Serves 4

The bocconcini can also be served as a light luncheon dish.

Crostini di Polenta ai Funghi

Crostini of Polenta and Mushrooms

In this dish, small slices of polenta are broiled and then topped with a delicious mixture of porcini and white cultivated mushrooms that have been cooked in a rich wine–cream sauce. A lovely, elegant way to start a meal.

For the Polenta

6 cups water
1½ tablespoons salt
1 cup coarsely ground cornmeal mixed
    with 1 cup finely ground cornmeal

For the Mushrooms

1 ounce imported dried porcini mushrooms
2 to 3 tablespoons unsalted butter
1 pound small fresh white cultivated
    mushrooms, cleaned and thinly sliced
½ cup dry Marsala, preferably Florio
    brand
⅓ cup heavy cream
Salt and freshly ground black pepper

SERVES 8 TO 10

Prepare the Basic Polenta (page 210). Pour it onto a large wooden board or platter and cool completely. (When completely cooled, the polenta will become quite firm.)

Soak the dried mushrooms in 2 cups of water for 20 minutes. Strain and rinse well to get rid of sandy deposits. Reserve the soaking water for another use, such as stews.

Melt the butter in a medium-size skillet. When the butter foams, add the sliced fresh mushrooms, and sauté over high heat until they are golden. Add the dried mushrooms and Marsala. Cook over high heat until the Marsala is almost all reduced. Stir in the cream. Cook gently for a few minutes longer. At this point, only a few tablespoons of sauce should be left in the skillet. Season lightly with salt and pepper. Keep warm over very low heat.

Cut the polenta into slices ½ inch thick and about 4 inches long. Preheat the broiler. Broil the polenta until golden and crisp on both sides. Top each crostino with some mushrooms and serve.

Cozze Gratinate al Forno

Stuffed Baked Mussels

Eating fish was not an everyday event while I was growing up in Bologna. My mother prepared it two or three times a month. Perhaps that is why it took me some time before I learned to like fish and to positively love mussels. During the summer months, we would vacation at the nearby Adriatic shore and, when at the beach, did what the locals did—ate fish. The fresh catch of the day was prepared by the chef of the small family-style pensione where we regularly stayed. I must have been fourteen or fifteen the first time

I tried stuffed mussels and I vividly recall that I simply couldn't swallow it. How we do change! Today, I adore mussels.

This delicious appetizer can be prepared with clams when mussels are unavailable.

Soak the mussels in cool salted water for 15 to 20 minutes. Wash and scrub the mussels thoroughly under cool running water. Put the mussels in a large saucepan or skillet. Add 2 tablespoons of the oil, the wine, and 1 cup of water. Cover and cook over high heat until the mussels open. Some might take a little longer to open than others. However, if they fail to open altogether, discard them.

Remove the mussels with a slotted spoon to a large bowl. Line a strainer with paper towels and strain the mussels' cooking liquid. Return the liquid to the same saucepan or skillet and boil over high heat until it is reduced to only 3 to 4 tablespoons.

Put the reduced liquid into a bowl. Add the parsley, garlic, bread crumbs, parmigiano, and remaining 2 tablespoons of oil. Season with salt and pepper. Mix everything well; the mixture should be moist.

Preheat the broiler. Lightly oil a baking dish.

Discard one shell from each mussel and leave the mussel meat in the other half shell. Put about 1 teaspoon of the stuffing loosely over each mussel. Put the stuffed mussels in the baking dish. Broil until the stuffing is lightly golden, 2 to 3 minutes. Serve with lemon slices.

Do not use store-bought bread crumbs, but make your own with leftover hard-crusted bread. If the bread is still too moist, place it in the oven set at a low temperature until dried and lightly toasted; in a pinch, use regular sliced bread that has been toasted. Place the bread pieces in a food processor fitted with a metal blade and process until you have fine bread crumbs. Bread crumbs freeze very well.

1½ pounds mussels (about 20)
4 tablespoons olive oil
½ cup dry white wine
2 tablespoons chopped fresh parsley leaves
2 garlic cloves, finely chopped
⅓ cup unseasoned bread crumbs
¼ cup freshly grated parmigiano
Salt and freshly ground black pepper
Lemon slices

SERVES 4

Spuma di Melanzane

Eggplant Mousse

Here is a tasty, light appetizer produced by first cooking eggplants in a traditional Italian manner. The eggplants are sautéed with parsley and garlic and then they are puréed and combined with a little whipped cream into a soft, light mousse. A bit of gelatin is added to give the spuma some firmness. This appetizer could be served elegantly on individual plates or it can be spread on triangles of toasted white bread and served informally with drinks.

For the Mousse

2 medium-size firm eggplants
4 tablespoons olive oil
3 tablespoons chopped fresh parsley leaves
3 garlic cloves, finely chopped
Salt and freshly ground black pepper
1 envelope unflavored gelatin
½ cup whipping cream, beaten to stiff peaks
Several white crisp lettuce leaves

For the Garnish

Capers, chopped parsley, or strips of roasted red peppers
8 to 12 slices thinly cut Italian bread, or 6 slices toasted white bread, cut into triangles

SERVES 4 TO 6

Peel the eggplants and cut them lengthwise into ½-inch-thick slices. Put the slices on a large platter and sprinkle with salt. Let stand for about 1 hour. Pat the slices dry with paper towels and cut them into small cubes.

Heat the oil in a large skillet. Add the parsley and garlic and sauté briefly. Before the garlic takes on color, add the eggplant slices. Season with salt and pepper. Cover the skillet and cook for 10 to 12 minutes, stirring a few times during cooking. Add a bit of water if the eggplants stick to the bottom of the skillet. Transfer the eggplants to a food processor or a blender and process until smooth. Transfer to a bowl and taste and adjust the seasoning. Cool.

Dissolve the gelatin in ⅓ cup of lukewarm water and stir into the eggplant mixture. Fold the whipped cream into the eggplant mixture. Cover and refrigerate for several hours or overnight.

When ready to serve, line individual serving dishes with a few slices of tender and crisp lettuce. Spoon some mousse in a mound in the center of the plate. Decorate with a few capers, a bit of chopped parsley, or with thin small strips of broiled red pepper. Serve slightly chilled with thin slices of Italian bread or with triangles of toasted white bread.

Caponatina di Melanzane in Agrodolce

Medley of Sweet and Sour Eggplants, Raisins, Pine Nuts, and Tomatoes

Caponatina di Melanzane is a traditional Sicilian dish made with eggplants and various other vegetables that are cooked together. In this version, pine nuts, raisins, sugar, vinegar, and capers are also added. The result is a sweet and sour, very appetizing dish. Serve caponatina at room temperature as an appetizer or, if you are a vegetable lover, as an entrée. This dish keeps well for several days in the refrigerator. It also freezes well.

Soak the raisins in warm water for 30 minutes. Drain and pat dry with paper towels.

Wash the eggplants and then cut them into 1-inch cubes. Put the cubes in a colander and sprinkle with salt. Let stand for about 1 hour. Rinse the eggplants quickly and pat them dry with paper towels.

Pour 1 inch of olive oil into a large skillet. When the oil is hot, add the eggplant cubes without crowding the skillet; fry, turning, to a nice golden color all around.

Remove the eggplant with a slotted spoon to paper towels. Continue frying until all the eggplant is done. Pat the eggplant cubes well with paper towels to remove as much oil as possible.

Discard some of the oil, leaving only enough to barely cover the bottom of the skillet. Add the onion and celery and sauté over medium heat until the onion is pale yellow.

Press the tomatoes through a food mill or a strainer to remove the seeds. Add strained tomatoes, eggplant, olives, capers, pine nuts, vinegar, and raisins to the skillet. Season with salt and pepper and bring the mixture to a boil. Lower the heat and cook, uncovered, for 10 to 15 minutes, stirring a few times. Taste for seasoning. Transfer the caponatina to a large bowl to cool. Serve at room temperature.

⅓ cup golden raisins
2 medium-size eggplants
Salt
Olive oil
1 onion, thinly sliced
3 inner white celery stalks, diced
3 cups drained canned imported Italian
  plum tomatoes
½ cup black olives, sliced
¼ cup rinsed and dried capers
¼ cup pine nuts
2 tablespoons sugar
2 tablespoons red wine vinegar
Salt and freshly ground black pepper

SERVES 8 TO 10

If you omit the raisins, sugar, and vinegar, the caponatina becomes a lovely sauce for pasta.

Spiedini con il Formaggio

Broiled Bread and Cheese Skewers

A delicious, if somewhat filling, Roman appetizer that was made originally with "provatura," a typical Roman cheese not unlike mozzarella. Spiedini could be the starter of a hearty winter meal, a simple tasty luncheon, or an appetizing late-night snack.

Slices of Italian bread cut into 16 pieces, 2½ inches wide and ½ inch thick
½ pound mozzarella, cut into 2½-inch wide and ½-inch-thick pieces
6 tablespoons unsalted butter
4 anchovy fillets, finely chopped
3 garlic cloves, finely chopped

SERVES 4

Preheat the oven to 375 degrees. Butter generously a large baking dish. Thread 4 pieces each of bread and mozzarella alternately on 4 wooden or metal skewers. Begin and end with a piece of bread. Arrange in the baking dish.

In a small saucepan, melt 3 tablespoons of the butter. Dribble the butter over the bread and cheese. Bake for 8 to 10 minutes, or until the bread is golden and the cheese begins to melt.

Meanwhle, melt the remaining 3 tablespoons of butter in a small saucepan. Add the anchovies and garlic. Cook over low heat for 2 to 3 minutes. As soon as the garlic begins to color, remove from the heat.

Place the skewers on individual serving dishes, spoon a bit of the anchovy sauce over each skewer, and serve.

Fondi di Carciofi Ripieni

Stuffed Artichoke Bottoms

Artichokes are very popular among Italians and specialty gourmet shops in Italy generally display artichokes in a variety of tempting preparations. Artichokes Roman Style, Deep-Fried Artichokes, and Stuffed Artichoke Bottoms are only some of the favorites. This dish will take 30 to 40 minutes to prepare. The bonus is, however, that it can be prepared completely ahead of time and refrigerated until ready to bake. Serve it as a lovely introduction to a meal.

If using fresh spinach, wash it in several changes of cool water. Discard the stems and any bruised tough leaves. Put the spinach in a large saucepan with only the water that clings to the leaves. Add a pinch of salt, cover the pan, and cook for 8 to 10 minutes, or until tender. Drain and squeeze out any excess moisture. If using frozen spinach, cook following the instructions on the package. Drain and squeeze dry.

Melt the butter in a medium-size skillet. When the butter foams, add the spinach. Season with salt and pepper and sauté for 1 to 2 minutes. Add the parmigiano and cream and stir well to incorporate. Cook over medium heat until the cream is completely reduced and no more moisture is left in the skillet. Set aside.

To prepare the artichokes, cut off the stems. Remove all outer leaves from the artichokes until you reach the tapering soft white inner leaves; cut off the top just above the heart. With a small knife, trim all green parts around artichoke's heart. Rub with lemon and place the bottoms in a medium-size saucepan. Cover the bottoms with water and add the lemon juice and olive oil. Bring to a gentle boil and cook for 8 to 10 minutes, or until bottoms are barely tender to the touch. Use a slotted spoon to transfer the artichoke bottoms to paper towels until cool.

Preheat the oven to 350 degrees. Butter a small baking dish.

With a spoon or a small knife, cleanly scoop out the fuzzy choke from each artichoke bottom. Fill the cavities with the spinach mixture and put the stuffed artichoke bottoms in the baking dish. Sprinkle each top with a bit of parmigiano. Bake for 10 to 12 minutes. The artichokes should be tender when pierced with the point of a thin knife. Serve hot.

3 to 3½ pounds fresh spinach, or 2 10-ounce packages frozen spinach
4 tablespoons unsalted butter
Salt and freshly ground black pepper
½ cup freshly grated parmigiano
½ cup heavy cream
6 medium-size artichokes
Juice of 1 lemon
2 tablespoons olive oil

SERVES 6

Crostini di Melanzane Trifolate

Crostini of Spicy Eggplant

In Italy, when we say *trifolar*, we always refer to the technique of sautéing vegetables in olive oil with parsley and garlic. Mushrooms are excellent done this way and so are eggplants.

2 medium-size firm eggplants
Salt
½ cup olive oil
3 anchovy fillets, finely chopped
A very small piece of a hot red chile pepper, finely chopped
2 garlic cloves, finely chopped
¼ cup chopped fresh parsley leaves
3 tablespoons rinsed and dried capers
12 slices crusty Italian bread, approximately 3 by 3 inches long and ½ inch thick

MAKES 12 CROSTINI

Peel and dice the eggplants. Place the eggplants in a colander, sprinkle with salt, and let stand for about 30 minutes. Pat the eggplants dry with paper towels.

Heat the oil in a large skillet. Add the anchovies, chile pepper, and garlic and sauté gently for 2 to 3 minutes. Add the eggplants and cook over medium heat for 10 to 12 minutes, or until the eggplants are tender. Add the parsley and capers and season lightly with salt. Cook for 1 to 2 minutes longer. Taste and adjust the seasoning. Set aside.

Meanwhile, broil the bread until golden on both sides. Top each slice of bread with some of the eggplant mixture, place the slices on a serving dish, and serve.

These eggplant trifolate can accompany a meat or a fowl.

Cape Sante Dorate

Marinated Deep-Fried Scallops

In this recipe, scallops are marinated for a short time in oil, garlic, and lemon juice. Then they are dipped in a light batter and deep-fried until golden and served with a sprinkling of chopped parsley. The temperature of the oil should be just about 370 degrees: Too much heat will scorch the scallops; too little heat will make them soggy.

Deep-fried food is, in a way, like pasta. Once it is ready it doesn't wait for anyone. So make sure your table is set and your salad or vegetables are ready. Then enjoy a lovely light meal.

Wash the scallops under cool running water and pat them dry with paper towels. Put the scallops in a bowl with the lemon juice, garlic, and olive oil. Marinate for about 1 hour at room temperature.

Prepare the batter. Beat the egg yolks in a medium-size bowl. Add the water and beat to blend. Gradually add the flour, mixing to prevent lumps from forming. Season with salt. Let stand at room temperature for 1 hour.

In a medium-size bowl, beat egg whites and a pinch of salt until stiff. Fold the whites into the batter.

Drain the scallops and pat them dry with paper towels.

Pour 2 inches of oil into a medium-size saucepan. Heat the oil. Holding each scallop with two forks, dip them into the batter, allowing any excess batter to drip off. Fry a few scallops at a time. When golden on both sides, about 1 minute, remove with a slotted spoon and drain on paper towels. Repeat with the remaining scallops.

Put the scallops on individual warm serving dishes, sprinkle with parsley, and serve hot accompanied by lemon wedges.

You will never find two Italians agreeing completely on how to prepare a classic dish: One will always have the most "authentic" recipe and will try to outdo the other. Even the ingredients are often known by different names in different parts of the country. Take the scallop. Here, a scallop is a scallop. But in Italy, scallops are called Cape Sante, canestrelli, Ventagli, and Pellegrini di San Giacomo, creating, it would seem, some confusion.

In any case serve the scallops as an entrée or an appetizer.

For the Marinade
1½ pounds sea scallops
1 tablespoon fresh lemon juice
2 garlic cloves, finely chopped
4 tablespoons olive oil

For the Batter
2 large eggs, separated and at room temperature
1½ cups water
1 cup all-purpose unbleached flour
1 teaspoon salt

To Complete the Dish
Oil for frying
2 tablespoons chopped fresh parsley leaves
Lemon wedges

SERVES 4

Pasta

Bucatini con i Fagioli Stufati

Bucatini with Stewed Beans

A very old country dish that is enjoying a revival throughout Italy is Pasta with Stewed Beans. In Bologna, the sauce is served over the favorite tagliatelle (noodles). In Mantua, it is served over the local delicious bigoli (homemade fat spaghetti). The beans are soaked overnight and then boiled gently. They are then stewed together with tomatoes, vegetables, and herbs.

Put the beans in a large bowl, cover with water, and let stand overnight. Drain and rinse the beans and put them in a medium-size saucepan with enough water to cover them. Bring the water to a boil, lower the heat and simmer for 30 to 40 minutes, stirring a few times. The beans should be tender but still a little firm to the bite. Drain the beans and set aside.

Put the tomatoes through a food mill or sieve to remove the seeds.

Heat the oil in a medium-size saucepan. Add the onion, carrot, and celery and sauté gently for 4 to 5 minutes. Add pancetta, garlic, and sage and sauté for 2 to 3 minutes longer. Add the beans, tomatoes, and chicken broth and season with salt and pepper. Simmer, uncovered, for 15 to 20 minutes. Stir in the parsley and cook 5 minutes longer. The sauce should have a medium-thick consistency. If it is too thin, cook a bit longer; if it is too thick, add a little more broth.

Bring a large pot of water to a boil. Add 1 tablespoon salt and the bucatini. Cook, uncovered, until the pasta is tender but firm to the bite. Drain the pasta and put it in a warm serving bowl. Add the sauce and toss well. Serve with a sprinkling of parmigiano.

1 cup dried red kidney beans, sorted and rinsed
2 cups canned imported Italian plum tomatoes with their juices
4 tablespoons olive oil
½ of a small onion, finely chopped
1 medium-size carrot, finely chopped
1 small celery stalk, finely chopped
2 ounces pancetta, sliced and then cut into small thin strips
1 garlic clove, finely chopped
4 fresh sage leaves, chopped, or a pinch of dried sage
½ cup homemade or canned chicken broth
Salt and freshly ground black pepper
1 tablespoon chopped fresh parsley leaves
1 pound bucatini or spaghetti
½ cup freshly grated parmigiano

SERVES 4

Now that we all know we should eat less meat and more complex carbohydrates, perhaps this humble satisfying winter dish will become as popular in this country as it is in Italy.

Ravioloni al Taleggio

Large Ravioli with Taleggio Cheese Sauce

Of all stuffed pastas, ravioli are the easiest to prepare, even simpler when they are oversized, because there are fewer pieces to assemble.

The stuffing for these ravioloni is made with Swiss chard, spinach, ricotta, and parmigiano, a classic but always loved preparation. When Swiss chard is not available, double the amount of spinach. The sauce is a wonderfully delicious preparation of butter, cream, and Taleggio cheese.

This is a filling dish, so I serve only four to five ravioloni to each person; however, they are so good that family and friends would rather have seconds of the ravioloni and skip anything else to be served after. A nice roast veal, pork, or chicken accompanied by a few fresh sautéed vegetables could follow the ravioloni.

For the Filling
1 pound fresh spinach, or 1 10-ounce package frozen spinach
1 pound fresh Swiss chard
2 tablespoons unsalted butter
½ cup freshly grated parmigiano
Salt and freshly ground black pepper
1 large egg yolk
½ pound ricotta

For the Basic Egg Pasta Dough
2 large eggs
1¼ cups all-purpose unbleached flour

For the Sauce
3 tablespoons unsalted butter
¾ cup heavy cream
2 to 3 ounces Taleggio cheese, cut into small pieces
Salt
¼ cup freshly grated parmigiano

SERVES 4

For the filling, remove the stems from the spinach and the chard leaves from the white stalks; reserve the stalks for another use, such as in vegetable soups. Wash the chard and spinach leaves very well in several changes of cool water. Put the leaves into a large saucepan with only the water that clings to the leaves. Add a pinch of salt, cover the saucepan, and cook over medium heat until tender, about 10 minutes. Drain and squeeze out any excess liquid from the leaves. Chop the leaves very fine.

In a small skillet, melt the butter. Add the chard and spinach together and ⅓ cup of the parmigiano. Season with salt and pepper and cook over medium heat, stirring, until everything is coated with the butter and cheese and all juices have evaporated. Transfer to a bowl. Add the egg yolk, ricotta, and remaining parmigiano. Mix thoroughly to blend. Taste and correct the seasoning. The stuffing at this point should have a somewhat "dry" consistency. If it is too moist, incorporate a bit more parmigiano. Cover the bowl and refrigerate the filling for 1 hour or longer.

Prepare the Basic Egg Pasta Dough following the instructions on page 63, using the proportions given here. Cut off one small piece of dough about the size of a large egg and work it through the pasta machine until you have a very fine sheet of pasta. (Keep the remaining dough covered with a kitchen towel.) Trim the sheet of pasta to a straight length (it doesn't matter how long) and to a width of 6 inches. Place large tablespoons of filling in the center of the pasta sheet, spacing the mounds 3 inches from each other. If the sheet of pasta is quite long, you might want to cut it in two or three pieces for easier folding. Fold the sheet in half over the filling toward you. Press the edges together firmly to seal them. If the dough is a bit dry, moisten lightly with a bit of water. Cut between the filling in a straight line with a scalloped pastry wheel. Put the ravioloni on a tray covered with a kitchen towel. Repeat these steps with another piece of dough until all dough and filling are used.

The ravioloni can be cooked immediately or they can be kept in the refrigerator, covered only with a kitchen towel, for several hours. In this case, they should be turned over at least once to allow the bottom part to dry evenly.

Bring a large pot of water to a boil. Meanwhile, prepare the sauce. Melt the butter in a small saucepan. Add the cream and Taleggio cheese and season with salt. Simmer gently until the cheese has melted and the cream has a thick consistency. Keep the sauce warm over very low heat while you cook the pasta.

Add 1 tablespoon of salt and the ravioloni to the boiling water. Cover the pot until the water returns to a boil. Then cook the ravioloni, uncovered, until tender but still firm to the bite. Drain the pasta and put it in a large warm bowl. Add the sauce and sprinkle with about ¼ cup of the parmigiano. Mix gently until the pasta is completely coated with the sauce. Serve immediately, accompanied by the remaining parmigiano, if desired.

Taleggio, a whole cow's milk cheese typical of Lombardy, has a mild, sweet, and creamy taste. It should be available in specialty Italian markets, but if it is not substitute a mild gorgonzola or simply serve these ravioloni with butter and parmigiano.

Spaghetti con i Frutti di Mare al Cartoccio

Spaghetti with Shellfish Baked in Aluminum Foil

I am still obsessed by the incomparable taste of a pasta with seafood in aluminum foil that I had two years ago at the Dante restaurant in Bologna. Maybe it was the fragrance and aroma of the very fresh fish, which had arrived that same morning from the nearby Adriatic, that permeated the air as soon as the foil was opened. Or maybe it was the special mood of the evening, relaxed and mellow, that made me appreciate and notice everything that was served to me, highlighting each flavor with a clean intensity. The fact is that I have never been able to duplicate the exact taste of that dish. I have been able, however, to reproduce a close second, because, very immodestly, I feel that this dish is simply excellent.

Because the washing, peeling, and scrubbing of shellfish in this recipe is a bit time-consuming, I wash and sauté my fish very briefly several hours ahead of time. I also peel, seed, and cut up the tomatoes and prepare the sauce several hours ahead; then I combine the fish with the sauce and leave it until I am ready to complete the dish. At dinner time while the pasta cooks, I warm the sauce over low heat and then proceed to complete the recipe. I open a chilled bottle of Chardonnay, take the first bite of pasta and shellfish, and, as by magic, I am back in Italy.

2 pounds clams, the smallest you can get
½ pound bay or sea scallops
½ pound medium-size shrimp
6 tablespoons olive oil
3 garlic cloves, finely chopped
1 cup dry white wine
6 large ripe tomatoes or 1 28-ounce can,
  imported Italian plum tomatoes, drained
¼ of a small red chile pepper, finely
  chopped
4 anchovy fillets, chopped
2 tablespoons chopped fresh parsley or
  chopped fresh basil leaves
Salt
1 pound spaghetti, preferably imported
  from Italy

SERVES 4 TO 6

Soak the clams in cool salted water for 30 minutes to draw out their sand. Scrub the clams with a brush and rinse thoroughly under cool running water.

Wash the scallops in cool water and pat them dry with paper towels; if they are very large, cut them in half.

Shell and devein the shrimp.

In a large skillet, heat 3 tablespoons of the oil. Add half of the garlic and all the shrimp and sauté until the shrimp are lightly colored, about 1 minute. Remove the shrimp with a slotted spoon to a bowl. Put the scallops into the same skillet and sauté for about 1 minute. Transfer the scallops to the bowl with the shrimp. Add the clams to the skillet. Then add ½ cup water and ½ cup wine. Cover and bring to a boil. Cook until the clams have opened. Remove them with a slotted spoon as they open. Some might take a little longer to open. However, if they fail to open, discard them. Remove the meat from the shells and put it in the bowl with the scallops and shrimp. Cover the bowl tightly with aluminum foil and set aside.

Boil the clam juice until it is reduced to about ½ cup. Strain through two layers of paper towels in a sieve to remove all sand. Set aside.

Peel and seed the tomatoes following the instructions on page 55. Dice the tomatoes and place them in a strainer over a bowl to drain off the excess juices. Reserve the juices for soup or stew. If using canned tomatoes, drain and dice them.

In a large skillet, heat the remaining 3 tablespoons of oil. Add the remaining garlic, chile pepper, and anchovies and sauté over medium heat until the garlic begins to color. Pour in the reserved clam juice and remaining ½ cup wine. Boil, uncovered, until the liquid is reduced by half. Add the tomatoes and parsley. Cook over high heat until the excess liquid has evaporated and the sauce begins to thicken, 4 to 5 minutes. Add the reserved shellfish and mix thoroughly with the tomatoes. Taste for seasoning and remove from the heat.

Preheat the oven to 375 degrees. Bring a large pot of water to a boil. Add 1 tablespoon of salt and the spaghetti. Cook, uncovered, for 5 to 6 minutes. The spaghetti should be quite firm to the bite as it will finish cooking in the oven. Drain the spaghetti and add it to the sauce in the skillet. Toss gently to mix.

Place a large sheet of aluminum foil on a baking sheet and brush it lightly with oil. Arrange the pasta and seafood in the center of the foil. Fold the foil over the pasta and seal the edges tightly. The pasta mixture should be enclosed loosely within the foil. Bake for 10 to 12 minutes. Unwrap the foil cautiously as steam will blast out when you open it. Serve immediately.

Cooking in foil is a relatively new and modern way of preparing food in Italy. The principle is to enclose and enlarge the flavor of food within a wrapping, to retain important nutritive elements, and to keep the food moist. Individual packages of pasta could also be prepared. Each guest would then unwrap his own bundle.

I Tortelloni di Melanzane Trifolate e Ricotta

Tortelloni Stuffed with Parsleyed Eggplants and Ricotta

Today, many of the restaurants cast in the *Nuova Cucina* style offer pasta dishes that are innovative, lighter, and absolutely delicious, like this feather-light pasta stuffed with eggplant and ricotta and topped by a delicate pink sauce.

When I make these tortelloni, I put the stuffing into a pastry bag fitted with a large round tip and fill the tortelloni in a matter of seconds. Remember that the stuffing and sealing should be done quickly or the dough will dry out. If this happens, moisten the dough lightly with water. To cut down on time, you might want to cook the eggplant ahead of time. However, assemble the eggplant and cheese just before you are ready to stuff the tortelloni for a drier, more interesting texture.

For the Filling
1 large eggplant
Salt
3 tablespoons olive oil
2 tablespoons chopped fresh parsley leaves
2 garlic cloves, finely chopped
Freshly ground black pepper
½ pound ricotta
½ cup freshly grated parmigiano
7 or 8 fresh basil leaves, chopped, or 1 tablespoon chopped fresh parsley leaves

Prepare the filling. Peel the eggplant and cut it into ¼-inch-thick slices. Put the slices on a large dish and sprinkle them with salt. Let stand for about 1 hour. Wipe the juices and salt off the eggplant slices with paper towels. Cut the slices into small cubes.

Heat the oil in a large skillet. Add the parsley and garlic and sauté gently for about 1 minute. Before the garlic changes color, add the eggplant cubes. Cook over medium heat, stirring for 2 to 3 minutes. Season lightly with salt and pepper. Add ½ cup water, cover the skillet, and cook for 10 to 15 minutes, or until the eggplant is thoroughly cooked. Remove the lid and cook, uncovered, until all the moisture has evaporated. Transfer the eggplant mixture to a bowl and cool to room temperature.

Mash the eggplant mixture against the side of the bowl, pressing with a large spoon. (Do not purée in a food processor or food mill or the eggplant will become too mushy.) Add the ricotta, parmigiano, and basil. Mix well; then taste and adjust the seasoning. Cover the bowl and refrigerate until ready to use.

Prepare the Basic Egg Pasta Dough, following the instructions on page 63. Cut one small piece of dough, about the size of an egg; cover the remaining dough with a kitchen towel. Work the small piece through the pasta machine until you have a thin sheet. Cut the pasta into

3-inch squares. Put 1 heaping teaspoon of filling in the center of each square. Fold one square at a time over the filling to form a triangle; press firmly to seal the edges. Bend a tortellone around your finger, pressing one pointed end slightly over the other. Repeat with the other squares and the additional dough until all the dough and filling have been used up. Arrange the tortelloni on a tray lined with a kitchen towel. If you are making the tortelloni a few hours ahead, keep them in the refrigerator covered with another kitchen towel. Turn them over once to allow the other side to dry.

Put the tomatoes through a food mill or a sieve to remove the seeds. Melt the butter in a large skillet. When the butter foams, add the tomatoes. Cook, uncovered, over medium heat for 10 to 15 minutes, or until the sauce is reduced to about 1½ cups. Season lightly with salt and pepper; stir in the cream and cook gently for 1 to 2 minutes.

While the sauce cooks, bring a large pot of water to a boil. Add 1 tablespoon of salt and the tortelloni. Cook uncovered, until the pasta is tender but still firm to the bite. Don't overcook or the filling will break out. As the tortelloni cook, they will rise to the surface of the water. Taste for doneness; then remove with a large slotted spoon. Add the tortelloni to the sauce in the skillet. Add ⅓ cup of the parmigiano and mix gently to combine. Serve at once with the remaining parmigiano.

A few years ago when *La Nuova Cucina Italiana* began to appear on the culinary scene, a few of the top Italian restaurants removed almost all the pasta dishes from their menus and offered instead dishes that tasted and looked suspiciously like French dishes. Curious patrons went, tasted, paid stiff prices, and left the restaurants hungry and upset at the absence of pasta. Soon these restaurants had to redefine their objectives for they realized that Italians would never give up their national treasure: pasta.

For the Basic Egg Pasta Dough
2 cups all-purpose unbleached flour
3 large eggs

For the Tomato–Cream Sauce
2 cups canned imported Italian plum tomatoes with their juices
2 tablespoons unsalted butter
Salt and freshly ground black pepper
⅓ cup heavy cream

To Complete the Dish
1 cup freshly grated parmigiano

SERVES 4 TO 6

Le Lasagne con i Funghi

Green Lasagne with Mushrooms

A few years ago one of the best and oldest restaurants in Bologna was Don Chisciotte. Located in the center of this beautiful medieval city, Don Chisciotte served some of the most outstanding and classic food of Bologna. There, I used to indulge from time to time in a dish of green lasagne and mushrooms that was positively sinful. The following is my adaptation of that mouthwatering dish. The original dish used fresh porcini for the lasagne filling. As fresh porcini are seldom available in this country, I use a mixture of fresh cultivated mushrooms and dried imported porcini. This dish should definitely be made with homemade pasta or it will lose all of its special delicate quality. If we have to indulge sometimes, then this is, unquestionably, the dish to indulge in.

For the Filling
2 ounces dried porcini mushrooms
2 pounds fresh cultivated mushrooms
¼ cup olive oil
3 tablespoons chopped fresh parsley leaves
3 garlic cloves, finely chopped
Salt and freshly ground black pepper

For the Béchamel Sauce
2 cups milk
4 tablespoons unsalted butter
4 tablespoons all-purpose unbleached flour
Salt
Pinch of saffron threads
1 large egg yolk

For the Basic Spinach Pasta Dough
3 cups all-purpose unbleached flour
4 large eggs
1 tablespoon very finely chopped cooked fresh or frozen spinach

To Complete the Dish
3 tablespoons unsalted butter
1 cup freshly grated parmigiano

SERVES 8

Soak the dried mushrooms in 2 cups of lukewarm water for 30 minutes; drain the mushrooms and reserve the soaking water. (The water can be used in stews or risotti.) Rinse the mushrooms under cool running water several times to get rid of the sandy deposits. Pat dry with paper towels and then dice the mushrooms.

Clean the fresh mushrooms with a damp cloth or wash them and then dry them quickly with paper towels. Cut the mushrooms into thin slices.

Heat the oil in a large skillet. Add enough fresh mushrooms to barely cover the bottom of the skillet. Do not overcrowd. (During cooking, the mushrooms will release their juices. If too many mushrooms are put in the skillet, there won't be enough evaporation of the juices and the mushrooms will stew instead of sautéing.) Sauté the mushrooms over high heat until lightly golden. With a slotted spoon transfer them to paper towels. While you are sautéing the last batch, add the parsley, garlic, and porcini mushrooms to the skillet and cook a few minutes longer. Transfer the mushrooms to paper towels and pat dry to remove the excess oil. Put the mushrooms in a bowl and season with salt and pepper.

Prepare the béchamel sauce, following the instructions on page 46. When the béchamel is slightly cooled, add the saffron and egg yolk. Whisk quickly to incorporate them. Set aside. Just before adding the béchamel to the lasagne, check its consistency. If it seems too thick, add a bit more milk. If too thin, return to the heat and cook a few minutes longer; it should have a medium-thick consistency.

Prepare the Basic Spinach Dough, following the instructions on page 64. Cut one small piece of dough, about the size of an egg, and work through the pasta machine until you have a thin sheet of pasta. Trim the pasta to fit your baking dish. Repeat with the remaining dough until all the dough has been rolled out.

Preheat the oven to 400 degrees. Bring a large pot of water to a boil. Add 1 tablespoon of salt and 3 or 4 sheets of pasta. When the water returns to a boil, cook the pasta for 30 to 40 seconds. Using a slotted spoon, transfer the pasta to a large bowl of cold water. Spread some kitchen towels on a countertop. Put the pasta on the towels and pat dry with another towel. Cook all the pasta sheets in this manner and dry well with towels.

Spread the bottom and sides of a large baking dish with butter. Cover the bottom of the baking dish with one layer of pasta. (You might have to trim off some of the pasta again to fit it in the dish since the pasta expands slightly during cooking.) Cover the pasta with a scant layer of mushrooms. Follow with a light layer of béchamel sauce and sprinkle with parmigiano. Repeat the layering of pasta, mushrooms, and parmigiano for a total of five to six layers. Dot the last layer with butter. Bake in the middle of the oven for 15 to 20 minutes, or until the top of the lasagne has a nice golden color.

Remove the lasagne from the oven and let stand for about 10 minutes before serving.

Rigatoni Casanova

Rigatoni with Mushrooms, Prosciutto, and Cream

Sauces that are fresh and fast, tasty and uncomplicated and eye-pleasing and pasta dishes that can be prepared literally in minutes are the trademarks of the modern Italian cook.

This dish could be the dominant course in a family meal or the beginning of a menu for entertaining, in which case remember to give small portions. While the mushrooms are being sautéed, the water for the pasta is being brought to a boil; while the cream is simmering, the pasta cooks and, like a great performance that is coming to an end in a strong crescendo, you will be tossing pasta and sauce together just in time for the enthusiastic applause of your loyal fans.

1 pound small fresh white cultivated mushrooms
3 tablespoons unsalted butter
2 tablespoons oil
2 tablespoons chopped fresh parsley leaves
2 garlic cloves, chopped
6 ounces prosciutto, sliced and then cut into small strips
½ cup heavy cream
Salt and freshly ground black pepper
1 pound rigatoni, preferably DeCecco or Spiga d'Oro
½ cup freshly grated parmigiano

SERVES 4 TO 6

Wipe the mushrooms clean with a damp towel, or, if they are very dirty, wash and dry them thoroughly. Cut the mushrooms into thin slices.

Heat the butter and oil in a large skillet. When the butter foams, add the mushrooms and sauté over high heat until lightly colored. Add the parsley, garlic, and prosciutto and sauté for 1 to 2 minutes longer. Add the cream and season with salt and pepper. Simmer gently for 2 to 3 minutes. Keep warm over very low heat.

Bring a large pot of water to a boil. Add 1 tablespoon of salt and the rigatoni. Cook, uncovered, until the pasta is tender but firm to the bite. Drain the pasta and add it to the sauce in the skillet. Sprinkle with the parmigiano. Mix well and serve immediately.

Fettuccine con Salsa di Funghi e Salsiccia

Fettuccine with Mushrooms, Sausage, and Cream

In Bologna, this sauce is used to top a special homemade local pasta called *gramigna* (crab grass), a thick, doughy spaghetti that resembles the kind made through a very old-fashioned extruder. Some of the old Bolognese families still have the original tool; however, this kind of pasta is seldom made at home today. It can be found in some of the old pasta and bread stores throughout Bologna.

The sauce for *gramigna* is too good to be forgotten, so I use it over home-made fettuccine. If I don't have time to make fresh pasta, I use it over penne or rigatoni. One pound of factory-made pasta will give you four generous portions. Choose a good brand, such as DeCecco, Agnesi, or Fini. As with most Italian sauces for pasta, this one takes only 15 to 20 minutes to prepare.

Prepare the Basic Egg Pasta Dough following the instructions on page 63 and roll out the pasta into fettuccine (page 64).

Soak the mushrooms in 1 cup of lukewarm water for 20 minutes.

Remove the casings from the sausages and chop the pork very fine. In a large skillet, melt the butter. When the butter foams, add the chopped sausage. Cook over medium heat until the sausage loses its raw color. Press down on the sausage with a large spoon as it cooks to prevent lumps from forming. Raise the heat and add the wine. Stir and cook until the wine has evaporated.

Drain the mushrooms and reserve the soaking water; rinse the mushrooms thoroughly under cool running water. Strain the mushroom soaking water several times through a few layers of paper towels to get rid of any sandy deposits. Add the water and the mushrooms to the sausage. Cook, uncovered, over medium heat until the mushroom water is almost all reduced. Add the cream, parsley, saffron, and several grindings of pepper. Season with salt. Simmer very gently until the sauce has a medium-thick consistency, about 3 to 5 minutes.

Bring a large pot of water to a boil. Add 1 tablespoon of salt and the fettuccine. Cook, uncovered, until the pasta is tender but firm to the bite.

Drain the pasta and add it to the sauce in the skillet. Sprinkle with the parmigiano. Mix gently over low heat until the pasta is well coated with the sauce. Serve immediately with additional cheese, if desired.

For the Fettuccine
2 cups all-purpose unbleached flour
3 large eggs

For the Sauce
1 ounce dried porcini mushrooms
2 Italian sweet sausages (about 5 ounces total weight)
3 tablespoons unsalted butter
1 cup dry white wine
1 cup heavy cream
1 tablespoon chopped fresh parsley leaves
Pinch of powdered saffron
Salt and freshly ground black pepper

To Complete the Dish
1 tablespoon salt
¾ cup freshly grated parmigiano

SERVES 4

Rotolo di Pasta Ripieno di Magro

Pasta Roll Stuffed with Spinach and Cheese

Nothing is more boring than repetitive habits. This is true even with food. We might grill some chops twice a week or sauté some scaloppine twice more. We might roast a chicken one night and prepare a lovely frittata another. But then comes the day that, time permitting, we need a new challenge. Perhaps it is a special occasion or we want to prove to ourselves that, indeed, we can cook something more complicated than a grilled dish. If you are in this mood, this is the dish for you. Stuffed pasta roll is as delicious as it is impressive. Even though it has many steps, with a good plan of attack this dish can become fairly simple.

Prepare the spinach stuffing and béchamel sauce in the morning. Even the tomato–cream sauce can be prepared several hours ahead. As the pasta has to be rolled out by hand with a rolling pin, I suggest you practice a few times before attempting to make this dish.

For the Spinach–Cheese Filling
3 pounds fresh spinach, or 2 10-ounce packages frozen spinach
2 large egg yolks
½ pound ricotta
½ cup freshly grated parmigiano
½ teaspoon ground nutmeg
Salt and freshly ground black pepper

For the Béchamel Sauce
2 cups milk
4 tablespoons unsalted butter
4 tablespoons all-purpose unbleached flour
Salt

For the Tomato–Cream Sauce
2 tablespoons unsalted butter
2 cups canned imported Italian plum tomatoes with their juices
⅓ cup heavy cream
Salt and freshly ground black pepper

If using fresh spinach, remove and discard the stems and bruised or tough leaves. Wash the spinach thoroughly in cool water. Put the wet spinach into a large saucepan, and add a pinch of salt. Cover the pan and cook over medium heat until tender, about 8 to 10 minutes. Drain well and cool slightly. Squeeze the spinach to remove as much moisture as possible. If using frozen spinach, cook according to the package instructions; then drain and squeeze dry.

Chop the spinach very fine. Beat the egg yolks in a large bowl. Add the spinach, ricotta, parmigiano, and nutmeg. Season with salt and pepper and mix to blend. Cover the bowl and refrigerate until ready to use.

Prepare the béchamel sauce following the instructions on page 46.

Prepare the tomato–cream sauce. Melt the butter in a medium-size saucepan. Press the tomatoes through a food mill or a sieve to remove the seeds. Add to the saucepan. Simmer, uncovered, for 10 to 12 minutes. Add the cream and simmer for 1 to 2 minutes longer. Season with salt and pepper. Remove from the heat and set aside.

Prepare the Basic Egg Pasta Dough following the instructions on page 63. Roll out the pasta by hand (see page 64). The sheet of pasta should be rolled out as thinly as possible to a diameter of approximately 16 inches. Leave the sheet on the table to dry for 10 to 15 minutes.

Bring a large pot of water to a boil. Add 1 tablespoon of salt and, if you wish, a bit of oil to prevent sticking. Lower the pasta sheet carefully into the boiling water and cook for 30 to 40 seconds from the moment the water returns to a boil.

Drain the pasta and place the colander immediately into a large bowl of cold water. This step will help "unravel" any sticky part of the pasta.

Dampen one or two cotton kitchen towels with cold water and spread on a working surface. Drain the pasta and spread gently on the damp towel. Dry the pasta with paper towels.

Preheat the oven to 375 degrees. Butter a large baking dish. With a fluted wheel or sharp knife, trim two edges of the pasta into straight lines. The other two sides of the pasta sheet should be no longer than your baking dish. Spread a thin layer of the spinach–cheese filling over the pasta sheet, leaving a border of about 1 inch free on three sides and a 4-inch border on the side near you. Fold the 4-inch border of pasta over the filling; then pick up the edges of the towel and roll the pasta over loosely, jelly roll style, until you have rolled up the entire sheet of pasta.

Very carefully place the roll into the buttered baking dish, seam side up. The dish can be prepared up to this point several hours ahead and kept tightly covered in the refrigerator.

Pour the tomato–cream sauce over the roll and spread about 1 to 1½ cups béchamel sauce over the top and sides of the roll. Sprinkle with the parmigiano and dot with the butter. Bake for 20 to 25 minutes, or until the top is lightly golden.

Remove from the oven and let stand for 10 minutes. Slice the roll into serving pieces and serve immediately.

For the Basic Egg Pasta Dough
2 cups all-purpose unbleached flour
3 large eggs

To Complete the Dish
½ cup freshly grated parmigiano
2 tablespoons unsalted butter

Serves 8

Tortelli di Zucca

Pumpkin Tortelli

Pumpkin Tortelli can be found in several northern Italian regions. The sweet and tangy taste of the stuffing is reminiscent of Renaissance dishes. I love to make these tortelli at Christmastime and observe the look of surprise and delight as the first tortello disappear into the mouths of my guests. Like all pasta dishes, these tortelli are a bit lengthy to prepare, but they are worth every biteful.

Mostarda di Cremona is a medley of candied fruit which is preserved in a thick sugar syrup, seasoned with a mustard oil. Mostarda is now easily available in many specialty Italian markets or gourmet stores. If unavailable, use a good-quality mixed candied fruit.

For the Filling
2 pounds pumpkin or butternut squash
¼ pound imported Italian Mostarda di Cremona or good-quality candied fruit, finely diced
4 Amaretti di Saronno (imported Italian almond cookies), or 4 regular almond cookies
½ cup freshly grated parmigiano
A few tablespoons unseasoned bread crumbs
Salt

For the Basic Egg Pasta Dough
2 cups all-purpose unbleached flour
3 large eggs

For the Sauce
4 tablespoons unsalted butter
½ cup freshly grated parmigiano

SERVES 4

Preheat the oven to 350 degrees.

Prepare the filling. Cut the pumpkin into large pieces and remove the seeds. Put the pieces on a baking sheet and bake for 30 to 40 minutes, or until tender. Cool slightly; then remove the skin and put the pumpkin on a cutting board. Chop into small, mushy pieces or put the pieces into a bowl and mash them with a large spoon. Do not purée in a food processor or the pumpkin will become too soupy. Put the mashed pumpkin in a large bowl with the Mostarda di Cremora.

Put the almond cookies in a food processor and process into small pieces. Add to the pumpkin with the parmigiano and 2 or 3 tablespoons of bread crumbs. Season lightly with salt. The filling should be firm enough to hold together. If the mixture is too soft or runny, add a little more parmigiano and an extra sprinkling of bread crumbs. Cover the bowl and refrigerate until ready to use. The filling can be prepared several hours ahead of time.

Prepare the Basic Egg Pasta Dough following the instructions on page 63. Use the pumpkin filling to make tortelli following the instructions on page 180.

Bring a large pot of water to a boil. Add 2 tablespoons of salt and the tortelli. Cook, uncovered, until the pasta is tender but still firm to the bite. As the tortelli cook, they will rise to the surface of the water. Remove them with a large slotted spoon, draining off the excess water.

While the pasta cooks, put the 4 tablespoons of butter in a shallow serving dish and warm the dish briefly in the oven. Put the drained tortelli in the warm serving dish. Add the parmigiano and mix gently to combine. Serve immediately with additional parmigiano, if desired.

Once, I attended a class given by Jacques Pépin, the famous French chef and cookbook author. The food he was teaching was extraordinary but also lengthy to prepare and quite elaborate. A student asked whether he cooked so elaborately for himself on a daily basis, and he replied: "Absolutely not. I like to eat good, but very simple food, which is better for my waistline. However, occasionally I like to cook something special." This is also my philosophy and the philosophy of many modern Italian women. Good, simple, quickly prepared food as a general rule, but for a special occasion, let's put on the ritz.

The cooking time will depend on how "fresh" and thin your pasta is. Always remember that fresh pasta cooks very quickly. The best way to judge for doneness is to taste it.

Because the stuffing for tortelli is quite moist and tends to make the pasta a bit wet, I never prepare my tortelli more than 2 or 3 hours ahead of time. They can be kept in a towel-lined tray in the refrigerator, uncovered, until ready to cook. They should be turned over at least once to allow the bottom part to dry evenly.

Linguine col Sugo di Aragosta

Linguine with Lobster Sauce

My husband's family comes from Salerno, a lovely city on the Mediterranean coast, south of Naples. A few years ago, during our yearly visit, aunt Rosalba prepared a most unforgettable pasta dish, linguine with lobster sauce. A savory tomato sauce was prepared and the lobster was cooked directly in the sauce. We then sat on the large terrace overlooking the city and the sea, eating informally and drinking good local wine. It was pure heaven.

Needless to say, I have made that dish many times since, changing the recipe slightly to fit our own needs. Because fresh lobster is not always available, I have substituted frozen lobster tail quite successfully.

For the Sauce

1 28-ounce can imported Italian plum tomatoes

4 tablespoons olive oil

3 anchovy fillets

A small piece of red hot chile pepper, finely chopped

2 garlic cloves, finely chopped

1 12- to 14-ounce frozen lobster tail

Salt

1 tablespoon chopped fresh parsley leaves

¼ cup fresh oregano leaves, or ½ teaspoon dried oregano

For the Pasta

1 tablespoon salt

1 pound linguine

Serves 4 to 6

To prepare the sauce, put the tomatoes through a food mill or press them through a strainer to remove the seeds.

In a medium-size saucepan heat the oil. Add the anchovies, chile pepper, and garlic and sauté over medium heat until the garlic begins to color. Add the strained tomatoes and season with salt. Cook, uncovered, for 15 to 20 minutes.

Add the lobster tail and cook for 5 to 10 minutes. Transfer the lobster to a cutting board. Remove the meat from the shell by cutting through the back of the tail with a sharp knife; then cut the meat into small pieces about the size of a grape. Return the pieces to the saucepan. Add the parsley and oregano. Cook for 2 to 3 minutes over very low heat. Taste for seasoning.

Bring a large pot of water to the boil. Add the salt and linguine. Cook until tender but firm to the bite. Drain the pasta and put it in a warm serving dish. Add the sauce and toss gently to mix. Serve immediately.

If you want to cook a whole live lobster, plunge it, head first, into a large pot of rapidly boiling water. This will kill the lobster instantly. Remove the lobster from the water and transfer it to the tomato sauce and simmer it gently, uncovered, for 12 minutes per pound. Then proceed as directed in recipe.

Fusilli col Sugo di Carne alla Napoletana

Fusilli with Meat Sauce Neapolitan Style

Most Neapolitan pasta sauces are based on tomatoes and are generally cooked very briefly to preserve their freshness and fragrance. The only exception is when fresh or canned tomatoes are used in conjunction with meat sauces, such as in this recipe. Then the long cooking time is needed to tenderize the meat. The sauce, which becomes very thick and dark, is served over pasta, while the meat is sliced and served as the next course.

This is another example of wonderfully uncomplicated Italian food.

Dust the meat lightly with flour. Heat the oil in a large casserole. Add the meat and sauté over medium heat until lightly browned on all sides. Add the onion and garlic and cook until wilted, stirring. Stir in the wine and cook until it is reduced by half. Add the tomatoes and tomato paste and season with salt and pepper. Simmer for 3 to 3½ hours. Add the oregano during the last 5 minutes of cooking.

Bring a large pot of water to a boil. Add the salt and fusilli. Cook the pasta, uncovered, until it is tender but firm to the bite, 8 to 10 minutes. Drain the fusilli and transfer it to a warm deep serving dish. Add the ricotta and half of the meat sauce. Toss to blend. Add ⅓ cup of the grated cheese and mix. Serve with the remaining cheese, if desired.

Fusilli are short spiral-shaped pasta, which are very popular in several southern Italian regions. Spaghetti, penne, or shells can also be used.

I generally prepare this sauce in the morning so that the only things left to do at dinner time are to cook the pasta and put a green salad together.

For the Meat Sauce

1 cup all-purpose unbleached flour
4 pounds bottom round or eye round
4 tablespoons olive oil
2 large onions, thinly sliced
2 garlic cloves, chopped
1 cup dry white wine
3 cups canned imported Italian plum tomatoes, strained through a food mill
2 tablespoons tomato paste
Salt and freshly ground black pepper
3 tablespoons fresh oregano leaves or 1 teaspoon dried oregano

To Complete the Dish

1 tablespoon salt
1 pound fusilli
1 cup ricotta
1 cup freshly grated Romano or parmigiano cheese

Serves 4

Penne con la Peperonata al Cartoccio

Penne with Pepper Sauce in Foil

This pasta dish is prepared with a minimal amount of fat. The peppers, onions, and tomatoes are sautéed, then stewed together. The pasta is cooked and then added to the sauce. Everything is then put in foil and baked.

4 teaspoons olive oil

2 medium-size onions, thinly sliced

4 sweet red peppers, seeded and cut into medium-size strips

4 medium-size ripe tomatoes, cut into chunks

Salt and freshly ground black pepper

½ cup chicken broth (all fat removed) or water

½ pound whole-wheat (or regular) penne or rigatoni

SERVES 4

Heat the oil in a large skillet. Add the onions and peppers and sauté them over medium heat until they are lightly golden, but not browned, about 15 minutes. Add the tomatoes and season lightly with salt and pepper. Cover skillet, leaving the lid slightly askew and cook for another 15 minutes, stirring a few times. At the end of cooking time there should be about ⅓ cup of natural juices left in the skillet. If not, add the chicken broth and cook it down a bit over high heat.

Bring a large pot of water to a boil. Add the pasta. Cook, uncovered, until the pasta is tender but still quite firm to the bite. Drain the pasta and add it to the sauce in the skillet. Mix well.

Preheat the oven to 375 degrees. Prepare 4 large pieces of parchment or aluminum foil and spread them out on a working surface. Divide the pasta into 4 parts and place each portion individually on the pieces of foil. Close the foil tightly and fold it over. Place the bundles on a baking sheet and bake 10 to 15 minutes. Open each bundle carefully since the steam will escape quickly. Serve at once, in foil if desired.

Cooking in foil enhances the flavor of food while retaining important nutritive elements and keeping the food moist. Make sure to undercook your pasta since it will continue to cook in the oven.

Penne ai Peperoni

Penne with Red Pepper Sauce

During the fall and winter months, when tomatoes are not at their best, I use canned imported plum tomatoes from Italy. For the dish below, I drain off the juices and use only the meat of the tomatoes. Sweet red peppers are now easily available in supermarkets, and the yellow ones are often found in small specialized markets. This recipe calls for red *or* yellow peppers, but if both are available, I use both.

My family and I eat considerably less meat than we used to; therefore, when I make a pasta dish that we all love, such as this, I increase the proportions. We can then have seconds and, sometimes, third helpings, without even blushing.

If using fresh tomatoes, peel and seed them following the instructions on page 55.

With a vegetable peeler, peel the peppers using a side-to-side motion as you peel down the pepper. Cut the peppers in half and remove the seeds; then cut the peppers into thin strips no longer than the length of your pasta.

In a medium-size skillet, heat the oil. Add the pepper strips and onion and sauté over medium heat until the vegetables are wilted. Add the garlic and parsley and stir and cook for 1 minute longer. Add the tomatoes and broth and season with salt and pepper. Cook, uncovered, over medium heat for 20 to 25 minutes, or until the sauce has a medium-thick consistency. Purée half the sauce through a food mill and return it to the skillet. Taste and adjust the seasoning. Keep the sauce warm over very low heat.

Bring a large pot of water to a boil. Add 1 tablespoon of salt and the pasta. Cook, uncovered, for 8 to 10 minutes or until the pasta is tender but firm to the bite. Drain the pasta and add it to the sauce in the skillet. Add the cheese, if using, and mix to blend. Serve immediately.

5 ripe tomatoes, or 1 28-ounce can imported Italian plum tomatoes, drained
4 large sweet red or yellow peppers
1 onion, thinly sliced
4 tablespoons olive oil
1 garlic clove, finely chopped
2 tablespoons chopped fresh parsley leaves
½ cup homemade or canned chicken broth
Salt and freshly ground black pepper
1 pound short macaroni, such as penne or rigatoni
⅓ cup Pecorino cheese (optional)

SERVES 4 TO 6

Pasta Tre Colori

Tricolor Pasta

For centuries, Italian peasants have relied on pasta and vegetables for sustenance, since meat was expensive and unaffordable on a regular basis. Now these simple, high-carbohydrate, appetizing dishes have been reappraised and hailed for their wholesome, healthy qualities. Finally, we can eat our pasta with total abandonment and, most important, without guilt.

½ medium-size cauliflower, separated into florets
2 small carrots, peeled
8 or 10 small brussels sprouts, root end and bruised outer leaves removed
4 tablespoons olive oil, preferably virgin olive oil
1 medium onion, thinly sliced
¼ pound pancetta, sliced and then cut into small julienne
2 garlic cloves, finely chopped
Salt and freshly ground black pepper
1 pound shells, penne, or rigatoni

SERVES 4

Boil or steam the vegetables until tender but still firm to the touch. When cool enough to handle, cut the cauliflower florets and brussel sprouts into halves (or into fourths if too large) and dice the carrots into pieces about the size of small olives.

Heat the oil in a large, heavy skillet. Add the onion and sauté over gentle heat until the onion becomes pale yellow, about 7 to 8 minutes. Stir in the pancetta and garlic. Sauté a few minutes longer. Season with salt and several twists of pepper. Add the boiled or steamed vegetables and mix.

Bring a large pot of water to a boil. Add 1 tablespoon salt and then the pasta. Cook, stirring a few times, until the pasta is tender but still firm to the bite. Scoop out ¼ cup of the pasta water and add it to the vegetables. Drain the pasta and add it to the vegetables in the skillet. Stir over low heat until well combined. Serve at once.

Soups

Zuppa di Riso e Verza

Cabbage and Rice Soup

This cabbage and rice soup is very easy to prepare. It is also inexpensive and delicious. Because rice keeps cooking even after the heat is turned off, it is best to undercook it slightly. This soup does not quite fall into the category of "thick soups." It should have a nice dense quality, but also a soupy consistency.

Chop the celery and its leaves very fine. Chop the pancetta. Heat the oil in a large saucepan. Add the parsley, garlic, celery, and pancetta and cook over medium heat for 3 to 4 minutes. Add the cut-up cabbage, stir, and cook a few minutes longer. Add the broth and season with salt and several grindings of pepper. (Use less salt or none at all if you are using canned broth, since it is already quite salty.)

Cover the pan, lower the heat, and cook gently for 15 to 20 minutes. Add the rice and cook for 10 to 15 minutes longer, or until the rice is tender but still firm to the bite. Just before serving, dribble a little olive oil into soup and add ⅓ cup of the parmigiano. Stir to blend. Taste for seasoning and serve hot with the remaining parmigiano.

Without the rice added, this soup freezes well. Make the rice before serving or it will be unappealingly soggy.

1 inner white part of a small celery, with its tender leaves
¼ pound pancetta, sliced
4 tablespoons olive oil, preferably virgin olive oil
2 tablespoons chopped fresh parsley leaves
2 garlic cloves, finely chopped
½ of a medium-size cabbage (about 1 pound) cut into small pieces
6 to 8 cups Basic Chicken Broth (page 45) or 4 cups canned chicken broth mixed with 4 cups water
Salt and freshly ground black pepper
¾ cup rice, preferably Italian Arborio rice
Olive oil
1 cup freshly grated parmigiano

SERVES 6 TO 8

Pasta is definitively Italian, but soups served and appreciated especially as part of the evening meal are also a very important element in Italian cooking. When an Italian has had a considerable lunch, a light soup is what he seeks for dinner. When a person is a bit under the weather or a child is sick, a light "brodino," a meat broth, is very much appreciated. When the temperature dips and the weather turns cold, a thick hearty soup will restore the glow to one's cheeks. Most often, Italian soups contain pasta or rice, and in many cases a particularly rich soup might become a whole meal.

Taglioline in Brodo

Taglioline in Broth

When the weather gets cold, a nice bowl of steaming homemade broth with thin noodles is a jolly treat.

Taglioline or tagliarini, homemade or store-bought, are thin noodles, used almost exclusively in broth. Because they are quite thin they cook very quickly.

10 to 12 cups Homemade Meat Broth
  (page 44)
½ pound taglioline or tagliarini
1 cup freshly grated parmigiano

SERVES 6

Bring the broth to a low boil and add the taglioline. Raise the heat and cook, uncovered, until the pasta is just tender but still firm to the bite. Serve with a generous sprinkling of parmigiano.

Stracciatella alla Romana

Egg Soup Roman Style

Stracciatella literally means "shredded." This is exactly what happens to the eggs when they are beaten into the hot broth. They shred. Good, homemade meat broth is essential to this soup. The result is light and delicious.

9 cups Homemade Meat Broth (page 44)
4 large eggs
Salt
⅓ cup freshly grated parmigiano
1 teaspoon chopped fresh parsley leaves
Pinch of ground nutmeg
Additional freshly grated parmigiano

SERVES 4

Prepare the meat broth and reserve 1 cup until cool. In a medium-size bowl, beat the eggs with a pinch of salt. Add the parmigiano, parsley, and nutmeg. Combine with the cold meat broth.

Bring the remaining meat broth to a low simmer. Add the egg mixture and stir quickly with a wire whisk. Simmer for 3 to 4 minutes, beating constantly. The eggs will cook and shred. Serve with additional parmigiano.

A good choice for a second course to follow this would be Roasted Leg of Lamb the Tuscan Way (page 232) or Paola's Boned Roasted Rabbit (page 239) with Sweet and Sour Zucchini (page 263).

La Zuppa di Fagioli della Franca

Franca's Country Bean Soup

Franca, the housekeeper of the country home of Marchesi Antinori, whose wines and olive oil are renowned throughout Italy and the rest of the world, prepared this delicious hearty soup when I was on a television assignment in Tuscany in 1983. It is a soup that needs no introductions or explanations, for it is the kind of basic food that we all crave and seek for comfort and sustenance.

Put the beans in a large bowl and cover with cold water; soak the beans overnight. Drain and rinse thoroughly.

Heat the oil in a large saucepan. Add the onion, garlic, and parsley and sauté over medium heat for 4 to 5 minutes. Add the beans, potatoes, tomatoes, prosciutto, and broth. Cover the saucepan and bring to a boil. Lower the heat and simmer for about 1 hour, or until the beans are tender, stirring a few times during the cooking. Season with salt and pepper.

Use a slotted spoon to transfer half of the beans to a blender or food processor and process until smooth. Return to the saucepan. Taste the soup and adjust for seasoning.

Broil the bread until golden on both sides. Place the bread slices in individual soup dishes and sprinkle generously with the parmigiano. Ladle the soup into the dishes, pour on a few drops of olive oil, and serve.

2 cups dried cannellini beans, sorted and rinsed
4 tablespoons olive oil
1 onion, finely chopped
2 garlic cloves, finely chopped
2 tablespoons chopped fresh parsley leaves
1 large potato, peeled and diced
1 cup canned imported Italian plum tomatoes with their juices
2 slices prosciutto rind
12 cups Homemade Meat Broth (page 44) or 6 cups canned meat broth mixed with 6 cups water
Salt and freshly ground black pepper
6 large thick slices Italian bread
1 cup freshly grated parmigiano
Olive oil

SERVES 8

This is a good recipe to double, as it is even better the second day and it also freezes very well.

To sort out beans or lentils that are infested with parasites, place them in a large saucepan full of water; discard any that rise to the surface of the water.

In preparing bean or lentil soup it is smart to cook more beans than you need. They can be used later in salads or stews.

La Zuppa della Val D'Aosta

Cabbage Soup Val d'Aosta Style

This is a substantial thick soup that will become even thicker after it is baked and will leave you with little desire for anything else other than, perhaps, a salad. This soup freezes extremely well, so it makes sense to double the recipe and freeze half of it.

3 tablespoons unsalted butter
2 onions, finely sliced
¼ pound pancetta, sliced and then cut into small strips
1 medium-size cabbage, about 2 pounds
10 to 12 cups Homemade Meat Broth (page 44) or 5 to 6 cups canned meat broth mixed with 5 to 6 cups water
Salt
6 slices whole wheat bread
½ pound Italian fontina, sliced
1 cup freshly grated parmigiano

SERVES 6

Melt the butter in a large saucepan. When the butter foams, add the onions and sauté for 3 to 4 minutes over medium heat. Add the pancetta and sauté for 3 to 4 minutes, stirring, until the pancetta is lightly golden and the onions are pale yellow.

Slice the cabbage into thin strips. Add to the onions and mix and cook, uncovered, for 8 to 10 minutes over low heat. Add the broth and season lightly with salt. Cover the saucepan and simmer for about 1 hour.

Preheat the oven to 350 degrees. Toast the bread until golden on both sides. Place 1 slice of bread in each of 6 individual ovenproof bowls. Cover the bread with 1 or 2 slices of fontina. Ladle the soup into the bowls and sprinkle generously with the parmigiano.

Bake for 10 to 15 minutes, or until the cheese has melted. For a lightly golden crust, place the bowls briefly under the broiler. Serve hot.

Never throw away the rind of parmigiano. It should be scraped and cooked in hearty soups to improve their taste.

Pasta e Ceci

Pasta and Chick-pea Soup

Generally, I prepare this soup in the morning since the taste and consistency improves when it is made several hours or a day ahead of time. The pasta is cooked separately and then added to the soup. Whether you are using freshly made or factory-made pasta, remember to undercook it slightly as it will continue to cook in the soup.

At dinner time I warm up the soup over low heat, taste it for seasoning, and serve it accompanied by a generous sprinkling of parmigiano and a few drops of virgin olive oil. If the soup becomes too thick, simply add a bit more broth.

Put the chick-peas in a large bowl, cover with water, and soak overnight. Drain and rinse, put in a large pot, and add the broth. Add enough water to cover the peas by 2 or 3 inches. Cover the pot and bring to a boil. Lower the heat and simmer for about 1 hour, stirring a few times during the cooking.

While the chick-peas cook, prepare the tomato sauce. Heat the oil in a medium-size saucepan. Add the garlic, anchovies, rosemary, and parsley and sauté gently for a few minutes.

Put tomatoes through a food mill or sieve to remove the seeds. Add to the garlic–rosemary mixture. Season with salt and several grindings of pepper and simmer, uncovered, for 15 to 20 minutes.

Place a third of the cooked chick-peas into a blender or food processor. Process until smooth and then return to the pot. Add the tomato sauce, stir, and cook for 10 minutes longer.

Bring a medium-size saucepan of water to a boil. Add the salt and pasta. Cook, uncovered, until pasta is tender but still firm to the bite. Drain the pasta and add it to the soup. Taste and correct the seasoning. Serve with a generous sprinkling of parmigiano and a few drops of good olive oil, if you wish.

It seems that hearty mountain dishes are also straightforward and uncomplicated to prepare. Like the people of the Val d'Aosta themselves, a beautiful mountain area bordered by France and Switzerland, this soup has an honest and direct quality.

For the Chick-peas

1 pound dried chick-peas (garbanzo beans), sorted and rinsed
5 cups Basic Chicken Broth (page 45) or canned broth
Water

For the Tomatoes

4 tablespoons olive oil
2 garlic cloves, finely chopped
2 anchovy fillets, finely chopped
1 tablespoon chopped fresh rosemary leaves
2 tablespoons chopped fresh parsley leaves
1 28-ounce can imported Italian plum tomatoes with their juices
Salt and freshly ground black pepper

To Complete the Soup

1 tablespoon salt
½ pound small pasta, such as ditalini or conchigliette (small shells)
1 cup freshly grated parmigiano
A few tablespoons virgin olive oil (optional)

SERVES 4 TO 6

La Zuppa di Lenticchie Semplice

Easy Lentil Soup

Another wonderful winter soup. Lentil, just like bean and vegetable soup, is one of those dishes that has a hundred different interpretations; mine is extremely simple to prepare. But be ready, because its divine flavor will remove your willpower, and you will find yourself yearning for soup at 10 o'clock in the morning.

For the Lentils

2 cups dried lentils, sorted and rinsed
5 cups Basic Chicken Broth (page 45) or canned broth
5 cups water
1 smoked ham shank (optional)

For the Tomato Sauce

1 28-ounce can imported Italian plum tomatoes
¼ cup olive oil
1 onion, finely chopped
3 garlic cloves, finely chopped
2 tablespoons chopped fresh parsley leaves
Salt and freshly ground black pepper

To Complete the Soup

1 cup freshly grated parmigiano
A few tablespoons virgin olive oil (optional)

Serves 6 to 8

Put the lentils in a large bowl, cover with water, and soak for several hours or overnight; discard any lentils that float to the surface. Drain and rinse. Put the lentils, broth, water, and ham shank, if using, into a stockpot or a large saucepan. Cover and simmer gently for 40 to 50 minutes, stirring a few times during the cooking.

While the lentils are cooking, prepare the tomato sauce. Press the tomatoes through a food mill or sieve to remove the seeds. In a medium-size saucepan, heat the oil. Add the onion and sauté gently for 3 to 5 minutes, until the onion begins to color. Add the garlic and parsley and cook a few minutes longer. Stir in the tomatoes and season with salt and pepper. Simmer, uncovered, for 15 to 20 minutes.

Transfer half of the lentils to a food processor or blender and purée until smooth. Return to the pot and add the tomato sauce. Cook for 10 minutes longer. Taste and adjust the seasoning. Serve with a generous sprinkling of parmigiano and a few drops of good olive oil, if you wish.

This soup can be made in large quantities and frozen. Pasta or rice can be added. It can also be served with slices of broiled Italian bread.

Crema di Zucca

Cream of Pumpkin Soup

This cream of pumpkin soup is extremely simple to prepare and thoroughly delicious. My husband, who is a hearty eater, and not at all inclined toward creamy soups, always has several bowls. Then he pats his stomach and says, "Gee, I wonder why I'm not hungry anymore."

Melt the butter in a medium-size saucepan. When the butter foams, add the onion and sauté gently for 4 to 8 minutes, or until the onion is pale yellow.

Cut the pumpkin into small pieces and remove the skin and seeds. Add the pumpkin and broth to the onion. Cover and cook over medium heat, until the pumpkin is tender, about 25 to 35 minutes.

Purée everything through a food mill, a sieve, or a food processor directly into another saucepan. Bring the soup to a boil. Add the cream, lower the heat, and simmer for 5 to 10 minutes longer. Serve hot, accompanied by a generous sprinkling of parmigiano.

For a thicker soup, reduce the amount of broth. For a thinner soup, increase it. To garnish the soup, you may want to toast a few slices of white bread, cut them into small pieces, and sauté them a little in butter. Then sprinkle the soup with the bread and some chopped parsley.

Soup, tortelli, risotto, and dumplings are among the treats we can create with pumpkin. But when pumpkin is unavailable, what do we do? We simply use a different squash. According to author and food scholar Giuliano Bugialli, butternut squash is the "real" squash used in Italy. I find that pumpkin and butternut squash can be used interchangeably and that, in a pinch, banana squash and acorn squash also will do.

4 tablespoons unsalted butter
1 onion, finely chopped
3 pounds pumpkin or butternut squash
8 to 10 cups Basic Chicken Broth (page 45) or canned broth
⅓ cup heavy cream
½ cup freshly grated parmigiano

SERVES 4

Zuppa Rustica di Funghi

Mushroom Soup with Porcini

Fortunately, porcini can be dried and their intense flavor is preserved and even magnified by drying. Dried porcini are easily found in Italian supermarkets all over the country. This hearty mushroom soup combines reconstituted dried porcini with ordinary white cultivated mushrooms. The result is a soup that has a woodsy fragrance and taste.

3 ounces dried porcini mushrooms
2 medium-size potatoes
1 pound small fresh white cultivated
  mushrooms
3 tablespoons unsalted butter
1 onion, finely chopped
3 ounces prosciutto, sliced and then diced
1 garlic clove, finely chopped
2 tablespoons chopped fresh parsley leaves
Salt and freshly ground black pepper
8 cups Basic Chicken Broth (page 45) or
  4 cups canned chicken broth mixed with
  4 cups water
4 to 6 slices Italian bread, cut ½ inch
  thick
Butter (optional)
½ cup freshly grated parmigiano

SERVES 4 TO 6

Break the porcini into small pieces and soak them in 2 cups of lukewarm water for 20 minutes. Drain the mushrooms and reserve the water. Rinse the mushrooms under cool running water. Line a strainer with two layers of paper towels and strain the mushroom soaking water well to rid it of any sandy deposits. Set aside.

Peel the potatoes and dice them. With a damp cloth, clean the mushrooms and then cut them into thin slices.

In a medium-size saucepan, melt the butter. When the butter foams, add the onion and sauté gently until the onion begins to color, about 5 minutes. Add the mushrooms, prosciutto, potatoes, garlic, and 1 tablespoon of the chopped parsley. Season with salt and pepper. Add reserved mushroom soaking water and broth. Cover the saucepan and cook for 25 to 30 minutes over medium heat. Transfer half of the soup to a food processor or a blender and blend until smooth. Return to the saucepan and add the remaining parsley. Taste and adjust the seasoning.

Preheat the broiler. Broil the bread slices until golden on both sides, buttered or not. Cut the slices into small rough pieces and put them in individual bowls. Ladle the soup into the bowls and serve hot or at room temperature with a generous sprinkling of parmigiano.

Like most soups, this one freezes well.

Wild Italian mushrooms are very popular in Italy, plentiful in spring and fall especially, when they find their way into innumerable dishes. A soup of wild porcini is an ultimate experience, though fresh porcini are virtually unavailable here in local markets. However, some lucky people, such as my good friends Beppe and Paola Bagnatori of San Francisco, know where to find them. The Bagnatoris get up at four o'clock in the morning to go hunting mushrooms; they also keep these excursions a well-guarded secret.

Gnocchi, Polenta, and Risotti

Cavatelli al Burro e Formaggio

Cavatelli with Butter and Cheese

My mother-in-law, a wonderful cook from southern Italy, taught me how to make this dish.

Instead of making the classic cavatelli with flour and water, she uses a combination of flour and ricotta. The result is a delicate, light, and tasty cavatelli which my family and I have grown to love.

In a large bowl, combine the ricotta with the flour and, with a wooden spoon or your hands, mix to incorporate.

Put the mixture on a wooden board and knead into a ball. Add a little extra flour if the dough is sticky. The dough should be soft and pliable.

Lightly flour your working surface. Break the dough into pieces the size of an egg. Shape the pieces into rolls about the size of your little finger. Cut the rolls into ½-inch pieces. With your index and middle fingers press one small piece of dough, pulling it toward you on the board. The pressure made by your fingers will give the pieces of dough the shape of little shells. Repeat with the remaining dough.

Arrange the cavatelli on a tray lined with a kitchen towel. Place in the refrigerator until you are ready to cook. Bring a large saucepan two-thirds full of water to a boil. Add the salt and cavatelli. Return the water to a boil and cook the cavatelli until tender but firm to the bite. (Because of the ricotta, the cavatelli will cook very fast, 2 to 3 minutes.)

Drain the cavatelli and transfer them to a warm dish. Add the butter and cheese and mix to blend. Serve immediately with additional cheese, if you wish.

1 pound ricotta
1 to 1½ cups all-purpose unbleached flour
1 tablespoon salt
3 to 4 tablespoons unsalted butter at room temperature
½ cup freshly grated Pecorino Romano or parmigiano

SERVES 4 TO 6

I serve this dish simply with butter and cheese or with a light tomato sauce (page 48). The cavatelli can be prepared several hours ahead. Place them on a tray lined with a kitchen towel, cover with another towel, and refrigerate until ready to cook.

Gnocchi di Zucca e Formaggio

Squash and Cheese Gnocchi

My first experience with these gnocchi brought me close to tears. The dough was so moist I kept adding flour and tried to knead the dough just like regular potato gnocchi. As a result, the dough stuck heavily to the board and to my hands. When I finally cooked and ate one of these lovely, golden gnocchi, I almost broke a tooth—they were as hard as a rock. Well, we all know that practice makes perfect. This is what I learned:

- After the squash is cooked and puréed, some of its juices must be removed or the dough will be very sticky. In the end, this dough will not be as firm as the dough for potato gnocchi; it will be stickier and softer, but resist the urge to keep adding more and more flour. The amount given in the recipe is more or less right.
- Do not knead the dough energetically; use only a gentle kneading.
- When rolling out the gnocchi, dust the surface very lightly with flour: Too much flour will make the gnocchi hard to roll.

- When rolling out the gnocchi, use a light back-and-forth motion. Do not press down on the dough, but rather gently stretch it sideways. If, after all this your cooked gnocchi are too hard, too much flour was added. If, on the other hand, they fall apart while cooking, chances are that not enough flour was added.

All that said, this dish is really simpler than it seems and worth the bit of effort involved.

1 2½-pound pumpkin or butternut squash
Salt
1 large egg yolk
1 to 1½ cups all-purpose unbleached flour
1 cup freshly grated parmigiano
3 to 4 tablespoons unsalted butter

MAKES 4 SERVINGS

Preheat the oven to 350 degrees.

Cut the pumpkin into large pieces and bake until tender when pricked with a fork. Cool slightly; then remove the pulp and discard the seeds and skin. Put the pulp through a ricer, a food mill, or in a food processor, in which case, turn the machine on and off just until the squash is puréed or it will become too soupy. Put the purée in a large kitchen towel and gently squeeze out about ½ cup of the squash juices. Do not remove too much or the gnocchi will be tough and dry.

Put the purée in a large bowl. Add 1 tablespoon of salt and the egg yolk. Mix with a wooden spoon. Add 1 cup of the flour and ⅓ cup of the parmigiano. Mix well with a wooden spoon or your hands. Put the mixture on a floured wooden board and knead lightly, adding more flour if dough sticks heavily to the board and your hands: The mixture should be soft, pliable, and just a little sticky.

Cut the dough into pieces the size of an egg. Using a light back-and-forth motion, shape each piece into a roll about the thickness of your thumb. Cut each roll into 1-inch pieces.

Hold a fork with its tines firmly against a work board. Starting from the bottom of the curve, press each piece of dough firmly upward along the length of the tines, pressing with the index finger of your other hand. Let the dumpling fall back onto the work surface. Repeat with remaining pieces.

Line a large platter or baking sheet with a kitchen towel. Arrange the dumplings on the towel and refrigerate, uncovered or covered loosely with another towel, until ready to cook. Do not use plastic or aluminum foil or the dumplings will become soft and sticky.

Put the butter in a shallow serving dish and keep the dish warm in the oven until gnocchi are ready.

Bring a large pot of water to a boil. Add 1 tablespoon of salt and the dumplings. When the dumplings rise to the surface of the water, after less than a minute, cook for 8 to 10 *seconds* longer. Remove the dumplings with a large slotted spoon, draining off all the excess water, and place them in the warm serving dish. Sprinkle with the remaining parmigiano, mix gently, and serve at once with additional parmigiano, if you wish.

Gnocchi can be prepared several hours ahead of time and kept in the refrigerator, covered only with a kitchen cloth. Although the gnocchi can be frozen, I personally do not recommend it, because their texture will change considerably.

Gnocchi Verdi di Patate con Salsa di Pancetta e Salvia

Green Potato Gnocchi with Pancetta and Fresh Sage

Green potato gnocchi are made exactly as potato gnocchi, but with the addition of chopped spinach and parmigiano kneaded into the dough.

Green gnocchi, just like potato gnocchi, can be cooked immediately or kept in the refrigerator covered only with a kitchen towel, for several hours.

For the Gnocchi
4 medium-size potatoes, preferably russets
2 large egg yolks
2 tablespoons cooked chopped fresh or frozen spinach, squeezed dry
Salt
½ cup freshly grated parmigiano
1 to 1½ cups all-purpose unbleached flour

For the Sauce
¼ pound pancetta, sliced
4 tablespoons unsalted butter
7 to 8 small fresh sage leaves, or a small pinch of dried sage
½ cup freshly grated parmigiano

SERVES 4

Preheat the oven to 350 degrees. Wash and dry the potatoes. With a knife, make a long incision in the potatoes lengthwise, about ½ inch deep. Put the potatoes in the oven and bake until tender.

Cool the potatoes slightly, peel them, and, while they are still warm, put them through a ricer into a large bowl.

Beat the egg yolks in a small bowl. Add the spinach and 1 teaspoon salt, mix well, and add to potatoes, with the parmigiano and flour. Mix energetically with a wooden spoon or your hands to incorporate. Transfer the mixture to a wooden board and knead, adding more flour if the dough sticks to the board and to your hands. The mixture should be soft, pliable, and just a bit sticky. Cut and shape the dough following the instructions for Squash and Cheese Gnocchi on page 206.

Line a large platter or baking sheet with a kitchen towel. Arrange the dumplings on the towel and refrigerate until ready to cook.

Bring a large pot of water to a boil. To prepare the sauce, cut the pancetta into small thin strips. Melt the butter in a small saucepan. When the butter foams, add the pancetta and sage. Cook over medium heat until the pancetta turns light golden. Keep warm over very low heat.

Add 1 tablespoon of salt and the dumplings to the pot of boiling water. When the dumplings rise to the surface of the water, cook for 8 to 10 *seconds* longer. Remove the dumplings with a large slotted spoon, draining off the excess water. Place the dumplings in a warm serving dish. Add the pancetta sauce and parmigiano. Mix gently to blend. Serve with additional parmigiano, if you wish.

Gnocchi are available frozen in specialty markets, but I never freeze mine. I find that the texture of frozen gnocchi, when cooked, is softer and mushier and, to my taste, quite unappealing.

Polenta

Polenta is made from maize which is ground into meal. Originally, it was prepared in a large copper pot called a *paiolo*; in country homes, the paiolo was suspended with a thick chain directly over a burning fire in the fireplace, while in the cities a charcoal or wooden stove was used.

During the long winter months, when I was growing up in Bologna, polenta was a regular staple in our house. My mother used to stir it endlessly, reaching inside the paiolo with a special long wooden spoon, while all of us would gather around to watch and to help with the stirring. Then my father would pour the polenta onto a large wooden board, scraping inside the paiolo to get every bit of that marvelous sustenance. Polenta is still central to the diet of many northern Italians, especially in the Veneto and Friuli regions, where it is preferred over bread or pasta.

Because cornmeal comes coarsely ground and finely ground, the texture of your polenta will depend on the cornmeal you use. I use a mixture of the two, which results in a well-balanced combination. I simply adore polenta and when I make it I generally double the recipe. Fresh, steaming polenta is heavenly with stews, game, or braised meats. Leftover polenta can be baked with butter and cheese or with meat sauces; it can be fried or broiled or sliced into small squares for crostini and topped with a variety of ingredients, such as wild mushrooms or gorgonzola. I even love it cold, with just a pat of butter. Polenta is a highly satisfying food with gusto, good for serious eaters, cold winter nights, and good company.

Basic Polenta

9 cups water

2 tablespoons salt

2 cups coarsely ground cornmeal mixed
  with 1 cup finely ground cornmeal

SERVES 6 TO 8

Bring the water to a boil in a large heavy saucepan. Add the salt. Lower the heat and start pouring in the corn-meal very slowly by the handful, stirring with a long wooden spoon. It is extremely important to add the cornmeal very slowly and to stir constantly in order to avoid lumps. Cook, stirring constantly, for 25 to 35 minutes.

The polenta will gradually become very thick as it cooks, and it will bubble and spit back to you. Crush any lumps that might form against the side of the pan. The polenta is done when it comes away cleanly from the side of the pan.

Pour the polenta onto a large wooden board, baking sheet, or platter. Wet your hands or wet a large spatula and pat the polenta down into a compact, smooth round, about 2 inches thick. Cool for 5 to 10 minutes or until firm. Cut the polenta into slices and serve topped with your favorite sauce.

As the polenta cooks, some of it will stick to the bottom of the pot. To clean, just soak the pot with cold water and detergent for about 1 hour and you will be able to remove the polenta very easily.

Risotto alla Chioggiotta

Risotto with Creamed Seafood

This is a classic dish from the Veneto region. As is often the case with classic old recipes, there are several slightly different versions.

As a general rule, Italians don't use cheese in conjunction with fish. There are, however, some exceptions, as in the case of this risotto. Even the people of Veneto are divided whether to add a bit of parmigiano or not. I will simply leave the choice up to you.

Sometimes, just before finishing the risotto, I add a few shrimp which have been sautéed in butter and garlic for extra color and texture. This is simply a personal preference.

Because this risotto is cooked in a broth that is rich and creamy, it acquires a wonderfully delicate and rich texture. It could be served as a meal all by itself. For a formal dinner, it should be served in moderate portions as a first course. A second course of broiled fish would be excellent.

To prepare the fish, heat the oil in a medium-size saucepan. Add the onion, garlic, and parsley and sauté gently for 2 to 3 minutes. Add the cut-up fish and pour in enough water to cover the fish completely by about 2 inches. Season with salt and cover the saucepan. Cook over medium heat for 25 to 30 minutes. Put the fish and broth into a blender or food processor and process until smooth.

Pour the puréed fish mixture into a clean saucepan—it should have a loose, soupy consistency. If it is too thick, add a bit more water. The cream of fish can be prepared several hours or a day ahead of time and kept tightly covered in the refrigerator.

To prepare the risotto, melt 3 tablespoons of the butter in a large saucepan. Add the onion and sauté over medium heat until the onion is pale yellow. Add the rice and stir. When the rice is coated with butter, add the wine. Cook, stirring, until the wine has evaporated. Add a few ladles of cream of fish or just enough to barely cover the rice. Cook and stir, until the cream has been absorbed. Add a little more cream of fish. Continue cooking the rice in this manner, adding the cream of fish when needed, until the rice is cooked, about 15 to 20 minutes. The rice should be tender but firm to the bite.

Remove from the heat, add the remaining tablespoon of butter and the cheese, if using. Season with salt and pepper and sprinkle with the parsley. Serve immediately.

As a variation, ½ pound medium-size whole or cut-up shrimp can be added to this risotto. Sauté the shrimp in butter and a bit of garlic very briefly; then add to the risotto 3 to 4 minutes before it is ready to be served.

For the Cream of Fish
3 tablespoons olive oil
1 small onion, finely chopped
2 garlic cloves, finely chopped
1 tablespoon chopped fresh parsley leaves
1 pound assorted fish pieces, such as halibut, sea bass or trout with all bones removed
Salt

For the Risotto
4 tablespoons unsalted butter
1 onion, finely chopped
2 cups Italian Arborio rice
1 cup dry white wine
½ cup freshly grated parmigiano (optional)
Salt and freshly ground black pepper
2 tablespoons chopped fresh parsley leaves

SERVES 4 TO 6

Polenta col Mascarpone

Polenta with Mascarpone

Luscious is the word for this polenta dish. Steaming polenta and sweet, creamy mascarpone—an unbeatable combination. Serve it as an appetizer, as a snack, or as a side dish to a nice simply roasted meat.

For Polenta
6 cups water or broth (see Note)
1½ tablespoons salt
1 cup coarsely ground cornmeal combined
 with 1 cup finely ground cornmeal

For the Topping
¼ pound mascarpone

SERVES 4 TO 6

Follow the instructions for Basic Polenta (page 210), using the quantities listed here. Pour the polenta onto a large wooden board or platter and cool for about 5 minutes. Cut the polenta into medium-size slices and place 1 or 2 slices onto individual serving dishes. Spread some mascarpone over each slice of polenta and serve while hot.

The polenta could be cooked in Chicken Broth (page 45) instead of water. If you are using canned broth instead of homemade, use 3 cans of broth and 3 cans of water, and reduce or omit the salt.

Polenta Pasticciata con i Funghi e la Pancetta

Polenta with Dried Wild Mushrooms and Pancetta

Polenta can be cooked in water, broth, or milk. When it is cooked in milk, polenta becomes deliciously tasty and delicate. In this dish, a sauce of mushrooms and pancetta is stirred directly into the polenta and everything is cooked together to the proper consistency.

Soak the mushrooms in lukewarm water for 20 minutes. Drain the mushrooms and reserve the water. Rinse the mushrooms under cool running water. Strain the mushroom soaking water several times through a few layers of paper towels to get rid of any sand. Reserve the water for another use, such as soups or sauces.

Chop the mushrooms into small pieces. In a small saucepan, melt the butter. When the butter foams, add the pancetta, and sauté until lightly golden. Add the mushrooms and cook a few minutes longer. Set aside.

Combine the coarse and fine cornmeal. Heat the milk just short of a boil. Add the salt. Take the cornmeal by the handful and add to the milk in a very slow stream, letting it fall through your fingers. In order to avoid lumps, be sure to add the cornmeal very slowly and stir constantly with a long wooden spoon. After all the cornmeal is incorporated, you will have a somewhat thick mixture. Cook and stir for 20 to 30 minutes. As it cooks, the polenta will become thicker and thicker. During the last 5 minutes of cooking, add the mushroom and pancetta mixture together with the parmigiano and, if you wish, 1 or 2 chunks of butter. Stir vigorously to incorporate.

Pour the polenta onto a large wooden board or platter. With a large wet spatula or wet hands, flatten the polenta to a 2-inch thickness. Let cool for about 10 minutes. Cut the polenta into medium-size slices and serve hot.

For the Sauce
1 ounce dried porcini mushrooms
3 tablespoons unsalted butter
¼ pound pancetta
½ cup freshly grated parmigiano

For the Polenta
9 cups lowfat milk
1½ tablespoons salt
*2 cups coarsely ground cornmeal mixed
    with 1 cup finely ground cornmeal*

SERVES 8

This "stuffed" polenta is quite rich and tasty. Serve it in moderation as an accompaniment to a stewed or braised meat or fowl. Never serve bread when you serve polenta.

The morning after dining on polenta and Rabbit in Piquant Sauce (page 238), I played tennis and beat the daylights out of my opponent. Could the polenta have given me so much strength and energy? I don't know, but, just in case, I must remember to feast on polenta before a serious match.

Polenta al Gorgonzola

Polenta with Gorgonzola

Polenta, like pasta, is a vehicle for sauces. Technically, polenta could be eaten plain without any condiment. But that is almost never the case. Here we have a basic polenta that is sliced, topped with sweet gorgonzola, and then baked briefly. It is absolutely delicious. A small portion of this dish could be served as an appetizer, a large portion as a casual meal. If you are like me, however, and you love polenta, you will be snacking on this delicious dish at ten in the morning, around noon, of course at three in the afternoon, and again at night. I always preach moderation, but there are some dishes for which it is very hard to retain my self-control.

For the Polenta
6 cups water
1½ tablespoons salt
1 cup coarsely ground cornmeal mixed with 1 cup finely ground cornmeal

For the Topping
2 tablespoons unsalted butter
½ pound gorgonzola

SERVES 4 TO 6

Prepare the Basic Polenta following the instructions on page 210, using the quantities listed here. Pour the polenta onto a large wooden board or platter. With a large wet spatula or slightly wet hands, flatten the polenta to a 2-inch thickness. Cool for 5 to 10 minutes. Cut the polenta into medium-size short slices.

Preheat the oven to 375 degrees. Butter a baking dish lightly. Place the polenta slices in the buttered dish. Dot each slice generously with gorgonzola. Bake a few minutes until the cheese becomes soft and begins to melt. Serve at once.

Timballo di Risotto con Funghi e Piselli

Baked Molded Risotto with Mushrooms and Peas

Timballos are a whole category of dishes. Made with pasta, meat, vegetables, or rice, and generally enclosed in a pastry shell, these dishes make for very elegant presentations, though a risotto timballo does not require the pastry. Rather, the rice is pressed into a mold that has been buttered and coated with unseasoned bread crumbs. Unmolded, this timballo is truly impressive.

Soak the mushrooms in 1 cup of lukewarm water for 20 minutes. Drain the mushrooms and reserve the soaking water. Strain mushroom soaking water through paper towels several times to get rid of the sandy deposits. Set aside. Heat the chicken broth in a medium-size saucepan.

Melt 4 tablespoons of the butter in a large saucepan. When the butter foams, add the onion and sauté over medium heat until the onion is pale yellow. Add the rice and mix well. When rice is coated with the butter, add the wine. Cook, stirring constantly, until the wine has evaporated. Add the mushrooms and reserved soaking water. Stir in 1 or 2 ladles of broth, just enough to cover the rice. Cook and stir over medium heat until the broth has been absorbed. Continue cooking and stirring the rice, adding the broth a little at a time, for about 10 minutes. Add the fresh peas, if using, and cook for 5 to 10 minutes longer. The rice should be tender but firm to the bite. Stir in the parmigiano and remaining 2 tablespoons of butter. If frozen thawed peas are used, instead of fresh, add them to the rice at this point. Taste for seasoning.

Preheat the oven to 375 degrees. Butter generously a 10-inch mold with a hole in the center and with smooth sides and sprinkle the bottom and sides well with the bread crumbs, shaking off any excess. Pour risotto into the mold and fill up to the rim. Press the risotto into the mold lightly with your hands. Put the mold in the center of the oven and bake for 15 to 20 minutes.

Remove the mold from the oven and let stand for about 10 minutes.

Place a warm serving platter on top of the mold and turn the mold over the platter. Pat gently all around the mold to loosen the edges; then unmold. Serve immediately.

1 ounce dried porcini mushrooms
8 to 10 cups Chicken Broth (page 45) or 5 cups canned broth mixed with 5 cups water
6 tablespoons unsalted butter
1 onion, finely chopped
3½ cups Italian Arborio rice
¾ cup dry white wine
1 cup fresh peas or frozen thawed peas
1 cup freshly grated parmigiano
Additional butter
½ cup unseasoned bread crumbs

SERVES 6 TO 8

Meat and Poultry

Cappone Arrosto con Patate

Roasted Capon with Potatoes

Here, a capon is roasted with fresh herbs and garlic. Then potatoes are added to the pan to cook in the capon juices. Nothing could be simpler and tastier.

Preheat the oven to 400 degrees.

Wash the capon under cool running water; then pat dry with paper towels. Put the capon in a large heavy casserole. Rub it with the oil, garlic, sage, and rosemary. Put some of this mixture into capon cavity. Season with salt and pepper. Squeeze the lemon juice over the capon and roast for 15 to 20 minutes. Lower the oven temperature to 350 degrees and roast for 40 minutes longer, basting a few times during the cooking. Add a bit of wine if the sauce dries out too much.

Peel and cut the potatoes into medium-size chunks. Add to the casserole along with the additional sage and rosemary. Roast for 30 to 35 minutes longer, or until the juices run clear when the capon flesh is pierced with a thin knife. Transfer the capon to a cutting board and let it rest for 10 minutes. Use a large spoon to remove as much fat as possible from the sauce. Taste the potatoes for doneness. Put the capon on a cutting board to rest. If the potatoes are not done, return them to the oven to finish cooking. Slice the capon and serve it with some potatoes and a bit of the pan juices.

A capon is a neutered male chicken. This large, plump bird has a moist, delicate flesh. When cooked properly, it literally melts in your mouth. If you have never tasted one, I urge you to make a special effort to do so.

1 6- to 7-pound capon
¼ cup olive oil
2 garlic cloves, chopped
Several fresh sage leaves, chopped, or a
   pinch of dried sage
1 or 2 rosemary sprigs, or 1 teaspoon
   dried rosemary
Salt and freshly ground black pepper
Juice of 1 lemon
Dry white wine, optional
4 to 5 medium-size potatoes
Additional fresh sage and rosemary

SERVES 4 TO 6

Bollito Misto

Mixed Boiled Meats

A good Bollito Misto should always include beef, veal, chicken or capon, as well as that wonderful sausage called cotechino. Traditionally, beef or veal tongue and calf's head also are usually a part of Bollito Misto, but I leave the decision to add these two ingredients up to you. To produce meats that are moist and juicy, they must be placed into water that is already simmering. Start the cooking of Bollito Misto early in the day to allow the broth to simmer gently for 3½ to 4 hours. Strain enough broth into another saucepan, adding pasta, such as angel's hair, if you wish, to make a delicious soup. Keep the meats in the remaining broth so that they will remain warm and juicy.

1 ripe tomato, or 1 tablespoon tomato paste
2 carrots, cut into pieces
2 celery stalks, cut into pieces
1 onion, quartered
A few parsley sprigs
3 to 4 beef or veal knuckle bones
1 3½-pound beef brisket
1 3- to 3½-pound veal rump roast
1 2½- to 3-pound chicken, or 1 small capon
2 tablespoons salt
1 2- to 2½-pound cotechino sausage, pricked in several places with a fork

SERVES 8 TO 10

To measure how much water you need, put all the ingredients, except the cotechino and salt, in a large stockpot and cover by 3 inches with cold water. Remove the meats. Bring the liquid to a gentle simmer and add the beef. After a few minutes of cooking, remove the scum that rises to the surface of the liquid with a large spoon. Cover the pot and simmer gently for 1½ to 2 hours.

Add the veal and the chicken. Simmer for 1 to 1½ hours longer. During the last few minutes of cooking, add the salt. Leave the meats in their hot broth until ready to use. (If you prepare Bollito Misto a few hours or a day ahead, reheat the broth gently before serving the meats.)

While the meats are cooking, bring a medium-size saucepan of water to a boil. Add the cotechino sausage, lower the heat, and cover the saucepan. Simmer the cotechino for 1 to 1½ hours, depending on its size. Leave the cotechino in its broth until ready to use.

Slice the meats and sausage and arrange on a warm serving dish. (Keep any extra meat in the broth to stay warm and tender.) Serve at once with Piquant Green Sauce (page 47) and some mashed potatoes.

For a lovely first course, use the intensely flavored broth to cook some tagliarini or use the broth to prepare Egg Soup Roman Style (page 196).

There was a time when Bollito Misto was routinely made in many northern Italian households. Today with our hurried lifestyle we don't seem to be able to set aside the few hours it takes to prepare this wonderful classic dish. It is really too bad, because this one-pot dish produces two courses—rich, aromatic broth that can be served as a first course and juicy, tasty mixed boiled meats that are served as a second course accompanied by Salsa Verde. Actually, the preparation of Bollito Misto is quite simple, since it will cook all by itself with only a little supervision on your part. Depending on the quantity of meats you use, this one-pot dinner, can also feed a large group.

Leftover broth from Bollito Misto can be frozen; the leftover meats can be served cold the next day or cut into small cubes and served as an appetizing salad (see Salad of Roasted Meat and Red Onions, page 128).

Spiedini di Carne Mista

Skewers of Mixed Broiled Meats

These spiedini are brushed with a mixture of olive oil, balsamic vinegar, and a bit of mustard, seasoned with salt and pepper and placed on a hot grill or under a broiler until they are golden in color. They are simply delicious. Remember to oil your grill or your barbecue lightly so the meat won't stick to it. Also make sure to place spiedini about 4 inches from the heat source to avoid scorching.

For the Dressing
¼ cup balsamic vinegar
1 teaspoon Dijon mustard
½ cup olive oil

For the Spiedini
½ pound center-cut boneless pork loin
2 whole chicken breasts, skinned, split, and boned
½ pound veal, cut from the shoulder
½ pound sirloin steak
½ pound pancetta, cut into ⅛-inch-thick slices
Several fresh sage leaves, if available
Salt and freshly ground black pepper

SERVES 4 TO 6

Preheat the broiler or prepare a barbecue so that the coals are ready when you are ready to grill the meat. In a small bowl, combine the balsamic vinegar, mustard, and oil. Cut the meat into 2-inch cubes. Cut pancetta into 2-inch pieces. Thread the meats onto skewers, alternating with pancetta and sage leaves. Brush with the oil–vinegar mixture and season with salt and pepper.

Put the skewers under the broiler or on the barbecue. Broil for 4 to 5 minutes or until lightly golden. Turn the skewers and broil for 4 to 5 minutes longer. Brush again with the oil–vinegar mixture and serve hot.

Of course, if cooked on an outdoor grill, this is equally appetizing in summer

Traditionally, spiedini are Italian kebabs that are grilled or broiled; today they can also be cooked in a skillet. Spiedini generally consist of a mixture of morsel-size ingredients threaded on skewers. In Spiedini di Carne Mista, the meat alternates with pieces of pancetta that prevent it from drying out and also impart to it a special flavor. Aromatic fresh sage, when available, is also a lovely way to season the meat.

Spiedini are practical and appetizing: They can be prepared in the morning and grilled at night. Any number of vegetables can be served alongside the spiedini or threaded onto the skewers. Spiedini can be served with polenta or rice or simply with a mixed green or tomato salad.

Braciole alla Barese

Stuffed Savory Beef Bundles

This dish, typical of southern Italy, is as valid today as it was years ago. It is easy to prepare, tasty, and economical. After the initial browning, the meat is cooked slowly in a savory tomato sauce. The long slow cooking will produce a very tender meat. The sauce, which will thicken and darken in color as it cooks, is generally served over pasta. The meat is served after the pasta. Since this dish freezes well, I generally double the recipe, using half and freeze the other half.

Press the tomatoes through a food mill or sieve to remove the seeds. Set aside. Put the beef slices between two pieces of wax paper and pound until thin. Season each slice with salt and pepper.

In a small bowl, combine the parsley, garlic, and cheese. Spread some of this mixture over one side of each slice. Roll up each slice tightly and secure with string or toothpicks.

Heat the oil in a large saucepan. Add the beef and brown on all sides over medium heat. Add the wine and cook over high heat until the wine has almost all evaporated. Stir in the tomatoes and season with salt and pepper. Cover the saucepan and cook over very low heat for 1 to 1½ hours. During the last 5 minutes of cooking, add the oregano. Remove the string or toothpicks, slice the bundles into several pieces, and serve. Follow with the beef and a mixed green salad.

For a complete dinner, serve the sauce over rigatoni or penne.

1 28-ounce can imported Italian plum tomatoes with their juices
2 pounds top beef sirloin or top round, from the widest part of the cut, cut into 4 slices, ½-inch-thick
Salt and freshly ground black pepper
⅓ cup chopped fresh parsley leaves
3 garlic cloves, finely chopped
1 cup freshly grated parmigiano or pecorino cheese
4 tablespoons olive oil
1 cup dry white wine
2 tablespoons fresh oregano leaves, or a pinch of dried oregano

SERVES 4

Scaloppe di Maiale in Agrodolce

Sweet and Sour Medallions of Pork

Pork is a meat much loved by Italians. In my region of Emilia-Romagna, pork is almost always present on the table in one form or another. In this dish, thin slices of pork loin are quickly sautéed in butter; then they finish cooking in a delicious sweet-and-sour sauce. It will take only 10 to 12 minutes to cook this dish. Keep in mind that the slices of pork are quite thin, a prolonged cooking will make them tough.

1 cup all-purpose unbleached flour
Salt and freshly ground black pepper
2 pounds center-cut boneless pork loin, cut into ½-inch-thick slices, all fat removed
3 tablespoons unsalted butter
1 tablespoon oil
1 garlic clove, finely chopped
A few fresh sage leaves, or just a pinch of dried sage
¾ cup dry white wine
⅓ cup good-quality white wine vinegar
¼ cup sugar

SERVES 4 TO 6

Flour the pork slices slightly and season with salt and pepper. Heat the butter and oil in a large skillet. When the butter foams, add the pork and sauté over medium heat until golden on both sides (about 3 to 4 minutes). Transfer the meat to a platter.

Add the garlic and sage to the skillet and stir for about 1 minute. Do not let the garlic turn brown. Stir in the wine, vinegar, and sugar. Cook over medium heat until the sauce is reduced by half. Return the pork to the skillet and cook, uncovered, for 4 to 5 minutes longer, turning and basting the meat. Transfer the meat to a warm serving platter. Reduce the sauce by cooking it over high heat until it has a thick, syrupy consistency. Taste and adjust the seasoning. Spoon over the pork and serve immediately.

Baked Cauliflower with Onions and Cheese (page 253) will make a perfect accompaniment for these medallions of pork.

Stracotto di Manzo con i Fagiolini

Braised Beef with String Beans

Twice I have had the good fortune of being sent to Italy by Sacramento KCRA/TV3 to film some of Italy's best restaurants and to report on the Italian life-style. In 1983, one of our stops was in Tuscany in the Chianti region. There my colleagues and I were guests of the Marchesi Antinoris at their country villa. It was a particularly chilly day and we had been out all day filming up and down the Chianti region, carrying with us heavy pieces of equipment. We were exhausted. The moment we walked through the door we were engulfed by a wonderful aroma. Franca, the housekeeper, had prepared for us a country dinner. For the antipasto, we were served the Antinoris' own salamis and prosciutto; next, thick and hearty bean soup and, as the main course, an absolutely tender and delicious braised beef—all accompanied by some of the Marchese Antinori's finest wines. We were in heaven and ate everything in sight.

The time needed to prepare this braised beef is a bit long, because long, slow cooking is required to produce a perfect brasato. However, after the initial browning it will cook all by itself. Be prepared to increase the recipe because this dish tastes even better the day after.

Put the tomatoes through a food mill or sieve to remove the seeds. Set aside.

In a large heavy casserole, heat the oil. Add the meat and brown on all sides over medium heat. Add the diced vegetables and sauté until lightly browned. Raise the heat and add the wine. Stir well and cook until the wine has almost evaporated. Stir in the tomatoes. Cover the casserole, leaving the lid slightly askew. Lower the heat and simmer for 2½ to 3 hours. Turn and baste meat a few times during the cooking. If the sauce becomes too thick add a bit of broth.

While the meat is cooking, snap off the ends of beans and wash them under cool running water. Bring a large saucepan of water to a boil. Add the salt and beans. Cook, uncovered, for 5 to 10 minutes, depending on the size of the beans. The beans should be tender but still quite firm to the bite. Drain the beans and set aside.

Transfer the meat to a cutting board and let it rest for about 10 minutes while you finish the sauce.

Tilt the casserole and scoop off the excess fat with a large spoon. Add the boiled string beans to the sauce and cook gently for 2 to 3 minutes.

Slice the meat and arrange it on a warm platter. Taste the sauce and adjust the seasoning. Spoon the sauce and string beans over the meat and serve.

2 cups canned imported Italian plum tomatoes with their juices
4 tablespoons olive oil
1 3- to 3½-pound bottom round or rump roast
1 carrot, diced
1 onion, diced
1 celery stalk, diced
1 cup good full-bodied red wine
1 teaspoon salt
Freshly ground black pepper
1 pound small string beans

SERVES 6

For a first course I hope you will try Franca's Country Bean Soup (page 197). I wish I could have you taste some of those incredible local salamis. But I am afraid that in order to do that you will have to go to Tuscany yourself.

Cosciotto di Maiale alla Birra

Roasted Leg of Pork Marinated in Beer

Because a leg of pork might be a bit too overwhelming in size for an average family, I have adapted this recipe to a more standard roast. Don't be restricted, however, by my adaptation. Use a whole leg of pork if you wish. Increase the amount of vegetables a bit and, of course, the cooking time. Generally, it takes 25 to 30 minutes per pound to cook a pork roast, though, of course, a thin roast will cook faster than a thick one. To be safe, use a meat thermometer. I use an initial high temperature to seal the juices and give the roast a nice, crisp surface. Then I lower the heat. This way the roast will cook gently without drying out. Make sure to baste the roast several times during the cooking, and remove it from the oven when it is still slightly undercooked, since it will keep on cooking while it rests.

For the Marinade

1 4-pound boneless leg of pork roast, trimmed of all fat
2 large onions, cut into slices
2 garlic cloves, peeled and crushed
2 celery stalks, cut into small chunks
2 tablespoons fresh rosemary leaves, or 1 tablespoon dried rosemary
Beer

To Complete the Dish

7 tablespoons olive oil
Salt and freshly ground black pepper
1 pound fresh cultivated mushrooms, wiped clean and cut into thin slices
1 cup dry white wine or beer

SERVES 6 TO 8

In a large bowl, combine the pork, onions, garlic, celery, and rosemary. Add enough beer to barely cover the meat. Cover the bowl and refrigerate several hours or overnight. Drain the meat and pat it dry with paper towel. Strain the marinade. Discard the beer and reserve the vegetables.

Preheat the oven to 400 degrees at least 15 minutes before you put the roast in.

Put 4 tablespoons of the oil in a roasting pan. Add the meat and season with salt and pepper. Roast for 15 to 20 minutes; then lower the oven temperature to 350 degrees and roast for about 1 hour, basting several times. Add the reserved vegetables and roast 1 hour longer. Check for your preferred doneness with a meat thermometer.

While the pork is roasting, heat the remaining 3 tablespoons of oil in a large skillet. Add enough mushrooms to barely cover the bottom of the skillet. Sauté over high heat until lightly golden. Use a slotted spoon to transfer the mushrooms to a bowl. Sauté whatever mushrooms you have left in the same manner. Add the sautéed mushrooms to the roast 10 minutes before removing the roast from oven.

Put the meat on a cutting board and let it rest for about 10 minutes. Tilt the roasting pan and remove as much fat as possible. Deglaze the pan over high heat by adding the wine or beer. Stir to pick up the bits and pieces attached to the bottom of the pan. Cook until the sauce is thick.

Slice the roast and arrange it on a warm serving platter. Spoon the sauce over the meat and serve immediately.

I had this lovely dish at a friend's house in Parma, where pork is particularly sweet and tender because of the special feeding that prepares pigs to become prized hams. Because of the large number of guests, the hostess prepared a whole leg of pork, which had been trimmed of its thick rind and excess fat; it was then marinated overnight in beer and vegetables and finally cooked with the vegetable marinade and freshly sautéed mushrooms. Sensational!

Braciole di Maiale alla Salsa Piccante

Pork Chops in Piquant Sauce

Pork chops that are grilled, broiled, or pan-fried can easily become tough without proper attention, but braised pork chops are simple to prepare, juicy, and, depending on their sauce, downright tasty. In this dish, the chops are first browned over high heat to seal in the juices. Then they are cooked over very low heat in a mildly spicy tomato–capers–olive sauce.

At the end of the cooking time check the consistency of the sauce; it should be medium-thick. If the sauce is too thin, keep the chops warm in the oven while you cook down the sauce over high heat; if it is too thick, add a bit of water.

4 large ripe tomatoes
2 tablespoons unsalted butter
2 tablespoons olive oil
4 rib or top loin pork chops, cut ¾ inch thick
1 small onion, chopped
10 green pitted olives, chopped
3 tablespoons rinsed and dried capers
Salt and cayenne pepper
½ cup dry white wine

SERVES 4

Peel and seed tomatoes as instructed on page 55. Cut tomatoes into medium-size chunks, put them in a bowl, and set aside.

Heat the butter and oil in a large skillet. When the butter foams, add the pork chops and sauté for 2 to 3 minutes on each side, or until the chops are golden in color. Transfer the meat to a plate. Add the onion, garlic, olives, and capers to the skillet and sauté for 2 to 3 minutes. Return the chops to the skillet and season with salt and a bit of cayenne pepper. Raise the heat and add the wine. Stir until the wine has evaporated. Stir in the tomatoes. Cover the skillet, leaving the lid slightly askew, and simmer for 15 to 20 minutes. Turn the chops a few times during the cooking.

Transfer the meat to a warm serving dish, spoon the sauce over the chops, and serve immediately.

Because this sauce is so good, you will want to soak it up with good bread. Or you might want to serve a few slices of polenta or some boiled or steamed rice alongside the chops.

Involtini di Vitello Veloci

Fast Stuffed Veal Bundles

This tasty dish is perfect for a family meal or for an informal gathering.

The veal is cooked briefly over high heat which keeps it from drying out.

Put the scaloppine on a work surface. Cover each with 1 slice of prosciutto and 1 teaspoon of parmigiano; roll up and secure with 1 or 2 toothpicks.

Heat the butter and oil in a large skillet. When the butter foams, add the veal and cook over medium heat until golden brown on all sides. Do not overcrowd the skillet. If necessary, brown the bundles in a couple of batches. Stir in the Marsala and cook, uncovered, stirring to pick up the bits and pieces attached to the bottom of the skillet, until the wine is reduced by half.

Transfer the veal to a plate while you finish the sauce. Stir the tomato sauce, parsley, and garlic into the skillet. Season with salt and pepper and cook over medium heat for 5 to 7 minutes, or until the sauce has a medium-thick consistency (at the end of the cooking, only a few tablespoons of sauce should be left for each serving). Return the veal to the skillet. Cook just enough to warm the veal and to coat it with the sauce, about 1 minute.

Transfer the veal to a warm platter, spoon the sauce over it, and serve immediately.

2 pounds veal scaloppine, cut ⅛ inch thick
6 ounces prosciutto, sliced thin
½ cup freshly grated parmigiano
3 tablespoons unsalted butter
2 tablespoons oil
¾ cup dry Marsala, preferably Florio
2 cups plain tomato sauce (page 49)
1 tablespoon chopped fresh parsley leaves
1 garlic clove, finely chopped
Salt and freshly ground black pepper

Serves 6 to 8

When I cook this dish for my family, I serve some steamed rice alongside the veal. If I prepare it for company, I generally precede it with a Risotto with Fresh Peas and Chives (page 90), a Rigatoni Casanova (page 184), or Cavatelli with Butter and Cheese (page 205).

Saltimbocca alla Romana

Veal with Prosciutto and Sage

A classic Roman dish that is quintessentially modern because of the simplicity of its preparation. A few slices of good milk-fed veal, paired with prosciutto and a hint of fresh sage, become a tantalizing, savory dish.

Saltimbocca literally means "jump in the mouth."

8 ¼-inch-thick slices veal scaloppine (about
   1½ pounds total weight)
¼ pound prosciutto, sliced
8 fresh sage leaves, or ½ teaspoon dried
   sage
4 tablespoons unsalted butter
Salt
1 cup dry white wine

SERVES 4

Put the veal between two pieces of wax paper and pound lightly. Place 1 slice of prosciutto and 1 sage leaf over each scaloppine. Secure with a wooden toothpick. (Classic saltimbocca are never rolled up.)

Melt the butter in a large heavy skillet. When the butter foams, add the veal, sautéing the side with the prosciutto first. Season lightly with salt and cook over high heat for about 1 minute on each side. When veal is golden on both sides, put it on a warm serving platter. Add the wine to the skillet. Stir to dissolve the meat juices on the bottom of the skillet. When the wine is reduced by half and the sauce begins to thicken, spoon the sauce over veal and serve immediately.

If you use dried sage, put it between the veal slice and the prosciutto and secure in a couple of places with wooden toothpicks so that it won't spill out.

Arrosto di Vitello al profumo di Funghi Porcini

Pan-Roasted Veal with Porcini Mushrooms

Pan roasting is traditionally Italian. The meat is first browned on all sides, generally with some seasoning; then it is cooked over very low heat with a bit of wine or broth. This technique produces tender, juicy meats. In this recipe, we have a standard veal roast that is cooked with the addition of dried wild porcini mushrooms and some of the porcini's flavorful soaking water. The result is a beautifully tasty roast.

Soak the mushrooms in 1 cup lukewarm water for 20 minutes. Drain the mushrooms and reserve the mushroom soaking water. Rinse the mushrooms to remove any sandy deposits. Strain the mushroom soaking water several times through layers of paper towels to get rid of any sandy deposits. Set aside.

In a large heavy casserole, heat the butter and oil. When the butter foams, add the veal, garlic, and rosemary. Brown on all sides over medium heat. Season with salt and pepper and add the wine. Deglaze the casserole by stirring to dissolve the meat juices attached to the bottom of the casserole. Add half the mushroom soaking water and bring to a boil. Lower the heat and cover the casserole, leaving the lid slightly askew so that the liquid will evaporate slowly. Cook the veal for 2 to 2½ hours, basting it a few times during the cooking. The veal is done when the juices run clear when the meat is pierced with a thin knife. If the sauce looks too dry, add a bit more wine during the cooking; if it is too watery, cook, uncovered, until the sauce is reduced to about ½ a cup. At this point, the roast should have a nice glazy brown color. Transfer the veal to a cutting board and let it rest for about 10 minutes. Tilt the casserole and remove some of the fat.

Put the casserole back over the heat. Add the remaining mushroom soaking water and bring to a boil. Stir and cook until the sauce reaches a medium-thick consistency.

Slice the meat and arrange on a warm platter. Taste the sauce and adjust the seasoning. Spoon the sauce over the meat and serve immediately.

Glazed Small Onions (page 255) will make this a memorable meal. Precede the roast with Cavatelli with Butter and Cheese (page 205) and end the meal with Frozen Hazelnut Zabaglione Mousse with Hot Chocolate Sauce (page 280).

Leftover broiled, boiled, or roasted meats can be minced and used to make savory meatballs with the addition of a bit of béchamel sauce (which will keep them moist), parmigiano, and ground nutmeg. They also can become delicious stuffing for pasta, or delightful meat salads.

1 ounce dried porcini mushrooms
3 tablespoons unsalted butter
1 tablespoon oil
1 3- to 3½-pound veal shoulder roast
2 garlic cloves, peeled
A few rosemary sprigs, or 1 tablespoon dried rosemary
Salt and freshly ground black pepper
1 cup dry white wine

SERVES 6 TO 8

Ossobuco ai Peperoni

Veal Shanks with Red Pepper Sauce

Good ossobuco should come from milk-fed veal, and preferably the hind shanks because they are meatier. When properly cooked, ossobuco is extremely tender and delicate, and will fall away from the bone. The best known and classic Italian preparation is the one for Ossobuco alla Milanese. There are, however, lesser known, but equally exquisite, preparations, such as the recipe below, which involves onions and sweet red peppers.

4 large sweet red peppers
4 tablespoons olive oil
2 large onions, thinly sliced
6 veal shanks, cut (by your butcher) into 2-inch-thick slices, with bone
½ cup all-purpose unbleached flour
2 tablespoons unsalted butter
1 cup dry white wine
1 chicken bouillon cube, crushed
Salt and freshly ground black pepper
1 cup canned imported Italian plum tomatoes that have been put through a food mill or sieve to remove the seeds

SERVES 6

Wash and dry the peppers. Remove the seeds and cut the peppers into medium-size strips.

Heat the oil in a heavy casserole. Add the peppers and cook over medium-high heat for 4 to 5 minutes. Add the onions and cook, stirring several times, until the onions are wilted and peppers become lightly colored. Use a slotted spoon to transfer the vegetables to a bowl.

Put the veal shanks on aluminum foil and flour them lightly on both sides. Add the butter to the casserole. When the butter foams, add the veal shanks and sauté until the meat is brown on all sides. Add the wine and cook over high heat, stirring to pick up the bits and pieces attached to the bottom of the casserole. When the wine is reduced by half, add the chicken bouillon cube and season with salt and pepper.

Return the vegetables to the casserole and add the tomatoes. Cover the casserole, leaving the lid partially askew. Simmer for 1 to 1½ hours, or until the meat falls away from the bone.

Transfer the veal to a serving platter and keep warm in the oven while you finish the sauce.

Put half of the sauce through a food mill or purée in a food processor or a blender. Return to the casserole. Raise the heat and cook until the sauce has a medium-thick consistency. Spoon the sauce over the meat and serve immediately.

This ossobuco can be served with plain boiled rice, with a butter and cheese risotto, with a few slices of polenta, or simply by itself. Make sure, however, to have enough bread in the house, because you will be scooping up every bit of this delicious red pepper sauce.

Costolette di Vitello alla Parmigiana

Veal Chops with Cheese Parma S...

In ...
the ...
pai ...
the ...
cho ...

Put ...
pou ...
geth ...
on ...
ther ...
crur ...
chop ...
coat ...
duri ...

In ...
and ...
side, ...

Ti ...
add ...
tache ...
erous ...

bread crumbs;
...den. Slivers of
...e cooked until
...hese succulent

...h-thick veal rib chops
...eggs
...d freshly ground black pepper
...easoned bread crumbs
...poons unsalted butter, or 4 table-
...s olive oil
...omemade or canned chicken broth
...y Marsala wine
...mall parmigiano slivers

...4

and return to the heat for 2 to 3 minutes longer, or until the cheese has completely melted. Serve hot.

Parma is the beautiful city in Emilia-Romagna that produces the inimitable parmigiano. It is only understandable that this cheese is vastly used in local cooking.

Quick Broiled Tomatoes (page 255) and String Bean Salad with Lemon (page 139) would complement this dish very well.

Agnello Pilottato al Forno

Roasted Leg of Lamb the Tuscan Way

The lamb in this recipe is cooked at an initial high temperature, which seals in the juices; then the heat is lowered and the meat is cooked gently and basted throughout the cooking. For medium-rare, cook for 13 to 15 minutes per pound. When in doubt, use a meat thermometer.

*1 4- to 5-pound leg of lamb with the hind
    shank bone sawed off just above the
    break joint*
*3 rosemary sprigs, or 1 tablespoon dried
    rosemary, chopped*
2 garlic cloves, finely chopped
2 ounces pancetta, sliced and diced
Salt and freshly ground black pepper
½ cup olive oil
1½ cups dry white wine

SERVES 6 TO 8

Preheat the oven to 450 degrees. Trim the leg of lamb of any excess fat.

In a small bowl, combine the rosemary, garlic, and pancetta. With a knife, make several incisions about ½ inch deep all over the lamb. Fill the incisions with the rosemary–garlic mixture and season with salt and pepper. Put the lamb in a large heavy casserole and add the oil. Roast for 10 to 15 minutes. Lower the oven temperature to 350 degrees and add 1 cup of the wine. Roast, basting several times, until the meat is cooked to your preferred doneness. Transfer the lamb to a cutting board and let rest for 10 minutes.

Remove the excess fat from the casserole. Put the casserole over high heat and add the remaining wine. Cook until the sauce has a medium-thick consistency.

Slice the meat and arrange it on a warm serving platter. Spoon the sauce over and serve immediately.

Pilottare means to make small incisions into the meat and stuff them with a mixture of fresh herbs. This procedure is widely popular in Tuscany and it is used for pork, goat, and wild boar, as well as lamb.

La Salsicce con i Broccoli e il Peperoncino

Fried Sausage with Broccoli and Hot Pepper

Years ago, after we had only been in this country for a few months, my husband and I joined some friends for a weekend in a mountain cabin in Maine. It was cold and rainy. For breakfast our first morning there, there were sausages, pancakes, bacon, waffles, and hot chocolate. I was shocked to see that people could eat all that heavy food first thing in the morning. So I stubbornly refused everything and sipped on my coffee, feeling very civilized and very European. On the second morning, following a day and a night of intense cold, rain, and snow, I was the first to sit at the breakfast table and gulp down all that wonderful food that brought some life back to my frozen cheeks.

The moral of the story is that there is a time and a place for everything. When the temperature dips we need high-calorie food, such as this robust and satisfying sausage and broccoli dish.

Remove the large stalks from the broccoli and reserve them for another use. Divide the broccoli into florets and wash thoroughly.

Bring a saucepan of water to a boil. Add 1 teaspoon of salt and the broccoli florets. Cook, uncovered, over medium heat for 5 to 7 minutes, or until the florets are tender but still a little bit firm. Drain and set aside.

Prick the sausages in several places with a fork. Put them in a large skillet with about 1 inch of water. Cook, uncovered, over medium heat for 15 to 20 minutes, turning sausage a few times while they cook. Add a bit more water if it should evaporate too quickly. At the end of the cooking time, the water should have evaporated and only the sausage fat be left in the skillet. Gently brown the sausage on all sides in this fat. Transfer the sausage to a dish.

Add the garlic and hot pepper to the skillet; add a little bit of oil, if needed. Cook and stir until the garlic begins to color. Add the broccoli and stir until well coated with the garlic and oil.

Return the sausage to the skillet. Raise the heat and add the wine. Stir gently until the wine has evaporated. Serve at once.

Serve this with the crunchy, appetizing Mamma Lea's Roasted Potatoes (page 260), a nice loaf of bread, and a good bottle of full-bodied red wine.

1½ to 2 pounds broccoli
Salt
2 pounds Italian sweet sausage
2 garlic cloves, finely chopped
A small piece hot red chile pepper, finely chopped
Olive oil
½ cup dry white wine

SERVES 4 TO 6

Stufato di Agnello con Cipolline e Carote

Lamb Stew with Small Onions and Carrots

I can't even think of stew in summertime. But just give me one cold, rainy day and a stew will probably be cooking on the back burner of my stove. Here, long, slow cooking produces tender, succulent meat with a rich, gratifying sauce. Vegetables are added for taste, substance, and color. Wine gives the stew flavor and all with a minimal amount of fuss and expense.

2½ pounds boneless lamb shoulder
¼ cup olive oil
1 small onion, finely chopped
2 garlic cloves, finely chopped
1 celery stalk, finely chopped
½ cup Marsala
2 tablespoons all-purpose unbleached flour
3 tablespoons tomato paste
1½ cups Meat Broth (page 44) or canned
  chicken broth
Salt
A generous pinch of cayenne pepper
1 tablespoon crushed juniper berries
4 carrots
1 pound small white onions
2 tablespoons chopped fresh parsley leaves

SERVES 4 TO 6

Trim all the fat from the lamb and cut the meat into 2-inch cubes.

Heat the oil in a large casserole or skillet. Add the onion, garlic, and celery and sauté for 4 to 5 minutes. Add the lamb and sauté over high heat until the lamb begins to color. Sprinkle the flour over the lamb and stir. Add the Marsala and cook over high heat until the wine has almost reduced.

Dissolve the tomato paste in the broth and add to the lamb. Season with salt and cayenne pepper. Sprinkle with the juniper berries and cover the skillet, leaving the lid slightly askew. Simmer for 1 to 1½ hours, stirring occasionally during the cooking.

While the lamb cooks, peel and slice the carrots into ½-inch-thick rounds. Boil carrots in lightly salted water until tender but still firm to the touch. Drain and set aside.

Plunge the small onions into boiling water for 20 to 30 seconds. Drain the onions and remove the skins. Bring a medium-size saucepan of water to the boil. Add salt to taste and the onions. Boil gently for 15 to 20 minutes, or until the onions are tender but firm to the touch. Drain the onions and pat dry with paper towels.

Add the onions, carrots, and parsley to the lamb. Cook, uncovered, for 5 to 10 minutes longer. At this point, the lamb should be very tender and the sauce thick and dark red in color. Season to taste.

Because I find myself dipping bread into the sauce, I generally don't feel like eating anything more after a stew. However, to end the meal and to freshen the palate, a nice Orange and Fennel Salad (page 267) would be just perfect. Polenta can also be served with the stew.

Abbacchio Brodettato

Lamb in Egg–Lemon Sauce

For this dish, fairly young lamb should be used—between the ages of six months to one year. If an older lamb is used, marinate the meat cubes in dry white wine with some bay and sage leaves for several hours, so it will lose some of its distinctive taste.

Heat the oil in a large skillet. Add the meat, prosciutto, and onion and season with salt and pepper. Brown the meat on all sides over medium heat. Sprinkle the flour over the meat and stir to incorporate it. Add the wine and cook over high heat until the wine is reduced by half. Cover the skillet and lower the heat. Simmer for 40 to 50 minutes, stirring occasionally during the cooking. Add a bit of water if the sauce becomes too dry.

In a small bowl, beat the egg yolks. Add the lemon juice, lemon rind, parsley, and marjoram and stir to blend. Add the mixture to the lamb, stirring constantly over very low heat for 1 to 2 minutes. The sauce should have a creamy consistency. Remove from the heat and taste for seasoning. Arrange the meat on a warm serving dish and serve immediately.

4 tablespoons olive oil
2½ to 3 pounds boneless shoulder lamb,
  cut into 2-inch cubes
¼ pound prosciutto, sliced and then cut
  into thin, short julienne
1 onion, thinly sliced
Salt and freshly ground black pepper
1 tablespoon all-purpose unbleached flour
1 cup dry white wine
2 large egg yolks
Juice of 1 lemon
Grated rind of 1 lemon
1 tablespoon chopped fresh parsley leaves
Pinch of dried marjoram

SERVES 6

Abbacchio is milk-fed lamb that is just 1 month old. Needless to say, it is of an unsurpassed succulence and is a favorite of the people of Rome and the Lazio region. Abbacchio is not available in this country. What is sometimes available is "hothouse" lamb—milk-fed lamb that is produced by controlled breeding and generally slaughtered at 2 to 3 months old. Most of us, however, do not come across even hothouse lamb very often, so we must content ourselves with the youngest lamb available.

Spiedini di Agnello all'Aceto Balsamico

Lamb Skewers with Balsamic Vinegar

My mother used to make spiedini in a skillet, because our "modern" oven didn't have a broiler. My sister, my brother, and I weren't very fond of lamb, so my mother would marinate the lamb for several hours in a mixture of oil, vinegar, and fresh herbs, which imparted a delicious flavor to the meat. Today, I still marinate my lamb in this way. The only difference is that sometimes I add sweet Marsala to the marinade and my spiedini are broiled or grilled rather than pan-roasted. I also brush my spiedini with a delicious, perfectly aged balsamic vinegar just before serving, and I always thread the meat alternately with some pancetta, because I like the combination of flavors.

If the meat is cut into 2-inch cubes, it will cook pretty fast, in 5 to 6 minutes; it should be golden brown on the outside and pink and juicy on the inside.

2 pounds boneless leg of lamb cut from the sirloin
½ pound pancetta, sliced
balsamic vinegar (optional)

For the Marinade
1 cup sweet Marsala, preferably Florio
¼ cup white wine vinegar
Salt and freshly ground black pepper
Several rosemary sprigs, or 1 tablespoon dried rosemary
2 garlic cloves, lightly crushed and peeled

SERVES 4 TO 6

Trim all the fat from the lamb and cut the meat into 2-inch cubes. Put the meat in a large bowl. Add all the ingredients for the marinade. Cover and refrigerate several hours.

With a slotted spoon, transfer the meat to a plate and pat dry with paper towels. Thread the lamb on skewers alternately with the pancetta.

Preheat the broiler or prepare a barbecue so that the coals are ready when you are ready to grill the meat. Broil the spiedini to your preferred doneness, about 5 minutes on each side. Remove the meat from the broiler and brush with some balsamic vinegar. Serve immediately.

Balsamic vinegar is used in this dish as a delicious condiment. If the vinegar is hard to obtain, omit it.

These spiedini can be served alongside buttered boiled rice, with a saffron risotto, with roasted potatoes, or with vegetables.

Coniglio con Pomodori e Olive

Rabbit with Tomatoes and Olives

In this preparation, the rabbit is first sautéed in oil until brown and then cooked gently in wine. Fresh or canned tomatoes and olives complete the savory sauce for this dish. For non-rabbit lovers, chicken can be substituted for the rabbit.

Wash the rabbit thoroughly under cool running water and dry well with paper towels. Rub the rabbit pieces with the rosemary and garlic and season with salt and pepper.

In a large skillet, heat the oil. Add the rabbit and sauté over medium heat until the rabbit is lightly golden on all sides. Add the wine and cook until wine is half evaporated. Cover the skillet and cook over low heat for 40 to 50 minutes, turning and basting the rabbit pieces a few times during the cooking.

Bring a small saucepan of water to a boil. Add the tomatoes and cook until the skins begin to split, 40 to 50 seconds. Transfer the tomatoes to a bowl of cold water. Peel and seed tomatoes and chop them fine. Add the tomatoes and olives to the skillet and stir to blend. Cover the skillet, leaving the lid slightly askew. Cook for 10 to 15 minutes, or until the rabbit is tender.

Transfer the rabbit pieces to a warm platter. Taste the sauce and adjust the seasoning. Spoon the sauce over rabbit and serve.

1 3- to 4-pound rabbit, cut into serving
   pieces
2 tablespoons chopped fresh rosemary
   leaves or 1 tablespoon dried rosemary
2 garlic cloves, finely chopped
¼ cup olive oil
1 cup dry white wine
Salt and freshly ground black pepper
3 to 4 juicy ripe tomatoes, or 2 cups
   canned imported Italian plum tomatoes,
   with their juice, coarsely chopped
½ cup pitted and sliced green olives

SERVES 4 TO 6

In the mountainous part of northern Italy, good stewed rabbit is generally served with steaming hot polenta.

Coniglio in Salsa Piccante

Rabbit in Piquant Sauce

Italians are essentially white-meat lovers, with chicken and veal running neck and neck in preference. Rabbit is also a favorite. The taste of a young rabbit is not unlike the taste of chicken and, when cooked properly, its meat is tender and delicate. When I was growing up in Bologna, my mother used to cook strange-looking chickens in rich, tasty sauces. Only later I learned that those special chickens were really rabbits. While for years I avoided cooking rabbits, my family in Bologna still serves and enjoys it regularly.

This is my sister Carla's favorite dish; it takes its character from the anchovy–vinegar sauce which is added to the tomatoes during the last 5 minutes of cooking.

1 3- to 4-pound rabbit, cut into serving
  pieces
3 tablespoons olive oil
2 garlic cloves, finely chopped
A few rosemary sprigs, finely chopped, or
  1 teaspoon dried rosemary
Salt and freshly ground black pepper
¾ cup dry white wine
1 cup canned imported Italian plum tomatoes that have been put through a food mill or sieve to remove the seeds
½ cup good-quality white wine vinegar
2 anchovy fillets, finely chopped
1 tablespoon chopped fresh parsley leaves
2 tablespoons rinsed and dried capers

SERVES 4

Wash the rabbit and dry it thoroughly. Heat the oil in a large skillet. Add rabbit pieces and brown on one side; then turn to brown on the other side. Add garlic and rosemary and season with salt and pepper. Cook until golden. Add the wine and cook until it has evaporated, stirring to pick up bits and pieces attached to the bottom of the skillet. Stir in the tomatoes. Cover the skillet, leaving the lid slightly askew. Cook gently for 30 to 40 minutes, stirring a few times during the cooking.

In a small saucepan, cook the vinegar over high until it is reduced to only a few tablespoons. Remove from the heat and stir in the anchovies, parsley, and capers.

Transfer the rabbit to a warm serving platter while you finish the sauce. Add vinegar–anchovy mixture to the tomato sauce. Cook over medium-high heat until the sauce has a medium-thick consistency. Spoon over rabbit and serve immediately.

As is almost always the case, chicken can be substituted for the rabbit.

If you wish to serve a first course, Cavatelli with Butter and Cheese (page 205) or Pasta and Chick-pea Soup (page 198) would be quite appropriate. Follow with a mixed green salad.

Il Coniglio della Paola

Paola's Boned Roasted Rabbit

My good friend Paola Bagnatori served this delicious roast at one of her smashing dinner parties. It was so extremely delicate and light, we all thought it was veal. She gladly gave me the recipe but warned me about the time and patience it takes to bone a whole rabbit. To bone a whole rabbit is also a job not meant for finicky people. Ask your butcher to do it.

An average rabbit weighs between 3 and 3½ pounds. After all the bones are removed, there will be about 2 pounds of meat left. This will give you a small, skimpy roast. So I use 2 boned rabbits, overlap them slightly, stuff them with prosciutto and cheese, and secure them tightly with string. This roast is wonderful when served hot, and equally delicious served at room temperature.

Put the boned rabbit between two large pieces of wax paper and pound lightly to flatten the rabbit evenly. Put the rabbits on a board slightly overlapping each other. Spread a mixture of the garlic and rosemary over the rabbit and season with salt and pepper. Cover the rabbit with the prosciutto slices and sprinkle the parmigiano over the prosciutto. Starting from the neck side, roll up the rabbit and tie the roll securely with kitchen string.

Choose a casserole into which the roast will fit tightly. Heat the oil and butter in the casserole. When the butter foams, add the rabbit. Brown on all sides over low heat. Add the onion and cook until the onion begins to color. Add ½ cup of the wine. Stir and cook until the wine has evaporated. Stir in the remaining wine and the crushed bouillon cube. Cover the casserole, leaving the lid slightly askew. Cook over very low heat for 1 to 1½ hours, depending on the size and thickness of the roast, basting several times during the cooking. Add more wine if the sauce should dry out.

Remove the roast to a cutting board and let it rest for 10 minutes. Raise the heat under the casserole and add the brandy. Stir and cook until the sauce has a medium-thick consistency.

Cut the roast into thin slices and arrange them on a serving dish. Spoon the sauce over the slices and serve.

2 whole boned rabbits, about 2 to 2½ pounds each
1 garlic clove, finely chopped
1 tablespoon fresh rosemary leaves, finely chopped, or 1 teaspoon dried rosemary
Salt and freshly ground black pepper
¼ pounds prosciutto, thinly sliced
⅓ cup freshly grated parmigiano
2 tablespoons olive oil
3 tablespoons unsalted butter
1 onion, thinly sliced
1½ cups dry white wine
1 chicken bouillon cube, crushed
A splash of brandy (about ⅓ cup)

SERVES 6 TO 8

Le Quaglie in Tegame con la Polenta

Quails and Polenta in a Savory Tomato Sauce

Quails and polenta are a time-honored combination—a classic, like apple pie and ice cream in this country. Tender quails that are cooked in a savory tomato–wine sauce are simply divine over a few slices of hot polenta. Here, the polenta is cooked with broth instead of water, which imparts additional flavor. A wonderful winter dish that begs to be shared.

For the Polenta

9 cups Homemade Chicken Broth (page 45), or 4½ cups canned chicken broth mixed with 4½ cups water

Salt

1½ cups coarsely ground cornmeal

1½ cups finely ground cornmeal

For the Quails

8 quails

Salt and freshly ground black pepper

1 28-ounce can imported Italian plum tomatoes

4 tablespoons unsalted butter

¼ pound pancetta, sliced and then cut into small pieces

1 cup dry Marsala

SERVES 4

Prepare the polenta following the instructions on page 210. Cut the polenta into slices and place in a buttered baking dish. Cover the dish with aluminum foil and keep warm in the oven while you prepare the quails.

Wash the quails and dry them well with paper towels. Season the inside of each bird with salt and pepper.

Put the tomatoes through a food mill or sieve to remove the seeds.

Melt the butter in a large skillet. When the butter foams, add the pancetta and quails, making sure that the quails fit comfortably into the skillet. Sauté over medium heat for 5 to 6 minutes, turning gently to brown on all sides.

Stir in the Marsala. When the wine is reduced by half, add the tomatoes and season with salt and pepper. Cover the skillet and cook for 8 to 10 minutes longer, basting the quails a few times during the cooking. Taste and adjust the seasoning.

Place 2 slices of polenta on individual warm serving dishes. Place 2 quails over each serving and spoon the sauce over. Serve immediately.

Good wine, such as a Dolcetto d'Asti or a Barbera d'Asti, would be perfect with this dish.

Freshly made polenta has a texture and taste all its own, but it is often hard to prepare at the last moment. The polenta can be prepared in the morning and kept, sliced, in a buttered baking dish. Before serving, dot with some butter and warm in the oven; of course, the polenta can also be broiled.

Pollo in Umido alla Romana

Chicken with Peppers and Tomatoes the Roman Way

For this preparation, use red and, if possible, yellow peppers. Their sweetness will impart a special flavor to the chicken. When I cook this dish, I generally double the amount of peppers, so that I can use any leftover sauce over pasta or rice the next day.

Press the tomatoes through a food mill or sieve to remove the seeds. Wash and dry the chicken pieces thoroughly. Heat the oil in a large casserole or skillet and add the garlic. When the garlic turns brown, discard it. Add the chicken and brown it on all sides over medium heat.

While the chicken is browning, wash the peppers and remove the seeds. Cut the peppers into medium strips and add them to the chicken. Cook the peppers and chicken for 3 to 5 minutes, stirring; then add the wine. When the wine has reduced by half, add the tomatoes and season with salt and pepper. Cover the casserole and cook over low heat for 35 to 45 minutes, stirring occasionally.

Transfer the chicken to a warm serving platter and keep it warm in the oven, if necessary. If the sauce is too thin, boil it down, uncovered, over high heat, until the sauce has a medium-thick consistency. Spoon the sauce and peppers over the chicken and serve hot.

Chicken with peppers is a classic of the Roman table that is perfect for today's busy life-style. Chicken cooks fast, is low in calories and inexpensive.

2 cups canned imported Italian plum tomatoes with their juices
1 3- to 3½-pound frying chicken, cut into serving pieces
3 tablespoons olive oil
2 garlic cloves
3 large sweet red, yellow, or green bell peppers
½ cup dry white wine
Salt and freshly ground black pepper

SERVES 4

Costolette di Pollo al Vermouth

Chicken Breasts with Vermouth Sauce

Tasty, easy, economical, and fast, these are the prerequisites of this simple dish which time after time receives raves from my family.

1½ cups dry unseasoned bread crumbs
⅓ cup freshly grated parmigiano
2 large eggs
Salt and freshly ground black pepper
3 whole chicken breasts, skinned, boned, and split
3 tablespoons unsalted butter
1 tablespoon olive oil
¾ cup sweet red vermouth
¼ cup heavy cream

SERVES 6

Combine the bread crumbs and parmigiano in a medium-size bowl. Beat the eggs and salt and pepper together in a shallow dish. Dip the chicken breasts into the eggs and then coat them with the bread crumb mixture. Lightly press the crumbs onto the meat with the palm of your hand. Put the chicken on a large plate and refrigerate for at least 30 minutes. This step can be completed several hours ahead.

In a large heavy skillet, heat the butter with the oil. When the butter foams, add the chicken and cook over medium heat for 2 to 3 minutes on each side, or until the chicken has a nice, golden color. Add the vermouth to the skillet, cover, and lower the heat. Simmer for 10 to 12 minutes. At the end of cooking time only a few tablespoons of sauce should be left in the skillet.

Transfer the chicken to individual warm serving dishes. Raise the heat under the skillet and add the cream. Stir and cook briefly, just until thick. Spoon the sauce over the chicken and serve.

Good accompaniments for this would be Glazed Small Onions (page 255) and Mamma Lea's Roasted Potatoes (page 260). A nice soup, such as Taglioline in Broth (page 196), could precede this dish.

Let me show you how far a few *chicken breasts* can go. Bone the chicken breasts. With the meat of the breasts prepare lovely chicken cutlets as above. Save all the bones and freeze them. When you have enough chicken bones (and perhaps a few other scraps of meats and bones) prepare a Basic Meat Broth (page 44) in which you can cook some homemade or store-bought taglioline (see Taglioline in Broth, page 196). Now, before you throw away all the bones that have produced the broth, make sure to remove all the attached meat to make a banquet for your pets. Seldom can so little stretch so far.

Seafood

Baccalà Dorato

Fried Cod Roman Style

In Lazio and Rome, this dish is made with Baccalà, dried salted cod. Baccalà is often available in Italian markets in this country, but I choose to make this dish with fresh cod, because I prefer its milder taste.

This is a simple, and yet delicious, dish to prepare. Marinate the fish for 1 hour before dinner and also prepare the batter ahead of time. However, fry the fish at the last moment.

Combine all the ingredients for the marinade, except the fish, in a large bowl. Wash and dry the fish thoroughly with paper towels; then cut the fish into 1½- to 2-inch pieces and add to the marinade. Mix well. Cover the bowl and let stand for about 1 hour.

Prepare the batter. Beat the egg yolks and salt in a medium-size bowl. Beat in the cream. Add the flour slowly, beating to incorporate it. The batter should be thick and smooth and have the consistency of lightly whipped cream. Set aside for 1 hour. When you are ready to fry the fish, beat the egg whites until thick and fold them into the batter.

Line a large platter with paper towels. Preheat the oven to 200 degrees for about 10 minutes; then turn the heat off.

Pat the fish dry with paper towels. Pour 2 inches of oil into a deep skillet and heat the oil. Dip several pieces of fish into the batter. Lift each piece of fish from the batter with 2 forks and allow the excess batter to drip off. Fry the fish a few pieces at a time until golden on all sides, 4 to 5 minutes.

Remove the fish from the oil with a slotted spoon and place on the paper towel–lined platter to drain. Put the platter in the warm oven while you fry the rest of the fish.

When all the fish is done, remove the paper towels, sprinkle the fish lightly with salt, and serve with the lemon wedges.

For the Marinade
3 to 4 tablespoons olive oil
Juice of 1 large lemon
¼ cup fresh oregano leaves, if available
Freshly ground white pepper
2 pounds boneless and skinless fresh cod

For the Batter
2 large eggs, separated and at room temperature
Pinch of salt
2 cups heavy cream, milk, or beer
1½ cups all-purpose unbleached flour

To Complete the Dish
Oil for frying
Salt to taste
Lemon wedges

SERVES 4 TO 6

Any firm-fleshed fish can be prepared in this manner.

Some vegetables sautéed quickly in butter and a nice green salad would complement this dish quite well.

Filetti di Trota a Vapore

Steamed Trout Fillets

When I arrived in Bologna one year for my annual visit, I was surprised to see that my sister-in-law, Emma, had lost twenty pounds, and that my brother, Gianni, had also lost weight. After years of promises never fulfilled, they both decided to tackle the task of reducing—together. When I asked them what kind of crash diet they had adopted, they answered, none. They had simply decided to reduce their intake of fats; in Bologna that generally means butter and cream. Pasta was still eaten daily, but in smaller portions and with mostly fresh tomatoes or vegetable sauces. White meats and fish were eaten in abundance, especially grilled, poached, or steamed. Vegetables were also steamed or eaten raw. With a bit of willpower and good common sense they both managed to lose weight and still eat well.

One night Emma prepared an antipasto of fillet of trout. It was so delicious that I have made it many times since.

You can use either cut-up fish fillet or, if you wish, buy a whole fish and fillet it yourself. The best fish to use for the dish are trout, salmon trout, and small sole fillets. If you are using boneless trout, remove the head and tail. It is up to you whether you want to leave the skin on or not. This dish can be done either by steaming or by placing the fish fillet in a wrapping of aluminum foil and baking it. Either way, the fish fillet retains moisture and taste.

2 medium-size trout
Salt and freshly ground black pepper
2 tablespoons chopped fresh parsley leaves
1 garlic clove, finely chopped
2 tablespoons rinsed and dried capers
2 tablespoons olive oil
Juice of 1 lemon

SERVES 4

Wash and dry the fish thoroughly. If you are using fish fillets, put them in an ovenproof dish. If you are using whole trout, cut off heads and tails.

Starting from the head side, slice the fish through the entire backbone. Insert the blade of the knife below the top part of the fillet and above the backbone. Keep the knife parallel to the ribs and cut with short strokes all the way to the tail. When the top part of the fish is detached, lift the backbone with your hands and, starting at the head end, slice away in short strokes to remove the bone from the lower fillet.

Put the fillets in an ovenproof dish, slightly overlapping each other. Sprinkle with salt. Cover the dish completely with aluminum foil. Put the dish in a preheated 350-degree oven or on top of a large pot of simmering water and cook for 12 to 15 minutes, depending on the thickness of the fish.

Remove the dish from the oven or from the pot and cool for about 1 hour. Remove the aluminum foil and transfer the fillets gently to a serving platter. Season with salt and pepper and sprinkle with the parsley, garlic, and capers. Add the olive oil and lemon juice, cover with aluminum foil, and refrigerate for 1 hour, or until the fish is completely cooled. Serve chilled as an appetizer.

Of all the methods of cooking, steaming is still the least fashionable in Italy. It is, however, picking up, especially among those people who, for health reasons, have to reduce their intake of fats, or for those who have a renewed interest in food that retains most of its nutritive elements.

Zuppa di Cozze Piccanti

Spicy Mussel Soup

My memory goes back to a mussel soup still fragrant with sea odor, and as spicy as anything I had ever had in my life, which I had in Pugnochiuso, a small seaside town of Puglia. Everything was remarkable: the simplicity of the preparation, the freshness of the ingredients, and the spiciness of the tomatoes.

This is a simple dish to reproduce, provided you can get very fresh mussels; you can decide for yourself on the degree of spiciness. Remember, you can always add a little more hot pepper, but you can't take it out once it's in.

For the Mussels

5 pounds mussels
1 tablespoon olive oil
1 cup dry white wine

For the Sauce

1 28-ounce can imported Italian plum to-
   matoes with their juices
¼ cup olive oil
3 garlic cloves, finely chopped
3 anchovy fillets, chopped
A small piece of red hot chile pepper,
   finely chopped
Salt
2 tablespoons chopped fresh parsley leaves
8 slices Italian bread, broiled or toasted

SERVES 4 AS A MAIN COURSE

Soak the mussels in cool salted water for 20 minutes; remove the beards and scrub the mussels under cool running water thoroughly. Put the mussels in a large saucepan; add oil, wine, and 1 cup of water. Cook over high heat until the mussels open. Remove the mussels with a slotted spoon to a bowl as they open and discard any that won't open during the cooking. Bring the cooking liquid back to a boil and cook until it is reduced to about 1 cup. Strain the liquid through paper towels to remove any sandy deposit. Set aside. Remove half of the mussel meat from the shells and leave the other half in the shells.

Put the tomatoes through a food mill to remove the seeds. Wipe the saucepan in which the mussels were cooked with paper towels. Heat the oil in the cleaned saucepan. Add the garlic, anchovies, and chile pepper and sauté gently for 1 to 2 minutes. Before the garlic turns brown, add the reserved mussel cooking liquid and strained tomatoes. Season with salt. Cook, uncovered, over medium heat for 10 to 12 minutes. The sauce should have a medium-thick consistency. Add the mussel meat and mussels in their shells and sprinkle with parsley. Mix and cook for about 1 minute, or until everything is completely coated with the sauce. Serve with slices of broiled or toasted Italian bread.

The food of southern Italy is alive with color and taste; the pleasure of eating here is directly related to the impact of eye appeal. Nothing is bland or uncertain. The cooking of the South is done with a steady and secure hand.

Seafood soups, or leftover mussels or clams, can be served over pasta.

Pesce Spada alla Siciliana

Swordfish Sicilian Style

Fish is an extremely important element in the Sicilian diet, and the fine Sicilian swordfish is one of the best. This recipe embodies the simplicity and creativity of Sicilian cooking. Sometimes, when I cook this dish, I increase a bit the ingredients for the zesty sauce to use another time over a plate of linguine or spaghetti.

2 cups canned imported Italian plum tomatoes with their juices
½ cup all-purpose unbleached flour
2 pounds swordfish steaks, cut about ¾
   inch thick
4 tablespoons olive oil
1 small onion, thinly sliced
2 garlic cloves, finely chopped
4 anchovy fillets, chopped
1 cup dry white wine
Salt
Pinch of cayenne pepper
½ cup black olives, cut into halves
1 tablespoon rinsed and dried capers
1 tablespoon chopped fresh parsley leaves

SERVES 4

Press the tomatoes through a food mill or sieve to remove seeds. Set aside.

Spread the flour on a piece of aluminum foil. Coat fish lightly with the flour. Heat the oil in a large skillet. Add the fish and cook over medium heat for 2 to 3 minutes on each side, or until the fish is lightly browned. Transfer the fish to a plate.

Add the onion to skillet and sauté over medium heat until the onion is pale yellow, 4 to 5 minutes. Add the garlic and anchovies and stir to blend with the onion. Cook 1 minute longer. Add the wine and stir to pick up the bits and pieces attached to skillet. When the wine has evaporated, add the strained tomatoes. Season with salt and cayenne pepper and cook the sauce over low heat, uncovered, for 8 to 10 minutes.

Return the fish to the skillet and add the black olives and capers. Cover the skillet and cook for 5 minutes longer over low heat. Stir in the parsley. Serve the fish topped by a few tablespoons of its own sauce.

Frittatas

Frittata di Pasta

Pasta Frittata

Necessity is the mother of invention. When times were lean, Italians would rely on imagination for variety in the kitchen. Humble meats became succulent stews. Leftover boiled or roasted meats would turn into appetizing salads. Beans and lentil soups would feed a family for days and leftover pasta could always be turned into a savory frittata. Then Italy prospered and became an affluent, modern nation. Yet many of these dishes, born out of need, remained. Why? Because they were good.

Today, modern women find that many of these dishes save them time as well as money. My sister-in-law in Bologna has a demanding job in a small fashion company. Her time is precious, so she plans her menus carefully. When she cooks pasta she often doubles the amount so that the leftover pasta can be quickly turned into a frittata for another meal.

Almost any pasta dressed with any sauce can become a frittata, with the possible exception of cream sauces, as they become quite dry and sticky. Any cooked pasta that doesn't have a sauce can be sautéed briefly with some oil, garlic, and fresh herbs and then added to the eggs.

6 large eggs
½ cup freshly grated parmigiano
Salt and freshly ground black pepper
2 tablespoons olive oil, or 2 tablespoons unsalted butter
2 to 3 cups leftover cooked pasta

SERVES 4

Beat the eggs, cheese, and salt and pepper together in a bowl.

In a medium-size skillet, heat the oil. Add the pasta and cook over medium heat until the pasta is thoroughly warmed. Add the pasta to the egg mixture and mix to combine.

Add a bit more oil to the skillet, if necessary, and heat again. Add egg–pasta mixture and cook for 7 to 8 minutes, or until the bottom of the frittata is lightly golden and the top begins to solidify.

Put a plate over the skillet and quickly invert the frittata onto the plate. Slide the frittata back into the skillet to cook the other side. Cook for 4 to 5 minutes longer. Serve warm or at room temperature.

This may not be the greatest culinary invention of our times, but it is a tasty way to use that wonderful pasta you made yesterday.

Frittata di Spinaci

Spinach Frittata

1 pound fresh spinach, or 1 10-ounce package frozen leaf spinach
4 tablespoons unsalted butter
½ cup heavy cream
6 large eggs
Salt and freshly ground black pepper
½ cup freshly grated parmigiano

SERVES 4

If you are using fresh spinach discard the stems and any bruised leaves. Wash the spinach thoroughly under cool running water. Put the spinach in a large saucepan and cook with only the water that clings to the leaves. When the spinach is tender, 7 to 8 minutes, drain and then squeeze out any excess water. If you are using frozen spinach, cook it according to the package directions. Drain and squeeze out any excess water.

Melt the butter in a heavy 8- or 10-inch skillet. When the butter foams, add the spinach and cream. Cook over medium heat for 2 to 3 minutes, or until the cream is reduced and no more moisture is left in the skillet.

In a medium-size bowl, beat the eggs, salt and pepper, and parmigiano together. Add the contents of the skillet to the egg mixture and stir quickly to incorporate.

Add a bit more butter to the skillet, if necessary. When the butter foams, add the egg mixture and cook over medium heat for 7 to 8 minutes, or until the bottom of the frittata is lightly browned and the top begins to solidify. Put a large plate over the skillet and turn the frittata onto the plate. Slide the fritatta into the skillet to cook the other side. Cook for 4 to 5 minutes longer. Slide the frittata onto a serving dish, cut into wedges, and serve.

Frittata di Cipolle

Onion Frittata

This is, perhaps, the most common and, in my opinion, the best-tasting of all frittatas. The onions are sautéed slowly in oil until they are thoroughly wilted and have lost all of their "bite." The eggs and onions are then combined with grated parmigiano into a savory frittata.

Cold leftover frittata can make a tasty, delicious sandwich.

Heat the oil in a heavy 8- or 10-inch skillet. Add onions and sauté over low heat until the onions are pale yellow and wilted, about 10 to 15 minutes.

In a medium-size bowl, beat the eggs, cheese, and salt and pepper together. Remove the onions from the skillet with a slotted spoon and stir them into the egg mixture.

Add a few drops of oil to the skillet, if necessary. When the oil is hot, add the egg mixture. Cook over medium heat for 7 to 8 minutes, or until the bottom of the frittata is lightly browned and the top begins to solidify. Put a large plate over the skillet and turn frittata onto plate. Slide it back into the skillet to cook on the other side. Cook for 4 to 5 minutes longer. Slide frittata onto a serving dish. Cut into wedges and serve.

3 tablespoons olive oil
2 large onions, thinly sliced
6 large eggs
½ cup freshly grated parmigiano
Salt and freshly ground black pepper

SERVES 4

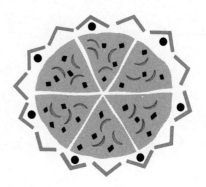

For a variation, take 4 ounces of diced pancetta and sauté it until golden. Drain on paper towels and add it to the beaten eggs when you add the wilted onions. Cook as instructed above.

Vegetables

Cavolfiore al Forno con le Cipolle

Baked Cauliflower with Onions and Cheese

Gratinéed vegetables can accompany virtually any dish. They are perfect for roasts, broiled meats, or fowl. Select a firm, compact head of cauliflower without bruises or discoloration. Boil or steam your cauliflower ahead of time and pop it in the oven just before serving.

Remove all the leaves from the cauliflower and detach the florets. Wash the florets under cool running water. Boil or steam the florets until tender but still firm to the touch.

Preheat the oven to 375 degrees. Butter a baking dish.

Melt the butter in a medium-size skillet. When the butter foams, add the onions and sauté over medium heat until the onions turn pale yellow. Add the parsley and cauliflower and season with salt and pepper. Cook and stir for about 1 minute.

Transfer the cauliflower to the baking dish. Sprinkle generously with the parmigiano and bake for 10 to 15 minutes. Serve hot.

To preserve the color of white vegetables, add some white wine vinegar to the cooking water.

1 2½- to 3-pound cauliflower
3 tablespoons unsalted butter
2 onions, thinly sliced
2 tablespoons chopped fresh parsley leaves
Salt and freshly ground black pepper
¾ cup freshly grated parmigiano

SERVES 8

Sedani al Forno Gratinati

Baked Celery with Butter and Cheese

Celery, with its mild delicate flavor, is a wonderful vegetable, vital to many stews, soups, and braised meat dishes, and its crunchiness is essential to many salads.

In this recipe, the celery is first boiled and then baked with butter and cheese. It makes a perfect accompaniment to Fast Stuffed Veal Bundles (page 227) or Veal Shank with Red Pepper Sauce (page 230).

2 large fresh heads celery
Juice of ½ lemon
1 teaspoon salt
1 cup freshly grated parmigiano
3 tablespoons unsalted butter
½ cup heavy cream

SERVES 8

Cut off the top leafy part of each celery head and reserve for soups or salads. Remove the outer bruised, tough leaves and reserve for another use. Cut the celery in half lengthwise and then cut into quarters. Remove the small tender leaves inside the celery. Wash celery under cold running water.

Bring a large pot of water to a boil. Add the lemon juice, salt, and celery and cook, uncovered, over medium heat for 25 to 35 minutes, depending on the size of the celery, or until the celery is tender but still firm to the touch. Drain and pat dry with paper towels.

Preheat the oven to 400 degrees. Butter a baking dish. Arrange the celery in the baking dish, cut parts up. Sprinkle generously with the parmigiano and dot with the butter. Pour the cream over the celery. Bake for 15 to 20 minutes, or until the cheese is completely melted.

Cipolline Glassate

Glazed Small Onions

This is a lovely accompaniment to most roasted meats or fowl. The onions can be prepared early in the morning and sautéed and glazed at the last moment. If fresh small onions are unavailable use small frozen onions.

Cut a cross at the root end of each onion. Bring a medium-size saucepan of water to a boil. Add the onions and cook for about 1 minute. Drain the onions and rinse under cool running water. Peel the onions and cut off the dangling tails. (The onion's skin will come off very easily after the quick boiling.)

Melt the butter in a large skillet. Add the onions and 2 cups of water. Cover the skillet and cook over medium heat for 20 to 25 minutes. Add more water, if needed. Remove the cover and add the sugar and season lightly with salt. Cook, stirring, until the onions are golden and glazed and can easily be pierced by a fork. Serve hot.

2 pounds small white boiling onions
3 to 4 tablespoons unsalted butter
2 tablespoons sugar
Salt

SERVES 4 TO 6

Pomodori Grigliati

Quick Broiled Tomatoes

This quick, delicious way to cook tomatoes makes a perfect accompaniment to a lamb roast or broiled skewered meat or fish.

Wash and dry the tomatoes. Cut them in half and remove the seeds. Put tomatoes, cut side down, on paper towels for 5 minutes to drain off any excess juices.

Preheat the broiler. Sprinkle the cut sides of the tomatoes with the basil, garlic, and parmigiano. Season with salt and pepper. Put the tomatoes on a broiler rack and broil 3 to 4 inches from the heat source for 4 to 5 minutes, or until the tops begin to brown and the skin begins to wrinkle.

4 firm ripe tomatoes
3 tablespoons chopped fresh basil or
*   chopped fresh parsley leaves*
2 garlic cloves, finely chopped
⅓ cup freshly grated parmigiano
Salt and freshly ground black pepper

SERVES 4

Radicchio Rosso alla Griglia

Grilled Red Chicory

Radicchio is a purplish-red, slightly bitter type of chicory that is typical of Treviso in the Veneto region in Italy; it is commonly called "Il Radicchio di Treviso."

Until recently radicchio was unknown in this country, except to a few well-traveled gourmands, but today it is not hard to find. It is available, imported from Italy, though the price is prohibitive and the quality, not always the very best. When selecting radicchio, make sure the head is compact and firm, with crisp leaves. Nevertheless, radicchio has also become very stylish. Suddenly, no good Italian restaurant can afford to be without radicchio, and where would the New American Cuisine be without radicchio?

This red chicory can be used simply in a salad by itself, or mixed with a variety of other lettuces. But it is a real treat when the radicchio is quartered, dressed with good virgin olive oil and salt and pepper, and grilled. Because most of us do not have indoor grills, this recipe is for broiling the radicchio rather than grilling it, but, of course, you can always grill radicchio outdoors over a charcoal fire.

Whatever method you choose, turn the radicchio so it becomes tender on both sides without burning.

1 head radicchio rosso, about 1 pound
Salt and freshly ground black pepper
⅓ cup olive oil, preferably virgin olive oil
1 tablespoon red wine vinegar (optional)

SERVES 4

Preheat the broiler. Discard the bruised outer leaves of the radicchio. Cut the radicchio in half lengthwise and then cut into quarters. Wash and dry each quarter thoroughly. Put the radicchio on a broiler pan and season with salt and pepper and a few drops of olive oil. Put the pan under the broiler about 5 inches from the heat source. When the radicchio begins to darken in color and becomes slightly soft, turn it to broil on the other side.

Serve with an additional sprinkling of oil and a few drops of vinegar, if you wish. Serve as an antipasto (but without the vinegar), as a side dish to any grilled meat, fish, or fowl, or instead of a salad.

Melanzane Dorate

Fried Eggplants

So often my students marvel at the simplicity of so many of the dishes I teach them. "How come we didn't think of this before?" they ask. Perhaps it's because the obvious is not always noticeable.

This dish is from southern Italy, where eggplants are particularly appreciated and are very often eaten in lieu of meat. The eggplants are sliced and seasoned with salt to draw out their bitter juices. Then they are sprinkled with flour, dipped in eggs, and fried until golden and crisp. The result is a crunchy dish that goes hand in hand with a lamb or pork roast.

Wash and dry the eggplants thoroughly. Trim off the ends but do not peel them. Slice the eggplants horizontally into disks about ⅛ inch thick. Put the slices on a large platter or baking sheet, sprinkle with salt, and let stand for about 1 hour to drain. Pat the slices dry with paper towels.

In a deep plate or small bowl beat the eggs and a pinch of salt together. Spread the flour on a piece of aluminum foil. Pour 2 inches of oil into a medium-size skillet. When the oil is hot, coat the eggplant slices lightly with flour and dip them into the beaten eggs. Fry the slices a few at a time until they are golden on both sides.

Remove the slices with a slotted spoon and drain on paper towels. Arrange the slices on a warm serving platter, season lightly with salt, and serve piping hot.

2 medium-size firm eggplants
Salt
2 large eggs
1 cup all-purpose unbleached flour
Oil for frying

Serves 6 to 8

Eggplant is delicious between two slices of bread. When I don't feel like having a salad for lunch and I have had enough fruit and cheese, I enjoy a vegetable sandwich. Fried eggplant or roasted peppers (page 59) make very tasty sandwiches.

Finocchi Dorati col Parmigiano

Fried Fennel with Parmigiano

In this recipe, the finocchio is first parboiled and then coated with bread crumbs and parmigiano and then fried until golden and crisp. If you can stop eating it as you cook it, you might want to serve fried fennel with any roasts of your liking.

4 medium-size heads of fennel
2½ cups dry unseasoned bread crumbs
¾ cup freshly grated parmigiano
2 large eggs
Salt
Vegetable oil

SERVES 6 TO 8

Trim off the long stalks from the fennel and remove any outer tough or bruised leaves; cut the fennel into thin slices about ½ inch thick. Put the slices in a large skillet and cover with water. Bring to a boil and cook over medium heat until tender but still firm to the touch, about 7 to 8 minutes. With a slotted spoon transfer the fennel to paper towels to dry. Cool completely.

In a bowl, combine bread crumbs and parmigiano. Beat the eggs and a pinch of salt in a shallow dish. Dip the fennel slices into the eggs and then into the bread crumb mixture. Press the mixture onto the fennel gently with the palm of your hand. Let stand for 15 to 20 minutes.

Pour 1 inch of oil into a large skillet and heat. Add the fennel slices and cook until they are golden brown on all sides. Drain on paper towels, season with salt, and serve piping hot.

Finocchio is a favorite vegetable among Italians and it is becoming more and more popular in this country. Fennel can be served raw by itself or mixed into salads, or it can be cooked in a variety of ways. Its delicious anise taste becomes milder when it is cooked and paired with other ingredients.

Cipolle al Forno Ripiene

Stuffed Baked Onions

Sometimes we take common vegetables for granted. The humble onion can become a real treat when prepared with a little bit of respect. Sweet or yellow onions (Bermuda or Spanish onions) are best for this preparation.

Slice off the ends of the onions and then peel the onions. Bring a large saucepan of water to a boil. Add the onions and cook, uncovered, over medium heat for 7 to 8 minutes, or until the onions are barely tender to the touch. Drain the onions and dry them with paper towels. Let the onions cool.

Preheat the oven to 375 degrees. Slice off the tops of the onions and set these slices aside. Using a sharp knife, remove the inner part of the onions. Chop inner parts as well as reserved slices. Put the chopped onions in a medium-size bowl. Add the cheese, 1 tablespoon of oil, nutmeg, and egg yolk. Season with salt and several grindings of pepper. Fill each onion with some of this mixture and dribble a bit of olive oil over the onions.

Pour 2 or 3 tablespoons of oil into a baking dish and put the stuffed onions in the dish. Bake for 15 to 20 minutes, or until the onions are lightly golden and are easily pierced with the tip of a thin knife. Serve hot.

6 medium-size sweet yellow onions
½ cup freshly grated Pecorino or parmigiano
Olive oil
1 teaspoon ground nutmeg
1 large egg yolk
Salt and freshly ground black pepper

SERVES 6

These tasty onions would be great with Roasted Leg of Lamb the Tuscan Way (page 232) or with Roasted Leg of Pork Marinated in Beer (page 224). Then again, they would also be perfect with Skewers of Mixed Broiled Meats (page 220).

Le Patate di Mamma Lea

Mamma Lea's Roasted Potatoes

Mamma Lea, the mother of my friend Milena, makes roasted potatoes better than anybody I know. These tasty, crunchy, aromatic potatoes are great next to any roasted meat or fowl.

1½ pounds boiling potatoes
4 tablespoons olive oil
1 tablespoon unsalted butter
Salt
A few rosemary or sage sprigs, or 1 tablespoon chopped dried rosemary
2 garlic cloves, finely chopped
2 to 3 ounces pancetta, sliced and then cut
  into small strips

SERVES 4 TO 6

Preheat the oven to 350 degrees.

Peel the potatoes and cut them into medium chunks. Put the potatoes into a large baking dish with the oil and butter. Season with salt and stir with a spoon until the potatoes are well coated with the oil. Bake for 15 to 20 minutes.

Add the rosemary, garlic, and pancetta and mix well. Bake for 15 to 20 minutes longer, or until the potatoes are golden in color. Serve hot.

Peperoni Arrosto Ripieni

Roasted Stuffed Peppers

Tasty ingredients with contrasting tastes are blended together and used to stuff sweet, meaty, red or yellow peppers. These delicious bundles can be prepared ahead of time and baked at the last moment. They can be served as an appetizer or as a light entrée. They are equally good warm or at room temperature.

Roast the peppers according to the directions on page 59.

Meanwhile, prepare the stuffing. Soak the raisins in water for 15 minutes. Drain the raisins and pat dry with paper towels. Put the raisins, pine nuts, capers, anchovies, bread, parsley, 3 tablespoons of the olive oil, and salt and pepper to taste in a food processor. Turn the machine on and off, only until the mixture is coarsely chopped. Do not purée.

Peel the peppers and open them flat, trying not to break them. Remove the seeds. Spread some stuffing on the inside part of each pepper. Roll the peppers up into loose bundles. Preheat the oven to 350 degrees. Place the bundles in a baking dish and sprinkle lightly with the remaining tablespoons of oil. Bake for 15 minutes. Serve hot or at room temperature.

8 large sweet red or yellow peppers
2 tablespoons golden raisins
2 tablespoons pine nuts
2 tablespoons capers, rinsed and dried
2 anchovy fillets
1 slice of white bread, crust removed
Several parsley sprigs
5 tablespoons olive oil
Salt and freshly ground black pepper

SERVES 4

Patate Fritte con la Cipolla

Fried Potatoes with Onions

Some of the memories from my childhood and adolescence in Italy are still so clear in my mind that it seems it all happened yesterday: a small, pleasant farm in the outskirts of Bologna; a loving aunt who would prepare delicious country food each time I went to visit her; loaves of bread still warm from the oven; country salamis and fresh cheese; trees heavy with ripe fruit.

My aunt would serve these wonderful potatoes after the soup, as a separate course, because meat was too expensive and the chickens were needed to provide eggs.

I generally parboil my potatoes ahead of time and fry them at the last moment, so that the potatoes and onions cook evenly.

5 medium-size potatoes
2 tablespoons unsalted butter
2 tablespoons olive oil
2 onions, thinly sliced
1 tablespoon chopped fresh parsley leaves
Salt

Serves 4 to 6

Peel and cut the potatoes into ½-inch-thick slices. Fill a large skillet halfway with water. Bring the water to a boil. Add the potatoes and boil for about 1 minute. Drain and dry thoroughly. Pour out the water and wipe the skillet dry with paper towels.

Put the butter and oil in the skillet and put it over medium heat. When the butter foams, add the potatoes and onions. Cook, uncovered, stirring, until the potatoes and onions are golden in color. Stir in the parsley, season with salt, and serve immediately.

Potatoes that have been peeled, sliced, and precooked briefly in boiling water can be kept in the refrigerator without spoiling or changing color for a few days. They will be ready on short notice to be sautéed or roasted quickly with some oil, garlic, and rosemary.

Zucchine in Agrodolce

Sweet and Sour Zucchini

In this dish, zucchini are quickly sautéed in a bit of oil until they are barely tender; then vinegar, raisins, sugar, and pine nuts are added and everything is cooked, over high heat for a short time.

Soak the raisins in 2 cups of warm water for 30 minutes. Drain and pat dry with paper towels.

Wash and dry the zucchini thoroughly. Cut off the ends and slice the zucchini into medium-size sticks, approximately 3 inches long and ½ inch wide.

Heat the oil in a large skillet. Add enough zucchini to fit comfortably into the skillet in a single layer. Do not overcrowd. Sauté over high heat until the zucchini begin to color. Using a slotted spoon, transfer the zucchini to paper towels. Repeat with whatever zucchini is left.

When all zucchini have been sautéed, return them to the skillet. Add the vinegar and stir. Add the raisins, pine nuts, and sugar and season lightly with salt. Stir and cook over high heat until the vinegar has evaporated, about 1 minute. Taste and adjust the seasoning. Serve hot.

½ cup golden raisins
4 medium-size zucchini
3 tablespoons olive oil
2 tablespoons red wine vinegar
⅓ cup pine nuts
1 teaspoon sugar
Salt

SERVES 4

I do not always like vegetables that are too crunchy or undercooked. The mania for crunchiness started in this country a few years back with the onset of a new wave of California cooking. I knew it had reached an extreme, when I bit into a practically uncooked vegetable.

A lovely dish to accompany broiled meats or broiled fish. Perfect with Skewers of Mixed Broiled Meats (page 220).

Salads

Cavolfiore con Salsa al Prezzemolo

Cauliflower with Parsley–Mustard Dressing

Both the cauliflower and dressing can be prepared ahead of time and kept tightly covered in separate containers in the refrigerator. The salad should be combined a short while before serving, so that it is served slightly chilled.

Remove all the leaves from the cauliflower and cut a cross at the stem end. Bring a large saucepan two-thirds full of water to a boil. Add the cauliflower and white vinegar (which will keep the cauliflower perfectly white). Cook, uncovered, over medium heat for 15 to 20 minutes, or until the cauliflower can be pierced with a thin knife. Drain the cauliflower and cool completely.

In a blender or food processor, combine the dressing ingredients and process until smooth. The sauce should be fairly liquid; add a bit more oil or vinegar, if needed. Taste and adjust the seasoning.

Put the whole cauliflower on a serving platter or separate the florets and put them in a salad bowl. Spoon half the dressing over the cauliflower and pass the remaining dressing at the table.

For the Cauliflower
1 head of cauliflower, about 2 to 2½ pounds
1 tablespoon white vinegar

For the Salad Dressing
1 slice white bread with crusts removed, soaked in 2 tablespoons red wine vinegar
2 cups loosely packed fresh parsley leaves
2 anchovy fillets
1 tablespoon Dijon mustard
½ of a medium-size red onion
½ cup olive oil
Salt and freshly ground black pepper

Serves 6 to 8

L'Insalata Mista

Mixed Raw Salad

Before writing this recipe I debated for a while. It seemed to me that anyone could make a mixed raw salad, and to write a recipe for something so basic would also seem to be a bit condescending. Then one night I prepared a salad combining curly chicory, radicchio, and yellow peppers that tasted and looked very good. I decided, then and there, that perhaps I could write a recipe giving "ideas" on how to compose a variety of salads, instead of just one basic salad with proportions. These are some of the possibilities. By changing and mixing the ingredients judiciously, it is possible to create a different salad for each day of the week.

These salads are best eaten when very fresh. Ideally, I would pick the greens and vegetables the same day I eat them, but for most of us this is a bit unrealistic. So go ahead and buy your lettuce and vegetables, but try not to leave them in the refrigerator too long or they will lose their freshness. For the suggestions given below you should:

- Wash all your greens and vegetables well and dry them thoroughly. Plan on using about a handful for each serving.
- Slice onions, celery, fennel, peppers, etc., very thinly.
- Do not serve salad that is cold; serve it slightly chilled or, better yet, at room temperature.

- Just before serving, dress the salad sparingly with salt, a nice coating of olive oil, and a little bit of good red wine vinegar. Pepper is optional; if you like it, use it.

Here are some of my favorite combinations:

- Boston lettuce, fennel, red onions, and carrots
- Curly chicory, radicchio, and yellow peppers
- Tomatoes, red onions, and fresh basil
- Butter lettuce, arugula, and red peppers
- Tomatoes, cucumbers, scallions, peppers, olives, and fresh basil
- Cabbage, zucchini, and radishes
- Spinach, Belgian endives, and fresh mushrooms
- Fresh mushrooms, red onions, and chopped parsley
- Arugula, cherry tomatoes, and cucumbers
- Belgian endives and red onions

As you prepare your salad, double or triple the amount so that you can store it in the refrigerator and have it ready on the spur of the moment. Wash your lettuce and pat it dry with paper towels; then wrap it in paper towels, place in a plastic bag, and refrigerate. It will keep fresh for several days.

Insalata di Arancie e Finocchi

Orange and Fennel Salad

In Sicilian cooking, fruit and vegetables are often paired in lovely, refreshing salad combinations. Today, this concept is very popular not only in Italy but also abroad. I particularly like the combination of fennel and oranges. The delicate anise taste of fennel blends beautifully with the sweetness of the oranges.

Remove the long stalks and bruised outer leaves of the fennel. Slice off the root ends of each bulb. Wash and dry the fennel bulbs thoroughly and cut them into quarters. Cut each quarter horizontally into thin slices. Put the slices in a salad bowl. Season with salt and pepper, olive oil, and lemon juice. Spoon the fennel slices onto individual salad dishes.

Peel the oranges, taking care to remove all the white membranes. Cut the oranges into thin rounds and remove the pits. Cut each round into quarters and lay over the fennel slices. Serve slightly chilled.

2 medium-size fennel bulbs
Salt and freshly ground black pepper
4 tablespoons olive oil, preferably virgin olive oil
Juice of 1 lemon
2 sweet oranges

SERVES 4

Fennel or anise, as it is interchangeably called, is a winter vegetable. Years ago, it was sometimes impossible to find it, but today it is available, in season, in supermarkets.

Insalata di Radicchio e Pancetta

Radicchio and Pancetta Salad

If radicchio is unavailable, substitute Belgian endives, arugula, or curly endive.

1 small head radicchio
3 tablespoons olive oil, preferably virgin olive oil
2 to 3 ounces pancetta, sliced and then cut into small strips
Salt and freshly ground black pepper
Balsamic vinegar

SERVES 4

Discard any bruised or wilted leaves from the radicchio. Wash the radicchio leaves under cool running water and dry well with paper towels. Cut or tear the leaves into small pieces and put them in a salad bowl.

Heat the oil in a small saucepan. Add the pancetta and sauté over medium heat until lightly golden and crisp. Pour the hot oil and pancetta over the radicchio and season with salt and pepper. Dribble a bit of balsamic vinegar over the salad and toss to combine. Taste for seasoning and serve.

Insalata di Radicchio e Pere

Radicchio and Pear Salad

Tart radicchio, sweet pears, and the delightful taste of anise are combined into a deliciously unusual salad. If radicchio is unavailable or too expensive, use Belgian endives. A few drops of good balsamic vinegar can be used instead of regular vinegar.

1 small head radicchio
1 medium-size fennel bulb
2 ripe pears, such as Bosc or Comice
⅓ cup of thinly sliced pieces of parmigiano
Salt and freshly ground black pepper
Olive oil, preferably virgin olive oil
Red wine vinegar

SERVES 4

Discard any bruised radicchio leaves. Wash the radicchio leaves well and pat dry with paper towels. Cut or tear the leaves into small pieces and put them in a salad bowl.

Remove the long stalks and bruised outer leaves of the fennel and trim the stem end. Wash and dry the fennel bulb, then slice it, across the bulb, as thinly as possible. Put these in the salad bowl.

Peel the pears and cut them into slim slices. Add these to the salad bowl together with the slivers of parmigiano. Season with salt and pepper. Add oil and vinegar. Toss well, taste, and adjust for seasoning. Chill slightly before serving.

Insalata di Indivia Belga e Radicchio

Belgian Endive and Radicchio Salad

At the end of a particularly filling meal Italians love a salad that has a slightly bitter and refreshing taste. Belgian endives and radicchio have those qualities. However, if this is not a taste you are fond of, substitute fresh spinach for one of these. The dressing is the classic Italian dressing of olive oil and vinegar with the addition of a touch of mustard.

The proportions given for the dressing are approximate; increase or decrease the ingredients according to your specific taste.

Wash and dry vegetables thoroughly. Cut the Belgian endives into strips and break the larger radicchio leaves into small pieces. Put everything into a large salad bowl.

In a small bowl, combine the vinegar and mustard. Add the olive oil, salt, and a few grindings of pepper. Mix to combine. Pour the dressing over the salad and toss. Taste and correct the seasoning.

½ pound Belgian endives
1 small head radicchio, or 1 bunch fresh spinach

For the Dressing
2 tablespoons good red wine vinegar
1 teaspoon Dijon mustard
⅓ cup olive oil (if using extra virgin olive oil, use only ¼ cup)
Salt and freshly ground black pepper

SERVES 4 TO 6

Insalata di Cetrioli e Popelmi Rosa

Cucumber and Pink Grapefruit Salad

If oranges and fennel, a classic Sicilian combination, is so good, why not cucumbers and grapefruit? I tried it and love it. I hope you will, too.

Peel the cucumbers and cut them into very thin rounds. Peel the grapefruit, taking care to remove all the white membranes. Cut the grapefruit into thin rounds and remove the pits. Cut each round into quarters. Put the cucumber slices onto individual salad dishes. Lay several pieces of grapefruit over cucumbers.

In a small bowl, combine the oil, lemon juice, and salt. Spoon the dressing over the salad and serve.

2 medium-size cucumbers
1 large pink grapefruit
¼ cup olive oil, preferably virgin olive oil
2 tablespoons fresh lemon juice
Salt

SERVES 4

Insalata di Sedano e Parmigiano

Celery and Parmigiano Salad

Crisp, white, tender celery and slivers of parmigiano are combined into a tasty salad. Serve as an appetizer or as a refreshing salad at the end of a meal; to serve as a light luncheon dish, double the ingredients.

2 heads crisp celery
¼ pound parmigiano
1 teaspoon Dijon mustard
Juice of 1 lemon
Salt and freshly ground black pepper
¼ cup olive oil, preferably virgin olive oil
1 tablespoon chopped fresh parsley leaves

SERVES 4

Remove the celery stalks until you reach the white, tender part of the celery; reserve the outer stalks for another use. Slice the celery hearts very thinly and put them in a salad bowl.

Use a potato peeler or a small knife to cut the parmigiano into slivers. Add the slivers to the salad bowl.

In a small bowl, combine the mustard, lemon juice, salt and pepper, and olive oil. Add the parsley and mix to combine. Pour the dressing over the celery and cheese in the salad bowl and toss well. Taste and adjust the seasoning. Serve the salad slightly chilled.

Insalata di Funghi e Gorgonzola

Mushroom and Gorgonzola Salad

The restaurant Abramo in Bolzano makes this wonderful salad with fresh porcini mushrooms. Fresh porcini mushrooms are virtually unavailable in this country, so I substituted white cultivated mushrooms. Serve this salad at the end of a lovely meal, or double the ingredients and serve it as a light luncheon.

1½ pound fresh white cultivated mushrooms
Juice of ½ of a large pink grapefruit
4 tablespoons olive oil
Salt and freshly ground black pepper
¼ pound gorgonzola

SERVES 4

Clean the mushrooms thoroughly and cut them into thin slices. Put the slices in a large salad bowl.

In a medium-size bowl, combine the grapefruit juice, oil, and salt and pepper. Beat until blended. With a spoon, crush the gorgonzola against the side of the bowl and beat it into the grapefruit–oil mixture until well blended. Do not worry if the gorgonzola is still a little chunky, it will give more character to the salad.

Pour the dressing over the mushrooms and toss lightly. Taste and correct the seasoning. Serve slightly chilled.

Desserts

Arancie Sciroppate

Oranges with Marsala Syrup

After eating fish I often yearn for something a bit sweet, yet refreshing, to cleanse my palate. Fresh fruit will always do. However, if I want to indulge a little, I prepare these oranges in Marsala syrup. It is an easy treat that doesn't require any special cooking skill. Be very careful, however, when you prepare the syrup, because you are boiling down alcohol and a little spill could start a fire. Make sure to boil the wine gently in a large saucepan. Keep careful watch over it, stir and check it for the right consistency. The syrup should be ready in less than 10 minutes.

Bring a saucepan half filled with water to a boil. Add the orange peel. Boil for 5 to 7 minutes. Drain and pat dry with paper towels.

Cut off the ends of the oranges. Slice away the orange peel, making sure to remove all the white membrane that clings to the oranges. Put the oranges in large dish. Cover and refrigerate until ready to use.

In a medium-size saucepan, combine the sugar, Marsala, and Cointreau. Bring to a gentle boil. Cook over medium heat, stirring, until the sauce has a medium-thick and syrupy consistency, about 10 minutes. Stir the orange rind into the syrup.

Place the oranges on chilled individual dessert dishes. Spoon the wine syrup and a few strips of orange peel over each orange and serve.

Peel of 1 orange, cut into thin strips
8 large oranges
1 cup sugar
2½ cups sweet Marsala
⅓ cup Cointreau or any other liqueur of your liking

SERVES 8

Le Pere al Forno col Marsala

Baked Pears with Marsala

These pears are baked with a bit of butter, wine, and sugar which, together with the pears' natural juice, make a delicious sauce to serve with the pears. Select firm but not rock-hard pears of uniform size for even cooking.

6 medium-size Bosc pears with stems attached
3 tablespoons unsalted butter
1 cup sweet Marsala, sherry, or port
3 cups white wine
1¼ cups sugar

SERVES 6

Preheat the oven to 375 degrees. Wash, dry, and core the pears. Cut off a thin slice from the bottom of each pear so that it will stand upright. Put the pears in a baking dish. Add the butter and wine. Sprinkle the pears with the sugar. Bake for 30 to 40 minutes, or until the pears can be pierced easily with a thin knife. Serve warm or at room temperature with a few spoonfuls of the sauce from the baking dish.

Torta di Pere

Pear Tart

In this pie, firm Bosc pears are cut into chunks and cooked in good red wine, Marsala, and sugar. The wine is then allowed to thicken into a syrup that coats the pears.

For the Pie Crust
2 cups all-purpose unbleached flour
4 ounces unsalted butter (at room temperature for hand mixing, or cold and cut in small pieces for the food processor)
1 large egg
2 tablespoons sugar
3 to 4 tablespoons chilled white wine

For the Filling
8 medium-size firm Bosc pears (about 2½ pounds total weight)
3 cups good red wine
1 cup sweet Marsala, preferably Florio
1 cup sugar

In a medium-size bowl or in a food processor fitted with a metal blade, mix the flour and butter until crumbly. Add the egg, sugar, and wine. Mix until the dough can be gathered loosely. Put the dough on a work surface and work lightly into two balls, one a little larger than the other. Wrap each ball in aluminum foil and refrigerate for 1 hour.

Peel the pears with a small sharp knife and cut them in half lengthwise. Use a melon baller to remove the cores. Cut the pears into chunks and put the chunks in a large skillet. Add the wine, Marsala, and sugar and bring to a boil. Cover the skillet and cook for 10 to 15 minutes, stirring a few times. The pears should be tender but still firm to the touch.

Place a large strainer in a bowl. Use a slotted spoon to

transfer the pears to the strainer; it will take about 5 minutes for most of the juices to drip into the bowl. Return the juice to the skillet and bring to a boil. Cook over high heat, until thick and syrupy.

Return the pears to the skillet and mix gently with the syrup. Cook a bit longer, until pears are thoroughly coated. Cool the mixture for 10 to 15 minutes.

Preheat the oven to 400 degrees at least 15 minutes before you are ready to bake the tart. On a lightly floured surface roll out the larger ball of dough to a 13-inch circle. Put the dough in a 10-inch tart pan with a removable bottom, pressing the dough to fit into the pan evenly. Prick the bottom of the dough with a fork so that the pastry will not puff up while it is baking. Fill the pastry shell with the pear mixture and smooth the top with a spatula.

Roll out the remaining dough and lay it over pear filling. Pinch the edges of the top and bottom crusts together to seal them. Brush the dough with the beaten egg and prick the top of the pie with a fork in several places to allow steam to escape while it is baking.

Bake for 40 to 50 minutes, or until the crust is golden in color. Let stand for 10 to 15 minutes; then remove from the pan and place on a serving platter. Let cool completely before serving.

It is important to cool the pears before filling the pastry shell, or the heat of the pears will cause the crust to become soft and limp. Also, this dessert should not be prepared more than several hours ahead, because the moisture in the filling will make the dough soggy.

1 large egg, lightly beaten, for glazing the pie

SERVES 8

Panettone Semplice Casalingo

Family-Style Panettone

Panettone is a traditional Christmas cake that originated in Milano. Today this tall, yeasty sweet bread is eaten all over Italy, and Christmas and New Year would not be the same without it.

When I was growing up, at the end of our Christmas meal we had a kind of ritual. My mother would slice the cake and my father would uncork a bottle of Spumante while we children would try to grab the largest slice. We were also allowed to have our own small glass of Spumante and sometimes, behind our parent's back, we would manage to go on sipping that lovely, sparkling sweet wine.

Panettone is not hard to make, though it does require a bit of time. With an electric mixer fitted with a dough hook, the task of making this delicious sweet bread is greatly simplified. Without the mixer there will be a little more work to do, but a real feeling of accomplishment comes with the end result.

For the Dough
2 ¼-ounce packages active dry yeast
Pinch of sugar
⅓ cup lukewarm water
4 cups all-purpose unbleached flour
½ cup sugar
Pinch of salt
6 ounces unsalted butter at room temperature, cut into pieces
6 large eggs at room temperature
1 large egg yolk, beaten with 1 teaspoon water for glazing

For the Filling
2 cups golden raisins soaked in dry Marsala
½ cup diced candied citron, soaked in dry Marsala

MAKES 2 PANETTONI

In a small bowl, combine the yeast, pinch of sugar, and ⅓ cup lukewarm water. Let stand for 10 minutes to activate the yeast. (When the surface of the water has small bubbles, you know that the yeast is alive and well.)

Put the flour, sugar, salt, butter, and eggs in the large bowl of an electric mixer. With the dough hook, beat at a low speed to mix. Add the yeast mixture slowly. When all the ingredients are well incorporated, beat at medium speed for 7 to 8 minutes. The dough should be shiny, pliable, and hold around the beater in a soft lump.

If you are making the dough by hand, combine all the ingredients in a large bowl. Then put the dough on a lightly floured surface and knead for about 10 to 12 minutes, slapping the dough down hard on the surface ten to fifteen times, until it is shiny and pliable. Dust lightly with flour if the dough sticks to the work surface.

Put the dough into a large bowl, cover with plastic wrap, and leave in a draft-free place to rise for 2 to 2½ hours, or until the dough has doubled in bulk. After dough has risen, punch it down a few times. Cover bowl with aluminum foil and let the dough rise until doubled in bulk, 2 to 2½ hours.

After the second rising, strain the raisins and citron

and dry thoroughly with paper towels. Mix with 1 table-spoon of flour to absorb any excess moisture. Lightly flour your hands and flatten out the dough. Sprinkle raisins and citron over the flattened dough. Fold the dough over the filling and knead until everything is well incorporated. If any of the raisins and citron fall out of the dough, knead them back in.

Butter the 1½-quart soufflé dishes. Divide the dough in half. Shape each half in a round and put the dough into the buttered soufflé dishes. Using a sharp, thin knife, cut a cross into the top of each ball of dough. Brush each ball of dough with the beaten egg yolk. Cover with foil and let rise in a warm place for about 1 hour.

Preheat the oven to 375 degrees for at least 15 minutes. Bake the panettoni for 35 to 45 minutes, or until golden brown. Unmold the panettoni and cool on a wire rack.

Panettone is now available in this country and, during the holidays, it can be found in many specialized food markets, Italian or otherwise. Homemade panettone is quite good, even though in my opinion it lacks that special lightness that the commercial product has.

The consistency of this dough is considerably stickier than a bread or pizza dough. If the dough sticks heavily to your hands or working surface, dust hands and surface *lightly* with flour. Do not add too much flour, however, or panettone will become heavy in texture.

La Ciambella Bolognese

Sweet Pastry Ring from Bologna

Many Italian regional desserts are simple and homey. They are also very good, which is why they have stood the test of time. La Ciambella was a standard item in our house. A good slice was our afternoon snack and we almost always had a slice of ciambella in our school bag. Every time I am in Bologna, I cannot resist the sight of this sweet pastry ring peeking through the windows of pastry shops. I buy it and eat it with the same avidity that I ate it as a child. Ciambella has a firm texture and a somewhat crumbly consistency. It is great when it is dunked into sweet wine at the end of a family meal.

This sweet pastry ring keeps well for several days. Wrap it in plastic wrap and leave at room temperature.

1 ¼-ounce envelope active dry yeast
½ cup lukewarm water
4 ounces unsalted butter
3 large eggs
1 cup plus 3 tablespoons sugar
Grated rind of 2 lemons
2 to 3 tablespoons milk
4 cups all-purpose unbleached flour
1 large egg yolk

MAKES 10 TO 12 SLICES

Dissolve the yeast in the lukewarm water. Let stand for 10 minutes to activate the yeast.

Preheat the oven to 375 degrees. Melt the butter over very low heat and cool it slightly. In a large bowl, beat the 3 eggs and 1 cup of the sugar until pale yellow. Add the grated lemon rind, melted butter, dissolved yeast, and milk. Mix to blend. Add the flour a little at a time and mix with your hands or a wooden spoon until well blended. Transfer the dough to a work surface and knead for 10 to 12 minutes. The dough should be smooth and pliable. Shape the dough into a long roll, about 4 inches in diameter.

Butter and flour a large baking sheet. Place the roll on the baking sheet and pinch the ends of the roll together to make a giant ring.

Beat the egg yolk with 2 of the remaining tablespoons of sugar and brush ring all over with this mixture. With a thin, sharp knife, make a few diagonal slashes over top of dough. Sprinkle dough with the remaining tablespoon of sugar. Bake for 30 to 35 minutes, or until the cake is golden in color and a wooden toothpick inserted in the center comes out dry. Cool on a wire rack before serving.

Pere con Zabaglione all'Champagne

Poached Pears with Champagne Zabaglione

In this dish, pears are poached in champagne and sugar; the liquid becomes a thick glaze that envelops the pears. A light, airy champagne zabaglione is served alongside each pear. This dish requires a minimal amount of fuss but produces a very delicious and eye-appealing dessert.

The consistency of this zabaglione is thinner than regular zabaglione because of the large quantity of champagne.

For the Pears
4 large Bosc pears
Juice of 1 lemon
¾ cup sugar
3 cups champagne

For the Zabaglione
4 large egg yolks
⅓ cup sugar
1½ cups champagne

SERVES 4

Peel the pears but leave the stems attached. Cut off a slice from the bottom of the pears so that they can stand upright and brush the pears with the lemon juice. Put the pears in a medium-size saucepan. Add the sugar and champagne and bring to a boil. Cover the saucepan, lower the heat, and cook for 20 to 30 minutes, or until the pears can be easily pierced with a thin knife. Baste the pears several times during the cooking. Leave the pears in the poaching liquid while you prepare the zabaglione.

In a large bowl or the top of a double boiler, beat the eggs and sugar until thick and pale yellow. Set the bowl or top of the double boiler over simmering water. Add the champagne slowly and beat energetically with a large wire whisk to incorporate. Cook and beat until the zabaglione has a nice thick consistency and is hot to the touch.

Cover the bottom of individual dessert plates with a thin layer of hot zabaglione. Place the pears on the plates.

Bring the remaining poaching liquid to a fast boil. Cook until the sauce is thick and syrupy. Dribble the thickened sauce over the pears and serve immediately.

Certosino

Bolognese Fruitcake

It seems that today we eat fewer desserts than we did years ago. There are times, however, when we sidestep resolutions. Christmas is such a time, and we all know that Christmas and fruitcake seem to go hand in hand. Try certosino with a glass of Spumante or with a nice dessert wine.

This is Bologna's celebrated fruitcake, made originally by the monks of the charterhouse of Bologna. Each year at Christmas, the monks would bake a very large fruitcake and send it to Rome to Pope Benedetto XIV, the former Cardinal Lambertini of Bologna, who had a passion for certosino. The word *certosino* means "Carthusian monk."

3 ounces golden raisins
¾ cup sweet Marsala, preferably Florio
6 ounces shelled fresh almonds
¼ pound candied citron
¼ pound candied cherries
2 1-ounce squares semisweet chocolate
½ cup pine nuts
1 teaspoon ground cinnamon
1 teaspoon anise seed
1 cup honey
¾ cup sugar
3 tablespoons unsalted butter
3 teaspoons baking soda
2 cups all-purpose unbleached flour

MAKES 10 TO 12

Soak the raisins in the Marsala for 20 minutes. Drain the raisins and reserve the wine. Bring a medium-size saucepan full of water to a boil. Add the almonds and boil for 30 to 40 seconds. Drain and rinse the almonds under cool running water. Put the almonds in a large kitchen towel and rub them against each other to remove most of their skins. Reserve about ⅓ cup of the almonds to decorate the top of the cake. Chop the remaining almonds into medium-size chunks and put them in a large bowl.

Chop the candied citron and cherries into medium-size pieces and add them to the chopped almonds. (Reserve ⅓ cup of the largest pieces to decorate the top of the cake.) Chop the chocolate into small pieces and add to the bowl with the pine nuts, drained raisins, cinnamon, and anise seed. Mix everything well.

Put the honey, reserved Marsala, sugar, and butter in a medium-size saucepan. Bring to a boil, lower the heat, and cook gently for 1 to 2 minutes, stirring, until the honey and butter are completely melted.

Mix the baking soda with the flour. Remove the saucepan with the honey from the heat. Add the flour mixture to the saucepan a little at a time, mixing well after each addition. Add the candied fruit mixture to the saucepan. Mix energetically until everything is thoroughly blended with the flour. The batter at this point will be very thick and hard to stir.

Preheat the oven to 350 degrees. Butter a 10-inch cake pan with a removable bottom.

With a wet spatula spread the mixture in the buttered cake pan. Arrange the reserved almonds and candied fruit over the cake to decorate it.

Bake for 40 to 50 minutes, or until the cake is golden and begins to pull away from the side of the pan. Cool to room temperature; then remove from the pan.

If the candied fruit and almonds do not stay on top of cake, but sink into the batter, it means that your batter is not firm enough, and a bit more flour should be added when the batter is still on the stove.

As you probably know, fruitcakes can be kept perfectly fresh for several weeks. Wrap them in aluminum foil and store at room temperature.

Sorbetto di Melone

Cantaloupe Sorbet

In a small saucepan, combine the sugar and water. Bring to a boil and cook until the sugar has dissolved completely, 1 to 2 minutes. Set aside to cool completely.

Peel and seed the cantaloupe. Cut it into pieces and put them in a food processor. Process until smooth.

Put 3 cups of the puréed cantaloupe through a sieve into a large bowl. Add the cooled syrup and lemon juice. Pour the mixture into the bowl of an ice-cream machine and freeze, following the manufacturer's directions, for 10 to 15 minutes. At this point sorbet should begin to have a thick consistency.

Beat the egg white until frothy. Add the sugar and beat until stiff. Add to the cantaloupe sorbet. Run the machine for 5 minutes longer, or until the sorbet has a thick, smooth consistency.

For the Simple Syrup
1 cup sugar
1 cup water

To Complete the Sorbet
1 large cantaloupe, about 3 to 4 pounds
Juice of 1 lemon
1 large egg white at room temperature
2 tablespoons sugar

MAKES ABOUT 1 QUART

Semifreddo di Nocciole al Cioccolato

Frozen Hazelnut Zabaglione Mousse with Hot Chocolate Sauce

This lovely frozen dessert is from Al Bersagliere restaurant in Goito, a small town near Mantua. The hazelnuts are roasted until their skins are blistered and darkened. Then they are put in a large kitchen towel and rubbed together to remove as much skin as possible. This is a tedious operation and it is often hard to remove all of the hazelnut's skin, but it doesn't matter if bits of skin remain.

For the Zabaglione

7 large egg yolks
¾ cup sugar
¼ cup hazelnut liqueur or any other liqueur of your liking

To Complete the Dish

2 ounces shelled hazelnuts
2 cups whipping cream
½ cup milk
4 1-ounce squares semisweet baking chocolate, cut into chunks

SERVES 8

Prepare the zabaglione. Put the egg yolks and sugar in the top of a double boiler. Beat until mixture is pale yellow and thick. (I do this with an electric beater.) Put the pan over the lower part of the double boiler which contains about 2 inches of simmering water. Add the hazelnut liqueur and beat with a large wire whisk until the mixture swells into a large, soft mass and doubles in volume. Remove from the heat and set the pan containing zabaglione over a bowl of ice water. Stir with a whisk until the zabaglione is completely cool.

Preheat the broiler. Spread the hazelnuts on a large baking sheet and toast until dark and the skin is blistered. Put the nuts in a large kitchen towel and rub them energetically against each other to remove the skins. Put the hazelnuts in a food processor or blender and process into very small pieces, but do not process to a powder.

Beat the cream until thick and fold it into the cooled zabaglione. Fold the chopped hazelnuts, a little at a time, into zabaglione–cream mixture until everything is well incorporated.

Butter the sides and bottom of an 8½- by 4½-inch loaf pan. Line the bottom and sides of the pan with plastic wrap, leaving about 5 inches of plastic wrap overhanging on each side. Pour the zabaglione mixture into the pan and smooth the top with a spatula. Fold up the overhanging plastic wrap to cover tightly. Freeze for at least 10 to 12 hours. Semifreddo can be prepared up to this point several days ahead.

One hour before serving, remove the semifreddo from freezer. Put a few inches of hot water into a sink. Dip the pan briefly into the hot water (for 2 to 3 seconds). Dry the outside of the pan. Using a serving dish that can be put safely into the freezer, place the dish over the loaf pan. Turn the pan upside down over the dish. Gently remove the pan and peel off the plastic wrap. Clean the dish of any running semifreddo. Put the dish back into the freezer, uncovered, until ready to serve.

About 30 minutes before serving the semifreddo, put the milk and chocolate in the top part of a double boiler. Put the pan over lower part of the double boiler which contains 2 inches of simmering water. Stir the chocolate as it melts. When completely melted, remove from the heat and keep warm in the double boiler until ready to use.

Cut the semifreddo into slices and place on chilled individual serving dishes. Serve with a bit of hot chocolate sauce over each slice.

Pere con lo Sciroppo di Vino e Limone

Pears Poached in Wine and Lemon

Of all the pear varieties, Bosc are my favorite. They have a firm consistency and a sweet flavor which makes them ideal for poaching.

When making this dish, try to select pears that have the same dimensions and consistency for even cooking. And select the ones that are free of blemishes and have nice, long stems.

4 firm Bosc pears
Juice of 2 lemons
5 cups of any good white wine
1 cup sugar
Peel of 1 lemon, removed with a vegetable peeler

SERVES 4

Peel the pears but leave the stems attached. Cut off a small slice from bottom of pears so they will stand up and brush the pears with lemon juice. Put the pears in a medium-size saucepan with the wine, lemon juice, and sugar. Cover the saucepan and bring the wine to a gentle boil. Cook the pears for 20 to 30 minutes, basting several times during the cooking. The pears are done when they can be pierced easily with a sharp knife.

Cut the lemon peel into very thin julienne. Place it in a small saucepan of boiling water and cook a few minutes to remove the acid taste of the lemon. Drain and dry with paper towels.

To serve, place the pears on a serving platter or on individual serving dishes. Add the julienned lemon peel to the poaching syrup and cook over high heat, until the syrup is thick. Spoon the sauce over the pears and serve warm.

Fresh fruit is almost always served at the end of an Italian meal. When we want to be fancy, or we crave something a bit sweet, we still turn to fruit.

Fresh succulent figs may be topped with brown sugar and broiled; tiny wild strawberries and berries of any kind are glorified with sugar and lemon; plump peaches and apricots are stuffed and baked; and pears are poached in wine and sugar.

Sorbetto al Barolo

Sorbet with Barolo Wine

Sometimes after a wonderful meal there is no place left for a rich dessert. Sorbet, therefore, is a perfect ending because it is light, delicate, and, when properly done, absolutely delicious.

This sorbet is made with a young Barolo wine, such as a Conterno, Ceretto, or Scarpa. Alcohol does not freeze; therefore, the wine must be boiled slowly to allow the alcohol to evaporate. When the sorbet has reached the proper thick consistency, then a few tablespoons of very cold Barolo can be added for extra flavor.

For the Simple Syrup
1½ cups sugar
1½ cups water

4 cups good young Barolo wine
Juice of 1 lemon
2 to 3 tablespoons very cold, good, young Barolo wine

Makes about 1 quart

In a small saucepan, combine the sugar and water. Bring to a boil and cook until the sugar has dissolved completely, 1 to 2 minutes. Set aside to cool completely.

In another saucepan, bring the wine to a boil. Lower the heat and simmer for 10 to 15 minutes. At this point, there should be about 2½ to 3 cups of wine left in the saucepan. Set aside to cool completely. Put the syrup and wine in the bowl of an ice-cream machine and add the lemon juice. Freeze, following the manufacturer's directions, for 15 to 20 minutes, or until the sorbet has a thick, smooth consistency. Slowly add 2 to 3 tablespoons of very cold wine. Run the machine for a few minutes longer, or until the sorbet has reached the stage of a finished product.

If not served immediately, the sorbet can be frozen. But make sure you allow enough time (about 1 hour) for the sorbet to soften in the refrigerator to a granular consistency before serving.

The simple syrup can be prepared several days ahead and kept tightly sealed in the refrigerator.

Struffoli

Neapolitan Honey Balls

This classic Neapolitan Christmas dessert employs ingredients much loved by southern Italians—honey and candied fruit. In many small villages throughout the South, women gather together to prepare and bake delicious treats for the holidays. My mother-in-law, who has been in this country for more than sixty years, still makes struffoli faithfully every Christmas. Making the dough by hand as my mother-in-law does is not hard, but it requires some time and patience; making it with a food processor is a snap. In this recipe, I will give you both methods. Then you can decide for yourself which method to use. The beautiful thing about this lovely dessert is that it can be prepared several days ahead of time and kept in the refrigerator. Serve it, however, at room temperature.

For the Dough
2 cups all-purpose unbleached flour
Pinch of salt
¼ cup sugar
Grated rind of 1 lemon
4 large eggs
1 large egg yolk
2 tablespoons unsalted butter, softened

To Finish the Cake
Oil for frying
1 cup honey
½ cup sugar
Grated rind of 2 oranges
¼ pound candied orange peel, finely diced

Serves 6 to 8

To make the Neapolitan honey balls by hand, combine the flour, salt, sugar, and grated lemon rind on a wooden board and make a well in the center. Break the eggs into the well and beat with a fork. Add the softened butter and mash down with the fork. Draw the flour from the inner rim of the well over the eggs a little at a time and beat with the fork to mix. Keep adding flour over the eggs until you have a soft dough. Knead for 6 to 8 minutes, or until you have a smooth pliable dough.

Cut off a piece of dough the size of an egg. Wrap the remaining dough in plastic wrap to prevent it from drying out. Shape the small piece of dough into a roll about the thickness of your little finger. Cut the roll into ½ inch pieces; then roll the pieces into small balls. Repeat with the remaining dough. Place the balls on a lightly floured dish until you are ready to fry them. Pour 3 inches of oil into a medium-size saucepan. When the oil is hot, fry as many balls as will fit loosely into the saucepan. When the balls are lightly golden, remove them with a slotted spoon to paper towels to drain.

Heat the honey and sugar in a wide skillet. When the honey is very hot and melted, remove the skillet from the heat and add the grated orange rind. Mix to incorporate. Add the balls and candied orange peel to the skillet. Mix gently with a wooden spoon until every ball is completely coated with honey. Pour out onto a large

round platter. Wet your hands and shape the mixture into a large cone, taking care not to burn yourself, since honey and balls will still be quite hot. Cool for several hours before serving.

To make the Neapolitan honey balls with a food processor, put the flour, sugar, salt, grated lemon rind, and butter in the bowl of a food processor fitted with a metal blade. Process lightly. Add the egg and turn the machine on and off several times, until you have a compact dough, but not a ball, around the blade. Remove the dough and knead it by hand for 2 to 3 minutes.

Take a ½-inch piece of dough and, with the palm of your hand, form a small ball. Repeat until you have used up all the dough. Place the balls on a lightly floured dish until you are ready to fry them. Fry and assemble as directed above.

Great, Fast Pasta Dishes Prepared in Less Than Twenty Minutes

If time is of the essence, this is the chapter for you. I still maintain that there is nothing more desirable when hunger strikes than a wonderful plate of pasta. And, when such a dish can be prepared with no fuss, virtually in a matter of minutes, and often at modest cost, we have a sure winner.

Sometimes we eat because we are hungry. Other times we eat because we must. Occasionally, we eat with indifference. There are certain dishes, however, that will make your gastric juices flow with anticipation because the aromas that pervade the kitchen when they are cooking are tantalizing.

The flavor and simplicity of Italian cooking is best exemplified in this chapter: great dishes without complicated techniques, sauces that can be prepared in the time it takes to put up and boil the water to cook the pasta. These sauces have flavors

287

that are direct yet elegant and harmonious and, in their simplicity, retain the character of their ingredients.

Trying to remain, in turn, with the overall mood of this book, I have selected for this chapter dishes that are not only good and quick, but also good for us. Many sauces are made with fresh vegetables and olive oil, which are the bases of the "Mediterranean Diet." A few dishes use butter and cream, judiciously. Some preparations, such as Spaghettini with Caviar, are decidedly elegant. Others like Spaghettini Aglio e Olio are quite humble. They are all, however, very appetizing.

As this chapter deals with "fast" pasta dishes, fresh pasta is omitted for the obvious reason of the considerably longer preparation time needed.

Bucatini al Pomodoro Fresco

Bucatini with Fresh Tomatoes

Sometimes we strive so much for originality in food that we forget that some of the best dishes are the simplest. A plate of pasta, dressed only with fragrant, fresh tomatoes will never go out of style. These are the basic and reassuring dishes that we go back to when we are saturated with "innovations."

2 pounds juicy ripe tomatoes, peeled, seeded, and diced (page 55)
1 tablespoon salt
1 pound bucatini or spaghetti
4 tablespoons olive oil
2 garlic cloves, finely chopped
Salt and freshly ground black pepper
Several fresh basil or oregano leaves, roughly shredded, or 1 tablespoon chopped fresh parsley leaves

SERVES 4

Put the tomatoes into a strainer to drain off the excess juices.

Bring a large pot of water to a boil. Add the salt and bucatini. Cook, uncovered, for 8 to 10 minutes, or until the pasta is tender but still firm to the bite. While the pasta is cooking, complete the sauce.

Heat the oil in a large skillet. Add the garlic and cook until the garlic begins to color. Add the tomatoes, season with salt and several grindings of pepper, and cook over high heat for 4 to 5 minutes. Stir in the fresh basil.

Strain bucatini and add it to the sauce in the skillet. Mix well and serve at once.

Orecchiette al Pomodoro e Ricotta

Orecchiette with Tomatoes and Ricotta Cheese

Good ricotta, a quick, tasty tomato sauce, and good pasta can be turned into a mouthwatering dish in no time at all. These are the dishes that are very popular in Italian households today, not only because they are easy to prepare, but also because they are tasty and economical. However, I urge you to go the extra mile to obtain good Italian ricotta, imported canned plum tomatoes, and 100 percent durum wheat pasta from southern Italy, because these basic ingredients are vital to good Italian cooking.

Put the tomatoes through a food mill or sieve to remove the seeds.

Heat the oil in a medium-size saucepan. Add the garlic and, when the garlic is golden on both sides, remove and discard it. Add the tomatoes to the oil and season with salt and several grindings of pepper. Cook, uncovered, over medium heat for 10 to 15 minutes, stirring a few times during the cooking.

Meanwhile, bring a large pot of water to a boil. Add 1 tablespoon of salt and the orecchiette. Cook, uncovered, until the pasta is tender but still firm to the bite.

Put half of the tomato sauce into a large warm bowl. Drain the pasta and add it to the bowl. Add the ricotta and mix well to incorporate. Add a bit more tomato sauce and ¼ cup of the cheese. Mix and serve at once with the remaining cheese, if you wish.

1 28-ounce can imported Italian plum tomatoes
3 tablespoons olive oil
2 garlic cloves, lightly crushed
Salt and freshly ground black pepper
1 pound orecchiette
¼ pound ricotta
¼ pound freshly grated Pecorino or parmigiano

SERVES 4

Orecchiette are small disks of pasta in the shape of earlobes. This pasta, which used to be made almost exclusively by hand, is a specialty of Puglia, a beautiful, sunny region that covers the heel of Italy. Penne, rigatoni, or conchiglie (shells) can be used instead of orecchiette.

Rigatoni con Tocco di Funghi alla Genovese

Rigatoni with Porcini Mushrooms Genoa Style

Dried wild mushrooms have a unique flavor and a distinctive fragrance. Here they are combined with onions and tomatoes into a lovely sauce that can be prepared in twenty minutes, kept tightly sealed in the refrigerator for several days, and also can be frozen.

1 ounce dried porcini mushrooms
2 cups canned imported Italian plum toma-
   toes with their juices
4 tablespoons olive oil
1 small onion, finely chopped
2 garlic cloves, lightly crushed
Salt and freshly ground black pepper
1 pound rigatoni
1 tablespoon chopped fresh parsley leaves
½ cup freshly grated parmigiano

SERVES 4

Soak the mushrooms in 1 cup lukewarm water for 20 minutes; drain and reserve the soaking water. Rinse the mushrooms under cold water. Strain the mushroom water through paper towels a few times to get rid of the sandy deposits. Set aside. Put the tomatoes through a food mill or a sieve.

Heat the oil in a medium-size saucepan. Add the onion and garlic and sauté over medium heat until lightly golden. Discard the garlic. Add the mushrooms and stir to blend. Add the strained mushroom soaking water and cook over high heat until the water is reduced by half. Stir in the tomatoes, season with salt and pepper, and cook over medium heat for 10 to 12 minutes.

While the sauce cooks, bring a large pot of water to a boil. Add 1 tablespoon of salt and the rigatoni. Cook until the pasta is tender but still firm to the bite, 8 to 10 minutes.

Stir the parsley into the sauce. Put half of the sauce in a large warm serving bowl. Drain the pasta and add it to the sauce in the bowl. Toss to combine. Serve with the additional sauce and a sprinkling of parmigiano.

Spaghettini al Caviale

Thin Spaghetti with Caviar

In this dish, onion, cream, mascarpone, and caviar are combined into a mouthwatering sauce. Since any kind of thin pasta when tossed in cream tends to become a bit dry, I generally reserve a little of the pasta cooking water and add it to the skillet while the pasta and sauce are tossed together.

Melt the butter in a large skillet. Add the onion and cook and stir over low heat until the onion is completely wilted, 12 to 15 minutes. Add the cream and mascarpone and season lightly with salt and pepper. Stir and cook for 1 to 2 minutes, or until the mascarpone is well blended with the cream. Turn the heat off under the skillet.

While the onion cooks, bring a large pot of water to a boil. Add 1 tablespoon of salt and the spaghettini. Cook until the pasta is tender but still firm to the bite. (Since spaghettini are quite thin, they will cook very fast. After a few minutes, taste for doneness.)

Drain the spaghettini and add it to the sauce in the skillet. Add the chives and half of the caviar. Toss well to incorporate. Put the pasta on individual warm serving dishes. Spoon a little caviar on each serving and serve at once.

4 tablespoons unsalted butter
1 small red onion, very thinly sliced
½ cup heavy cream
2 tablespoons mascarpone
Salt and freshly ground white pepper
1 pound thin spaghetti (spaghettini)
2 tablespoons finely diced chives
3 ounces golden caviar

Serves 4

Mascarpone is a soft, creamy cheese that has a high butterfat content and tastes somewhat sweet, not unlike a very thick whipped cream. In Italy, this cheese is used primarily in desserts and in elegant, delicate pasta dishes.

An alternate method: Melt the butter and put it in a large warm serving bowl. Cook the pasta and add it to the bowl. Add the mascarpone, caviar, and chives. Toss well and serve.

Penne alla Crudaiola

Penne with Uncooked Tomato Sauce

Here is a fresh, uncooked tomato sauce that is delightfully appetizing, highly aromatic, and quick to prepare. Ripe tomatoes, fresh basil, the scent of garlic, some capers, and a hint of anchovies—just close your eyes and these ingredients will transport you to the Italian Riviera. This great summer dish can be prepared also with spaghetti, linguine, shells, and fusilli.

For the Uncooked Tomato Sauce
1½ pounds juicy ripe tomatoes
12 to 15 small basil leaves, shredded into
*   small pieces, or 2 tablespoons chopped*
*   fresh parsley leaves*
2 garlic cloves, finely chopped
2 tablespoons rinsed and dried capers
2 anchovy fillets, finely chopped
¼ cup freshly grated pecorino, or 2 to 3
*   ounces mozzarella, diced*
¼ cup olive oil, preferably virgin olive oil
Salt and freshly ground black pepper

For the Pasta
1 tablespoon salt
1 pound penne

Serves 4

Prepare the uncooked tomato sauce. Peel, seed, and dice tomatoes following the instructions on page 55. Put the tomatoes in a colander over a bowl to drain off the excess juices. Put the drained tomatoes in a large serving bowl that can later accommodate the pasta. Add all the other ingredients and season lightly with salt and several grindings of pepper. Cover bowl and leave at room temperature for 2 hours.

Bring a large pot of water to a boil. Add the salt and penne. Cook, uncovered, until the pasta is tender but still firm to the bite. Drain the pasta well and add it to the sauce in the bowl. Mix well and serve at once.

Spaghetti con Zucchine e Prosciutto Affumicato

Spaghetti with Zucchini and Smoked Ham

Another wonderful, fast pasta dish. As the water heats up, the sauce is prepared. Firm zucchini, tasty pancetta, and smoked ham, a bit of garlic and hot chile pepper are tossed together with virgin olive oil to produce a mouthwatering sauce. Smoked mozzarella and fresh basil, when available, are added for extra flavor. Spaghetti, linguine, fusilli, or bucatini can be used interchangeably for this dish.

Wash the zucchini thoroughly under cool running water. Cut off both ends of the zucchini and slice lengthwise into small strips.

Heat the oil in a large skillet. Add garlic, chile pepper, and zucchini and sauté over medium heat for about 1 minute. Add the pancetta and smoked ham and cook for 2 to 3 minutes longer. Season lightly with salt. (Remember that the pancetta and ham are already quite salty.) Turn the heat off under the skillet.

Bring a large pot of water to a boil. Add 1 tablespoon of salt and the spaghetti. Cook until the pasta is tender but still firm to the bite. Turn the heat on again under the skillet. Add the basil. Scoop up ¼ cup of the pasta cooking water and add it to the sauce. Drain pasta and add it to the sauce in the skillet. Stir until the pasta and sauce are well combined and serve at once.

2 medium-size firm zucchini
¼ cup olive oil, preferably virgin olive oil
2 garlic cloves, finely chopped
A small piece of red hot chile pepper
3 ounces pancetta, sliced and then cut into small strips
3 ounces smoked ham, sliced and then cut into small strips
Salt
1 pound spaghetti
Several fresh basil leaves, shredded
3 ounces smoked mozzarella

SERVES 4

Pasta con i Broccoli, le Acciughe e il peperoncino

Pasta with Broccoli, Anchovies, and Hot Chile Pepper

Another peasant dish that now enjoys a resurgent popularity in Italy. Broccoli, anchovies, garlic, and good olive oil are the unassuming tasty ingredients of this dish, which is also quick to prepare, economical, and absolutely mouthwatering. After a movie, invite some friends over informally and dazzle them with this quick preparation.

Wash the broccoli. Remove ⅓ of the tough stalks and discard. Separate broccoli into florets. Peel the remaining stalks and slice them into rounds. Steam or boil florets and stalk rounds until they are barely tender to the touch.

In a large skillet, heat the oil. Add the hot chile pepper, anchovies, and garlic. Sauté gently for 1 to 2 minutes. Stir in the broccoli and season with salt and several grindings of pepper. Set aside.

Bring a large pot of water to a boil. Add the pasta and cook uncovered until the pasta is tender but still firm to the bite. Drain the pasta and add it to the broccoli in the skillet. Cook over low heat for 1 to 2 minutes, until the pasta and sauce are well combined. Serve at once.

1 bunch broccoli (about 2 pounds)
5 tablespoons olive oil, preferably virgin olive oil
A small piece of a red, hot chile pepper, finely chopped
4 anchovy fillets, rinsed and finely chopped
3 garlic cloves, finely chopped
Salt and freshly ground black pepper
1 pound pasta, such as orecchiette, penne, or shells

SERVES 4

Pennette al Burro, Oro e Prosciutto

Pennette with Cream–Tomato and Prosciutto Sauce

It is always amazing, even to me, to discover new sauces, or dishes, out of the same basic ingredients. Here a lovely, tasty sauce is prepared in a matter of minutes by combining a lightly cooked tomato sauce with some sautéed onions, prosciutto, and a bit of cream. The total cooking time for the sauce is about 15 minutes.

While the sauce cooks, bring a big pot of water to a boil and cook the pasta. Pennette are a smaller version of penne, a quill-shaped pasta that comes smooth or ridged. Choose a good brand of imported pasta, such as DeCecco or Del Verde, both from southern Italy.

2 cups canned imported Italian plum tomatoes with their juices
1 tablespoon olive oil
3 tablespoons unsalted butter
1 small onion, thinly sliced
¼ pound prosciutto, sliced and then cut into small thin strips
Salt and freshly ground black pepper
⅓ cup heavy cream
2 tablespoons chopped fresh parsley leaves
1 pound pennette or penne
½ cup freshly grated parmigiano (optional)

SERVES 4

Put the tomatoes through a food mill or sieve to remove the seeds. Heat the oil in a small saucepan. Add the tomatoes and cook, uncovered, over medium heat for 10 to 12 minutes. Set aside.

While the tomato sauce cooks, melt the butter in a large skillet. Add the onion and sauté over medium heat until the onion is pale yellow. Add the prosciutto and mix until the prosciutto is well coated with the butter and onion. Stir in the tomatoes and cream. Season with salt and a bit of pepper and simmer gently for 2 to 3 minutes. Stir in the parsley. Turn off the heat under the skillet.

While the sauce is cooking, bring a large pot of water to a boil. Add 1 tablespoon of salt and the pennette. Cook until the pasta is tender but still firm to the bite.

Turn on the heat again under the skillet. Drain the pasta and add it to the sauce in the skillet. Mix until the pasta and sauce are well combined. Serve at once, with a bit of parmigiano, if you wish.

Pasta al Salmone Affumicato

Pasta with Smoked Salmon and Cream

Sometimes, after a long day, the idea of having to prepare a meal is enough to make one slouch into a soft chair, pick up the phone, and order a pizza. And yet, it is precisely on days like these that we need something uplifting. Now, please follow me into the kitchen. Put a large pot of water on the stove. Uncork a bottle of wine, forget the television news, and, instead, listen to some soft music while you sip the wine and prepare the sauce. True to this chapter, the whole dish will be ready in minutes.

Melt the butter in a large skillet. When the butter foams, add the onion and sauté over medium heat until the onion turns lightly golden. Add the salmon and sauté a few minutes longer. Stir in brandy, if using. Cook until the brandy has evaporated. Add the cream and season lightly with salt and pepper. Simmer gently for 2 to 3 minutes. Turn the heat off under the skillet.

Meanwhile, bring a large pot of water to a boil. Add 1 tablespoon of salt and the pasta. Cook until the pasta is tender but still firm to the bite. Drain the pasta and add it to the sauce in the skillet. Turn the heat on again under the skillet. Add the parsley and parmigiano. Toss quickly until the pasta and sauce are thoroughly blended. (Do not leave it on the heat longer than 40 to 50 seconds or the sauce will dry out. If it should, add a bit more cream.) Serve immediately.

4 tablespoons unsalted butter

½ of a medium-size red onion, thinly sliced

¼ pound smoked salmon, sliced and then cut into small strips

¼ cup brandy (optional)

1 cup heavy cream

Salt and a bit of freshly ground white pepper

1 pound fettuccine, tagliatelle or tagliarini, preferably imported

1 tablespoon chopped fresh parsley leaves

¼ cup freshly grated parmigiano

SERVES 4

When possible, make this dish with homemade pasta.

Pasta con le Melanzane

Pasta with Eggplants

This is a classic Sicilian dish that uses a much-loved combination of pasta and vegetables. The original recipe calls for dicing and frying the eggplants. Since eggplants absorb a great deal of oil, I have opted to broil instead of fry them. The result is a delightfully lighter dish, without an excessive oily taste.

2 small firm eggplants
Salt
4 tablespoons olive oil
2 garlic cloves, finely chopped
2½ cups canned imported Italian plum to-
  matoes that have been put through a
  strainer or food mill to remove the seeds
Salt and freshly ground black pepper
2 tablespoons chopped fresh parsley or, if
  available, chopped basil leaves
1 cup ricotta
1 pound pasta, such as shells, penne, or
  tortiglioni
1 cup freshly grated parmigiano

SERVES 6

Wash and dry the eggplants and cut off both ends. Cut the eggplants into ¼-inch-thick slices. Put the slices on a large dish and sprinkle with salt. Leave for about 1 hour so that salt will draw out the bitter juices from the eggplants. Pat dry with paper towels.

Preheat the broiler. Brush the eggplants lightly with oil. Broil until the slices are golden on both sides. Cut the eggplant slices into pieces of about 1½ to 2 inches. Set aside.

In a medium-size saucepan, heat the oil. Add the garlic and sauté over medium heat until the garlic begins to color. Add the tomatoes and season with salt and several grindings of pepper. Cook, uncovered, for 8 to 10 minutes. Add the parsley and eggplants and cook a few minutes longer. Taste and adjust the seasoning and keep warm over very low heat.

Bring a large pot of water to a boil. Add 1 tablespoon of salt and the pasta. Cook until the pasta is tender but still firm to the bite, 8 to 10 minutes.

Drain the pasta and put it in a warm serving dish. Add the ricotta and mix. Stir in the sauce and ⅓ cup of the parmigiano. Serve at once with the remaining cheese, if you wish.

For a simpler version, omit the ricotta.

Linguine con Cape Sante e Acciughe

Linguine with Scallops and Anchovy Sauce

Improvising and doing with what you have at hand are characteristics of the good cook, Italian or otherwise.

Once a week my mother would find a way to use almost everything that was left over. With old bread she would make a bread soup called pancotto. With leftover vegetables, she would make a friggione (a mixture of stewed vegetables). And with leftover roasted meats, she would prepare salads or delicious stuffing for pasta. This dish came about because I had a surplus of scallops. Altogether the time needed to cook this dish is about 10 minutes.

Bring a large pot of water to a boil. Add the salt and linguine. Cook over high heat until the pasta is tender but firm to the bite, 8 to 10 minutes.

While the pasta is cooking, prepare the sauce. Wash scallops and pat them dry with paper towels. If the scallops are large, cut them in half or into quarters. Heat the oil in a large skillet. Add the garlic and anchovies and sauté gently for about 1 minute. Add the scallops and sauté over high heat for 1 minute longer. Season with salt and several grindings of pepper. Drain the pasta and add it to the sauce in the skillet. Stir in the parsley. Taste and adjust the seasoning and serve at once.

1 tablespoon salt
1 pound linguine or spaghetti
1 pound bay scallops
6 tablespoons olive oil
2 garlic cloves, finely chopped
3 anchovy fillets, finely chopped
1 tablespoon chopped fresh parsley leaves
* or chives*

SERVES 4

Spaghettini Aglio e Olio

Spaghettini with Garlic and Oil

Here is one of the most appetizing, tastiest, and easiest pasta dishes to prepare, a very humble and popular Neapolitan dish that needs only one ingredient to be outstanding—excellent olive oil. While the pasta cooks, the garlic is sautéed in the oil. Then the pasta and the sauce are combined and tossed together over low heat with a handful of freshly chopped parsley. Good food doesn't have to be expensive to be outstanding.

Salt

1 pound spaghettini (thin spaghetti) or regular spaghetti

6 tablespoons good olive oil, preferably virgin olive oil

4 garlic cloves, finely chopped

1 small piece hot red chile pepper or

Several grindings of black pepper

1 tablespoon chopped fresh parsley leaves

SERVES 4

Bring a large pot of water to a boil. Add 1 tablespoon of salt and the spaghettini. Cook, uncovered, over high heat, until tender but still firm to the bite.

While the pasta is cooking, prepare the sauce. In a large skillet, heat the oil. Add the garlic and hot pepper, if using. Sauté over very low heat until the garlic is lightly golden.

Drain the spaghettini and add it to the skillet with the sauce. Stir in the parsley and season with salt and pepper. Stir to blend thoroughly and serve immediately.

I know for sure that there are foods that make people happy. My husband works long, exhausting hours as the Director of the Sutter Community Hospital Cancer Center here in Sacramento. Yet, as he walks through the door and the aroma of well-prepared food hits him, he smiles and automatically begins to relax. This is one of his favorite dishes.

Bucatini con Salsa di Funghi e Acciughe

Bucatini with Mushrooms and Anchovy Sauce

Bucatini is a thick, hollow spaghetti that is generally associated with a very famous Roman dish, Bucatini all'Amatriciana, which is a zesty combination of tomatoes, pancetta, and hot red pepper. These chubby brothers of spaghetti are at their best when paired with hearty and satisfying sauces, such as the one below.

Soak the mushrooms in 1 cup of lukewarm water for 15 to 20 minutes. Drain the mushrooms and reserve the soaking water. Rinse the mushrooms under cold running water to get rid of all sandy deposits. Line a strainer with paper towels and strain the soaking water several times until completely clear.

Press the tomatoes through a food mill or sieve to remove the seeds.

Heat the oil in a medium-size saucepan. Add the garlic and anchovies and sauté gently for 1 to 2 minutes. Add the mushrooms and parsley and cook for a few minutes longer. Stir in mushroom soaking water. Cook over high heat until it is reduced by half. Stir in the tomatoes and season with salt and pepper. Cook, uncovered, over medium heat for 15 to 20 minutes, stirring a few times. The sauce should have a medium-thick consistency.

Bring a large pot of water to a boil. Add the salt and bucatini. Cook until the pasta is tender but still firm to the bite, about 8 to 10 minutes. Drain and put in a large serving dish or bowl. Add the sauce and mix thoroughly. Serve immediately.

1 ounce porcini mushrooms
1 28-ounce can imported Italian plum tomatoes with their juices
3 tablespoons olive oil
2 garlic cloves, finely chopped
2 anchovy fillets, finely chopped
1 tablespoon chopped fresh parsley leaves
1 tablespoon salt
1 pound bucatini

SERVES 4 TO 6

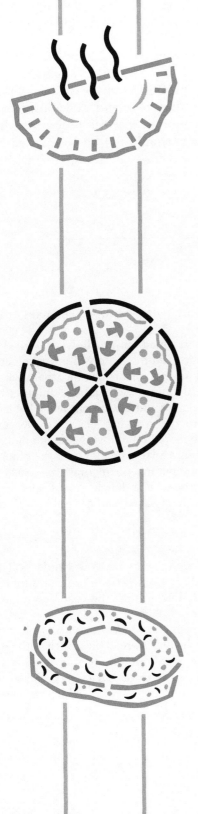

Pizza, Calzoni, Rustic Pies, and Savory Breads

Pizza

Years ago, when I was a teenager, there was a movie in Italy called *Pane Amore e Fantasia* (*Bread, Love, and Fantasy*). It depicted the story of two beautiful young people without money who lived solely on bread, love, and fantasy.

Those three words could also have been used quite successfully to identify a very popular Italian dish that originated out of the need of poor people to feed themselves. Pizza was full of love and fantasy and through the years became one of the most recognized and loved of all Italian dishes.

This ancient dish, made originally with a kind of rough dough, once had different names and was topped with various flavorful ingredients. Originally, it was made without tomato sauce, because tomatoes arrived in Italy much later—in the sixteenth century—from America.

In Italy, and throughout the world, pizza is instantly associated with Naples, where it originated. In this beautiful, sunny, and exuberant city, pizza tastes as nowhere else in the world. It was there that the first "Pizzeria" was opened in 1830. The rest is history.

Unfortunately, too often pizza has been abused. Good pizza should not be smorgasbord of contrasting and, very often, clashing ingredients, but rather an orchestration of well-balanced tastes that complement each other. To be good, pizza needs only three things: a crisp good dough, fresh-tasting ingredients, and a light hand in using them.

Following are the recipes for basic pizza dough and for seven different kinds of toppings, plus tips and ideas for making your dough foolproof and deliciously crunchy. Keep in mind that the proportions for the toppings should not be considered inflexible. Use them as general guidelines; then go on to create your own pizza.

Basic Pizza Dough

1 package active dry yeast
½ cup plus 2 tablespoons lukewarm water
1½ cups all-purpose unbleached flour
1 tablespoon olive oil
1 tablespoon salt

MAKES ONE 12-INCH PIZZA

Dissolve the yeast in the water for 10 minutes to activate the yeast.

Put the flour in a medium-size bowl or in the bowl of an electric mixer. Add the dissolved yeast, oil, and salt. Mix well until all ingredients are incorporated. Knead the dough for 10 minutes by hand or 5 minutes by machine. The dough should be smooth and pliable. If the dough sticks to the working surface or work bowl, knead in a little more flour. Dust the dough lightly with flour and place into a large bowl. Cover the bowl with a kitchen towel and put in a warm, draft-free place to rise, about 3 to 3½ hours. The dough should double in volume, be springy, and have small gas bubbles all over its surface.

Preheat the oven to 450 degrees 20 to 25 minutes before baking.

Flatten the dough down with your hands. Roll out the dough into a 10- or 11-inch circle, making sure to leave the edges a little thicker than the center so the topping won't spill over.

Grease a 12-inch pizza pan with a bit of olive oil and lay dough over the pan. Spread the dough with your fingertips to adjust evenly in pan. Spread topping over in the order given for each individual recipe. Bake for 15 to 20 minutes, or until the dough is golden brown. Serve hot.

Pizza dough can also be made in the food processor. Dissolve the yeast in the water and let stand for 10 minutes. Put the flour and salt in the bowl of the food processor fitted with a metal blade. Start the machine and pour the oil and yeast mixture through the feed tube. Process until a dough forms around the blade. Then process a few seconds longer. Knead 1 minute by hand and then proceed as instructed above.

For a crisp dough and a wonderful crust, place 1 large ovenproof unglazed terra-cotta tile, or several smaller ones in your oven and preheat the oven at least 20 minutes before baking. In any case, make sure to have a *very* hot oven before baking.

When dissolving the yeast in the water, make sure the water is lukewarm and not too hot. The ideal temperature would be 100 to 120 degrees. Too much heat will kill the yeast. Test the water with the inside of your wrist if you do not have a thermometer.

Active dry yeast, today, is highly reliable. However, it won't hurt to proof the yeast. Simply add a pinch of sugar to the dissolved yeast. If tiny bubbles appear on the surface of the water, the yeast is alive and well. *Always* check the expiration date on the yeast package before using it.

There is today on the market a "Rapid Rise" yeast that works 50 percent faster than regular yeast.

Basic pizza dough can be prepared in the morning, allowed to rise all day, and baked at night. Dough will also rise, at a much slower rate, in the refrigerator.

Fillings for a 12-inch pizza

Pizza alla Napoletana

5 to 6 fresh ripe plum tomatoes, cut into pieces
1 garlic clove, finely chopped
2 tablespoons fresh oregano leaves, or 1 teaspoon dried oregano
¾ cup shredded mozzarella
1 tablespoon olive oil

Spread on the pizza in the order given, sprinkle with the oil, and bake until golden.

Pizza Margherita

1 cup tomato sauce (page 48)
¾ cup shredded mozzarella
2 tablespoons fresh oregano leaves, or 1 teaspoon dried oregano
¼ cup freshly grated parmigiano
1 tablespoon olive oil

Spread on the pizza in the order given, sprinkle with the oil, and bake until golden.

Pizza con Prosciutto Cotto

Pizza with Ham

Same as Pizza Margherita with the addition of 2 to 3 ounces of boiled ham, cut into thin strips.

Pizza with Olives, Capers, and Anchovies

1 cup tomato sauce (page 48)
½ cup shredded mozzarella
½ cup black pitted olives, cut into quarters
¼ cup rinsed and dried capers
4 to 5 anchovy fillets, cut into small pieces
1 tablespoon olive oil

Spread on the pizza in the order given, sprinkle with the oil, and bake until golden.

Pizza con i Funghi

Pizza with Mushrooms

Heat the oil in a medium-size skillet. Add the garlic and mushrooms and cook over high heat for 1 to 2 minutes. Add the parsley and capers and season with salt and pepper. Cook for 1 minute longer. Spread the tomato sauce over the pizza dough and top with the mushroom mixture. Bake until golden.

2 tablespoons olive oil
2 garlic cloves, finely chopped
½ pound small white cultivated mush-
  rooms, thinly sliced
2 tablespoons chopped fresh parsley leaves
2 tablespoons rinsed and dried capers
Salt and freshly ground black pepper
1 cup tomato sauce (page 48)

Pizza con Le Melanzane

Pizza with Eggplant

Wash and dry the eggplant. Cut lengthwise into 1-inch-thick slices. Cut the slices into cubes. Put the cubes in a colander and sprinkle with salt. Let stand for about 1 hour. The salt will draw out eggplant's bitter juices. Pat dry with paper towels.

    Heat the oil in a medium-size skillet. Add the garlic, anchovies, and eggplant cubes and sauté for 5 to 6 minutes over medium heat, stirring a few times. Add the parsley and season with salt and pepper. Cook for 1 minute longer. Spread on the pizza and bake until golden.

1 large eggplant
Salt
3 to 4 tablespoons olive oil
2 garlic cloves, finely chopped
2 anchovy fillets, chopped
2 tablespoons chopped fresh parsley leaves
Freshly ground black pepper

Pizza con le Melanzane e Pomodoro

Pizza with Eggplant and Tomatoes

Same as Pizza with Eggplants, with the addition of 5 to 6 fresh ripe plum tomatoes, cut into pieces.

Torta di Zucchine e Cipolle

Zucchini and Onion Tart

When one doesn't know what to do with that last couple of zucchini, the pieces of onion, and the handful of mushrooms or other vegetables that are left in the refrigerator, one can always improvise and turn them into lovely soups or tasty vegetable tarts. A vegetable tart can be served as an appetizer, a luncheon, or can be enjoyed as a treat in between meals.

For the Pie Pastry

1⅓ cup all-purpose unbleached flour
6 tablespoons unsalted butter (at room temperature for hand mixing or cold and in small pieces for the food processor)
1 large egg
Pinch of salt
2 to 3 tablespoons chilled white wine
1 large egg white, lightly beaten to brush over the pastry shell

For the Filling

4 tablespoons unsalted butter
2 large onions, thinly sliced
1½ pounds small zucchini, cut into ¼-inch-thick rounds
½ cup heavy cream
¾ cup freshly grated parmigiano
Salt and freshly ground white pepper

SERVES 8

In a medium-size bowl or in the bowl of a food processor fitted with a metal blade, mix the flour and butter until crumbly. Add the egg, salt, and wine. Mix or process until the dough forms a ball. Put the dough on a working surface and work into a ball. Wrap in aluminum foil and refrigerate for at least 1 hour.

Preheat the oven to 400 degrees. On a lightly floured surface, roll out the dough to a 12-inch circle. Place the dough in a 10-inch tart pan with a removable bottom. Trim the edges of the dough by gently rolling the rolling pin over the top of the pan. Prick the bottom of pastry shell in several places with a fork. Line the pastry shell with aluminum foil. Fill the foil with uncooked rice or beans to prevent the pastry from shrinking while cooking. Bake for 15 minutes. Remove the foil and rice or

beans. Brush the dough with the beaten egg white and bake for 10 minutes longer, or until pastry is lightly golden in color. Cool in the tart pan.

Make the filling. Melt the butter in a large skillet. When the butter foams, add the onions and sauté over medium heat for 3 to 4 minutes. Add the zucchini and sauté for 3 to 4 minutes longer. Stir in the cream and simmer for 3 to 4 minutes, or until the cream is reduced by half. Season with salt and pepper and cheese. Stir and cook until the sauce is thick and coats the vegetables completely. Remove from the heat and cool slightly. Spoon the mixture into pastry shell, spreading evenly with a spatula. Cool at least 1 hour before serving.

The tart can be prepared completely several hours ahead of time and kept in the refrigerator, tightly covered, until ready to serve. Serve at room temperature.

Torta di Melanzane

Eggplant Tart

Sometimes it is by pure coincidence that we "discover" new dishes. Such was the case of this eggplant tart.

Every so often I look into my refrigerator and try to use everything that is left over before I do the shopping again. With leftovers of eggplants sautéed in oil with parsley and garlic and a butter pie pastry that had been frozen, I prepared a lovely eggplant tart. This proves that one needn't have genius in the kitchen, only a little imagination.

For the Pie Crust

1⅓ cups all-purpose unbleached flour
6 tablespoons unsalted butter (at room temperature for hand mixing or cold and in small pieces for the food processor)
1 large egg
Pinch of salt
2 to 3 tablespoons chilled dry white wine
1 large egg white, lightly beaten to brush over pastry shell

For the Filling

1 large eggplant
⅓ cup olive oil
4 anchovy fillets, chopped
2 garlic cloves, finely chopped
2 tablespoons chopped fresh parsley leaves
Salt and freshly ground black pepper
3 large eggs
¾ cup freshly grated parmigiano

SERVES 8

In a medium-size bowl or in a food processor fitted with a metal blade, mix the flour and butter until crumbly. Add the egg, salt, and wine. Mix until the dough forms a ball. Put the dough on a work surface and work lightly into a ball. Wrap in aluminum foil and refrigerate for 1 hour.

Preheat the oven to 400 degrees. On a lightly floured surface, roll out the dough to a 12-inch circle. Put the dough into a 10-inch tart pan with a removable bottom. Trim the edges of the dough by gently rolling the rolling pin over the top of the pan. Prick the bottom of the pastry shell in several places with a fork. Line the shell with aluminum foil. Fill the foil with uncooked beans or rice. Bake for 15 minutes. Remove the foil and beans or rice. Brush the dough with the beaten egg white and bake for 10 minutes longer, or until the pastry is lightly golden in color. Cool in the tart pan.

Peel eggplant and cut it into 1-inch cubes. Put the cubes in a colander, sprinkle with salt, and leave for about 30 minutes to allow the eggplant to discharge its bitter juices. Pat dry with paper towels.

Heat the oil in a large skillet. Add the anchovies and garlic and cook gently for 1 to 2 minutes. Add the eggplant cubes and cook over medium heat for 8 to 10 minutes, stirring. Add the parsley and season lightly with salt and pepper. Cook for 1 minute longer; then transfer the mixture to a bowl to cool.

Beat eggs, pinch of salt, and parmigiano together in a bowl. Add to the cooled eggplant mixture. Fill the pastry shell with the mixture. Bake in a preheated 375-degree oven for 15 to 20 minutes, or until top of filling is firm to the touch.

Cool for 10 to 15 minutes; then transfer the tart to a serving dish. Serve warm or at room temperature.

Tortino di Patate, Prosciutto, e Formaggio

Potato–Prosciutto and Cheese Cake

This tortino combines potatoes, sautéed sweet onions, ham, and fontina cheese in a baked, succulent dish. It is by no means the lightest dish in this book; it is meant to be served on a cold winter night, perhaps preceded by a soup such as Mushroom Soup with Porcini (page 202). Leftovers can be stored in the refrigerator and eaten for lunch the day after, served at room temperature.

Bring a large pot of water to the boil. Add the potatoes and cook until tender but still firm to the touch. Drain the potatoes and cool them. Peel the potatoes and cut them into medium-thin slices. Set aside.

Melt the butter in a large skillet. When the butter foams, add the onions and cook over medium-low heat until the onions are pale yellow and wilted.

Cut the fontina into thin slices or small pieces. Preheat the oven to 400 degrees. Butter a 10-inch spring-form pan and coat it with bread crumbs.

Line the bottom of the pan with slices of ham. Cover the ham with a layer of sautéed onions. Place potato slices over the onions and cover the potatoes with pieces of fontina. Repeat with layers of ham, onions, potatoes, and fontina until all the ingredients have been used up. Top the last layer with grated parmigiano and dot with a bit of butter. Bake for 30 to 40 minutes, or until the cheese has completely melted and the top of the cake is lightly golden.

Remove from the oven and cool for 15 to 20 minutes in the pan. Transfer to a serving platter and serve.

1½ pounds boiling potatoes
4 tablespoons unsalted butter
1½ pounds yellow onions
½ pound Italian fontina
2 to 3 tablespoons unseasoned bread crumbs
¾ pound boiled or baked ham
⅓ cup freshly grated parmigiano
Additional unsalted butter

SERVES 6 TO 8

Torta Rustica

Rustic Pie

Nothing goes to waste in an Italian kitchen. Leftover ingredients can be used successfully in a variety of ways. Leftover cheese and salami can be turned into rustic pies.

The filling of this rustic pie changes according to the season and the preference of the cook. It can be made with fresh ingredients or with leftovers. The dough for the crust employed here is the basic, easy-to-make, universal butter crust. The crust can also be made with a pizza dough.

For the Pie Pastry

2 cups all-purpose unbleached flour
4 ounces unsalted butter (at room temperature for hand mixing or cold and in small pieces for the food processor)
1 large egg
Pinch of salt
3 to 4 tablespoons chilled white wine

For the Filling

4 large eggs
1½ pounds ricotta
¼ pound mozzarella, diced
¼ pound Italian fontina, diced
¼ pound prosciutto, sliced and then cut into short strips
¼ pound Tuscan or Genoa salami, cut into short strips
2 tablespoons chopped fresh parsley leaves
½ to ¾ cup freshly grated parmigiano
Salt

For the Crust

1 large egg, lightly beaten

SERVES 8 TO 10

In a medium-size bowl or in the bowl of a food processor fitted with a metal blade, mix the flour and butter until crumbly. Add the egg, salt, and wine. Mix until the dough forms a ball. Put the dough on a work surface and work into two balls, one a little larger than the other. Wrap in aluminum foil and refrigerate for 1 hour.

Preheat the oven to 375 degrees. Butter a 10-inch springform pan.

Make the filling. In a medium-size bowl, beat the eggs until pale yellow. Put the ricotta through a sieve directly into the eggs. Add the mozzarella, fontina, prosciutto, salami, parsley, and parmigiano. Mix everything thoroughly, taste, and adjust the seasoning.

On a lightly floured surface roll out the larger ball of dough to a 13-inch circle. Place the dough in the buttered pan. Pour the cheese mixture into the pastry shell and level the filling with a spatula. Roll out the remaining dough and place it over the filling. Pinch the edges of the top and bottom doughs to seal the pie. Brush the top crust with the beaten egg. Prick the top of the pie in several places with a fork.

Bake for 50 minutes to 1 hour, or until the pastry is golden brown. Cool for 10 minutes; then transfer to a serving dish. Serve at room temperature.

Torta Rustica can also be made with only one crust. Follow the proportions and directions for the Torta Rustica above, but with the following changes:

Separate eggs;
Beat whites until stiff;
Fold into cheese mixture;
Roll out dough and place in pan;
Fill with ricotta mixture;
Bake.

Torta Salata ai Quattro Sapori

Savory Pie with Four Tastes

This pie is my interpretation of a classic theme. The "four tastes" are given by ham, spinach, fontina, and sweet red peppers. A fresh asparagus salad in spring or an Orange and Fennel Salad in winter (page 267) would be a perfect accompaniment to this delicious pie.

For the Pie Pastry
2 cups all-purpose unbleached flour
4 ounces butter (at room temperature for hand mixing or cold and in small pieces for the food processor)
1 large egg
Pinch of salt
3 to 4 tablespoons chilled white wine

For the Filling
2 pounds fresh spinach, or 1 10-ounce package frozen spinach
Salt to taste
2 tablespoons unsalted butter
⅓ cup heavy cream
⅓ cup freshly grated parmigiano
5 large sweet red peppers
¾ pound boiled or baked ham, sliced thin
1 pound Italian fontina, cut into medium strips

For the Crust
1 large egg, lightly beaten

Serves 8

In a medium-size bowl, or in a bowl of a food processor fitted with a metal blade, mix the flour and butter until crumbly. Add the egg, salt, and wine. Mix until dough forms a ball. Put the dough on a work surface and work into two balls, one a little larger than the other. Wrap in aluminum foil and refrigerate for 1 hour.

Preheat the oven to 400 degrees. Butter a 10-inch springform pan.

Roast the peppers according to the instructions on page 59. Peel the peppers, cut them in half, and remove the seeds. Pat the peppers dry with paper towels. Set aside.

Remove the stems from the spinach and wash the leaves thoroughly under cool running water. Place the wet spinach in a large saucepan. Add a pinch of salt and cook over medium heat until the spinach is tender. Drain well. If using frozen spinach, cook following the package directions and drain well.

Melt the butter in a small saucepan. Add the spinach, cream, and parmigiano and season lightly with salt. Cook over high heat, stirring, until the cream is reduced—the mixture should have a creamy consistency, but no liquid should be left in the pan. Set aside.

On a lightly floured surface, roll out the larger ball of dough to a 12-inch circle. Place the dough in buttered pan. Cover the bottom of the shell with a layer of ham. Follow with a layer of spinach. Place pieces of fontina over the spinach and top the fontina with the red peppers. Repeat with remaining ingredients. (You should not have more than three layers of each ingredient, and the pastry should only be two-thirds full.)

Roll out the remaining dough to a 10-inch circle. Place over the filling. Pinch the edges of the top and bottom doughs together to seal. Brush the surface with beaten egg. Prick the top of the pie in several places with a fork. Bake for 50 minutes to 1 hour, or until the crust is golden brown. Cool the pie for 10 minutes; then transfer to a serving dish. Allow the pie to cool to room temperature before serving.

Savory pies are found all over Italy in one form or another. Made with the basic butter crust or a yeast crust, the filling is often left to the imagination of the cook. These splendid preparations often solve the problem of what to prepare in advance for dinner for the working woman, as they can be kept very well in the refrigerator for several days waiting to become a light lunch or dinner. They are also perfect for buffets, for picnics, and delicious to lunch on while sunbathing on a beach or fishing by the river. But most of all they look and taste scrumptious.

Calzone al Formaggio

Calzone Stuffed with Cheese

Calzone is a Neapolitan specialty, but it can be found in many other southern Italian regions as well. It is made from pizza dough rolled out into circles and stuffed with a variety of locally available ingredients. Once a poor man's staple, it is now experiencing a revival all over Italy. And it is becoming increasingly popular, even a bit trendy, in this country.

For the Dough

2 packages active dry yeast
3½ cups all-purpose unbleached flour
1 cup plus 4 tablespoons lukewarm water
2 tablespoons olive oil
2 tablespoons salt

For the Filling

2 large eggs
1 pound ricotta
¼ pound prosciutto, cut into julienne
¼ pound mozzarella, diced
½ cup freshly grated parmigiano
Pinch of salt

MAKES 4 LARGE CALZONI

Prepare the dough. Dissolve the yeast in the water for 10 minutes to activate the yeast. Put the flour in a medium-size bowl or in the bowl of an electric mixer. Add the dissolved yeast, oil, and salt. Mix well until all the ingredients are incorporated. Knead the dough for about 10 minutes by hand or 5 minutes by machine. The dough should be smooth and pliable. If the dough sticks to the work surface or working bowl, knead in a bit more flour.

Dust the dough lightly with flour and place it in a large bowl. Cover the bowl with plastic wrap or aluminum foil and put it in a warm, draft-free place to rise for 3 to 3½ hours. The dough should double in volume and be springy with small gas bubbles over its surface.

Preheat the oven to 400 degrees at least 20 minutes before baking.

Prepare the filling. In a medium-size bowl, beat the eggs and pinch of salt together. Add the ricotta, prosciutto, mozzarella, and parmigiano. Mix thoroughly and taste for seasoning. Cover the bowl with aluminum foil and refrigerate until ready to use.

Divide the dough into four equal parts. Roll out into circles about 8 inches in diameter. Fill half of each circle with some of the cheese mixture. Fold the dough over the filling, pressing the edges together. Crimp the edges flat with a fork to seal them.

Place the calzoni on a baking sheet and bake for 30 to 35 minutes, or until golden in color. Cool slightly and serve.

Calzone alle Cipolle Rosse

Calzone with Red Onions

The original calzoni were all filled with humble ingredients and, to my mind, they are still the best-tasting ones. This one is filled with red onions that are sautéed gently until they become tender and almost sweet. Then tomatoes, olives, and capers are added and everything is held together by the distinctive taste of Pecorino Romano, a typical cheese of Rome that has a slightly spicy, quite salty taste.

Prepare the dough following the instructions for Calzone Stuffed with Cheese (page 314).

Preheat the oven to 400 degrees at least 20 minutes before baking.

Peel and seed the tomatoes (page 55) and cut them into chunks. Put the tomato chunks in a colander to drain off the excess juices.

Heat the oil in a large skillet. Add the onions and sauté, stirring, over medium-low heat for 15 to 20 minutes. The onions should be thoroughly cooked. Add the tomatoes, olives, and capers and cook, stirring, over high heat until all the moisture has evaporated from the skillet. Transfer the mixture to a bowl, cover, and refrigerate until ready to use. When the mixture is completely cool, add the cheese and mix to combine.

Divide dough into four equal parts. Roll out into circles about 8 inches in diameter. Fill half of each circle with some of the onion mixture. Fold the dough over the filling, pressing the edges together. Crimp the edges flat with a fork to seal them.

Place the calzoni on a baking sheet and bake for 30 to 35 minutes, or until golden in color. Cool slightly and serve.

Use salt sparingly, especially if you are using Pecorino. Parmigiano can be substituted for the Pecorino.

For the Dough

2 packages active dry yeast
3½ cups all-purpose unbleached flour
1 cup plus 4 tablespoons lukewarm water
2 tablespoons olive oil
2 tablespoons salt

For the Filling

4 ripe tomatoes
5 large red onions, thinly sliced
10 pitted black olives, cut into small pieces
2 tablespoons rinsed and dried capers
Salt and freshly ground black pepper
1 cup grated Pecorino Romano

SERVES 4

I Calzoni del Caffè San Domenico

Calzoni with Ham and Cheese of Café San Domenico

The calzoni of Café San Domenico are a bit different from the traditional calzoni of the south of Italy which are made from pizza dough. These are made with a classic butter pastry. The stuffing might vary, but often it includes cheese and ham; their shape is like large cannelloni.

I generally serve these calzoni as an appetizer with a good glass of sparkling wine. They are also perfect for a luncheon, a buffet, or as a special treat while watching a ball game or tennis match.

For the Butter Pastry

1 cup all-purpose unbleached flour
2 ounces unsalted butter (at room temperature for hand mixing, or cold and in small pieces for the food processor)
1 large egg
Pinch of salt
2 tablespoons chilled white wine

For the Filling

½ pound boiled or baked ham, sliced
6 ounces Italian fontina, roughly cut into slices
1 large egg, lightly beaten

MAKES 8 CALZONI

Prepare the pastry. In a medium-size bowl or in a food processor fitted with a metal blade, mix the flour and butter until crumbly. Add the egg, salt, and wine. Mix until the dough can be gathered loosely. Work the dough lightly into a ball, wrap it in aluminum foil and refrigerate for 1 hour.

Preheat the oven to 400 degrees.

On a lightly floured surface, roll out the dough. Cut the dough into 5½- by 5½-inch squares. Place 1 slice of ham over each square leaving a free border of about ½ inch on all sides. Cover the ham with 1 slice fontina. Fold two opposite edges of the pastry over the filling. Crimp the edges flat with a fork to seal them.

Place the calzoni on a baking dish and brush the dough with the beaten egg. Bake for 20 to 30 minutes, or until the dough is golden in color. Cool for 10 minutes before serving.

As a teenager growing up in Bologna, one of my best friends was a boy named Carlo whose father owned the Café San Domenico on the Piazza San Domenico. When his father was not around, Carlo would invite a bunch of friends to gorge on pastries, ice cream, pizzas, and delicious savory treats for which, needless to say, he got into trouble many times. On a recent visit to Café San Domenico, Carlo, who now owns and operates the café, treated me to samples of several of the old-fashioned treats the café still serves. As I bit into a small, hot calzone filled with ham and cheese, all the memories of my childhood came rushing back to me—nothing had ever tasted better than that delicious, fragrant calzone.

Schiacciata con Cipolle, Pancetta e Pomodori Secchi

Savory Bread with Onion, Pancetta, and Sun-Dried Tomatoes

This dough is not really too time-consuming to make if done by hand, but it is also very fast and quite easy if done by machine.

Serve this savory bread alongside a hearty soup, a stew, or, even better, by itself.

For the Dough

2 packages active dry yeast
1 teaspoon sugar
2 cups lukewarm water
4½ cups all-purpose unbleached flour
1 tablespoon salt

For the Filling

1 onion, thinly sliced
2 tablespoons fresh rosemary leaves
2 ounces pancetta, finely diced
4 to 5 sun-dried tomatoes, finely diced (optional)
2 tablespoons olive oil
1 teaspoon coarse salt

SERVES 12

Dissolve the yeast and sugar in the lukewarm water. Put 4 cups of the flour in a large bowl or in the bowl of an electric mixer. Add the salt and dissolved yeast and mix well. Knead the dough for about 10 to 12 minutes by hand or 5 to 6 minutes by machine. The dough should be smooth and pliable. Dust the dough lightly with flour and place in a large clean bowl. Cover the bowl with plastic wrap or aluminum foil or a kitchen towel and place in a warm, draft-free place to rise until double in bulk, about 1 to 1½ hours.

Remove the dough and flatten it out to a 15- to 16-inch circle, about 1 inch thick. Put the onion, rosemary, pancetta, and sun-dried tomatoes, if using, over the dough. Fold the dough over the filling and knead to incorporate, about 3 to 4 minutes. As you knead, some of the ingredients will fall off. Simply knead them back into the dough. Add up to ½ cup of the reserved flour if dough is too sticky.

Oil two 12-inch-round pizza pans. Divide the dough in half and place it in the pans. Starting from the center, use your fingers to push the dough to fit the pans. Prick dough with a fork in several places. Brush the dough with oil and sprinkle lightly with coarse salt.

Bake the schiacciata for 30 to 35 minutes, or until golden in color and crisp. Remove from the oven and cool for 10 to 20 minutes before serving. Serve warm.

These savory breads have their own distinctive names and identities from region to region: schiacciata in Tuscany; crescenta in Emilia-Romagna; focaccia in Liguria; and pizza in Campania and in every other part of Italy.

Made with flour and yeast, schiacciata are baked with only a hint of fresh herbs and oil. At other times, ingredients, such as onions, cheese, and salamis, are kneaded into the dough. Quite often, the dough is flattened and topped with a variety of ingredients, transforming them into delicious, tasty, and old-fashioned delicacies.

Once standard items in an Italian kitchen, schiacciata, today, are treats to prepare on a special occasion. For the unskilled baker, these delicious savory breads can still be found in bread shops all over the country.

La Crescenta Bolognese

Flat Bolognese Savory Bread with Bacon

I don't recall my mother ever making bread, perhaps because we lived in the city and had the choice of so much wonderful bread made daily by our favorite baker. However, she did make a savory bread called crescenta that was flavored with pancetta. The taste of that bread is unforgettable. When I make crescenta, I like to do the kneading by hand if I have time; I find it very relaxing and satisfying. If I am in a hurry, my electric mixer will do the work for me. Crescenta has two risings, which gives it a very interesting texture. To fully enjoy its flavor, serve the crescenta when it is still warm as an accompaniment to a bowl of steaming soup.

For the First Rising

1 teaspoon active dry yeast
½ cup lukewarm water
1 cup all-purpose unbleached flour

For the Second Rising

2 teaspoons active dry yeast
1 cup lukewarm water
2½ cups all-purpose unbleached flour
Salt
½ pound pancetta, chopped
2 tablespoons olive oil

SERVES 10 TO 12

For the first rising, dissolve the yeast in the lukewarm water for 10 minutes to activate the yeast. Put the flour in a medium-size bowl or in the bowl of an electric mixer. Add the dissolved yeast and mix with the flour. Knead the dough for about 10 minutes by hand or 5 minutes by machine. The dough should be smooth and pliable. Dust the dough lightly with flour and put it in a bowl. Cover the bowl with plastic wrap or aluminum foil and put in a warm, draft-free place to rise until double in bulk, about 2 to 2½ hours.

For the second rising, dissolve the yeast in the water. Put the flour into a large bowl or in the bowl of an electric mixer. Make a well in the flour and add the dissolved yeast, 1 tablespoon of salt, pancetta, and olive oil. Mix well.

Knead the dough from the first rising into dough for the second rising. Then knead energetically for 10 to 12 minutes by hand or 5 to 10 minutes by machine. The dough should be smooth and elastic. If it is too sticky, work in some additional flour. Dust the dough with flour lightly and place in a large bowl. Cover with aluminum foil and allow to rise in a warm, draft-free place for about 1½ to 2 hours. The dough should again double in bulk and have large gas bubbles all over its surface.

Preheat the oven to 400 degrees 20 to 30 minutes before baking.

Roll out the dough to about a ½-inch thickness. Lightly oil a 15- by 12-inch baking sheet. With your fingers, starting from the center, push the dough out to fit the baking sheet. Prick the dough with a fork in several places and sprinkle lightly with salt. Bake for 30 to 35 minutes, or until golden brown. Cool for about 10 minutes before serving.

Index

About the Author

A native of Bologna, Italy, Biba Caggiano is also the author of *Northern Italian Cooking*. She lives in Sacramento, California, where she is proprietor of the highly successful and critically acclaimed restaurant Biba.